USING TH |||||||||||||||||||||||||
CHILDCARE SOURCE D0970128
INCLUDED WITH THIS BOOK

The disk included with this book is formatted for use on IBM PC or compatible computer systems using Windows software, including WordPerfect® for Windows™ version 5.2, 6.0a, or 6.1; Microsoft® Word for Windows version 2.0 or 6.0; or Lotus® Ami Pro™ for Windows version 3.0 or 3.1.

INSTALLATION INSTRUCTIONS

To install the *ChildCare Sourcebook* software, follow these simple instructions:

1. Close all open Windows word processors.
2. Insert the *ChildCare Sourcebook* disk into drive A or B.
3. At the Windows Program Manager, choose **Run** from the File menu. The Run dialog box appears.
4. Type **a:install** or **b:install** and click OK. The installation process begins.
5. A dialog box will appear asking you to select your word processing program. Select the program you use and click **Continue.**

   Note: *If your default word processor is not listed here, simply type in its name.*

> *Once the installation process is complete, the ChildCare Sourcebook program is added to your Program Manager and can be selected at any time.*

USING THE DISK

Once you have decided what kind of child care you need, click on the appropriate icon, or use the icons in the book as your guide. The HotDocs system will automatically load into your computer.

1. A dialog box will appear containing the list of templates you may choose from (this window is labelled "Tree/List"). Note that the templates are numbered to correspond to the numbered templates in Chapter 10. Choose the template you wish to work with now and click "Assemble."

2. A dialog box will appear with "Assembly Options."

- Choose "Blank form" if you want to review the form or if you want to print out a blank version of the questions to fill out at a later date. If you choose "Blank form" you may also fill in the checklists on the screen, but the program will not prompt you with questions.

  Note: The blank forms contain all of the information in the templates located in Chapter 10 in the book, but are formatted differently.

  *If you want to print a blank form to fill out later, choose **Print** from the File menu or follow the instructions for printing in your word processor.*

- Choose "Assemble form" if you want to answer the questions or checklists now and print out a completed document. Follow the on-screen prompts to complete each template. If you need to go back to an earlier question or an earlier screen, click on the **Back-Up** button.

  When a question involves one or more fill-boxes, fill in each box by moving your mouse to the appropriate box and clicking on. You can edit any box on that screen this way. *Do not hit **Enter** or **Return*** (this will take you to the next screen). If you hit **Enter** or **Return** by mistake, simply click on the **Back-Up** button and continue answering the questions.

  If a template asks you for the date, click on the **"C"** button and a calendar will pop up for you to choose the date. Click **Okay** on the calendar to continue.

  You may click **Stop Asking** at any time and the program will assemble the document based on your existing responses.

  HotDocs will assemble the template and display a completed one in your word processing window. At this point, you may edit any question or response or insert comments directly on this screen.

  Once the document is assembled, you may print out the completed version by choosing Print from the File menu or by following the instructions for printing in your word processor.

3. To save the completed document choose **Save** from the File menu or follow the instructions for saving a document in your word processor.

4. To start a new template, choose **Switch To** from the button in the upper left-hand corner of your screen, or press **Alt+Tab** to switch windows(hold down the **Alt** key and press **Tab** to scroll through the windows). To get back to the list of templates in your category, select "HotDocs"; to get back to the original window and choose a different kind of child care, select "Program Manager."

If you need assistance or experience any problems, contact Technical Support at Macmillan Computer Publishing at (317) 581-3833 or fax them at (317) 581-4773. Please telephone between the hours of 9:00 A.M. and 5:00 P.M. Central Time (summer) or Eastern Time (winter).

The
CHILDCARE
SOURCEBOOK

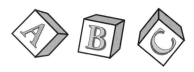

*The Complete Guide to Finding and Managing
Nannies, Au Pairs, Baby-sitters, Day Care,
and After-School Programs*

Ellen O. Tauscher,
President and CEO, The ChildCare Registry

with Kathleen Candy

Macmillan • USA

Macmillan

A Simon & Schuster Macmillan Company
1633 Broadway
New York, NY 10019

Library of Congress Cataloging-in-Publication Data

Tauscher, Ellen O.

The childcare sourcebook: the complete guide to finding and managing
nannies, au pairs, baby-sitters, day care, and after-school programs/Ellen O.
Tauscher and Kathleen Candy.

p. cm.

Includes bibliographical references and index.

ISBN 0-02-860818-6

1. Child-care services—United States. 2. Nannies—United States. 3. Au pairs—
United States. 4. Baby-sitters—United States. 5. Day-care centers—United
States. 6. School-age child care—United States.
I. Candy, Kathleen. II. Title.

HQ778.63.T38 1996

362.7' 12—dc20   95-50700
                                                         CIP

10 9 8 7 6 5 4 3 2 1

Printed in the United States of America

CONTENTS

INTRODUCTION

WHY THIS BOOK?

Before I begin, let me make it perfectly clear. I am not a professional "expert" in child care and make no claims to be. I am a forty-three-year-old former Wall Street investment banker who, after marrying a wonderful man six years ago, decided that I wasn't too old or set in my ways to start a family. Because my husband Bill has two children, Lauren and Joe, from a first marriage, I saw what a great father he was. Better yet, I had a chance to "drive with a learner's permit" by being a stepmother every other weekend.

Although I was lucky enough to have no problem getting pregnant, we suffered through two major disasters—the death of our first baby, Matthew, at birth, and the loss of our second in my sixteenth week of pregnancy. By the time I was pregnant with Katherine, I was within six months of my fortieth birthday and feeling as if this was our last chance.

All was not well in my tenth week of pregnancy, when we found out that although Katherine did not suffer from the same fatal bone disease that had claimed Matthew, a further complication endangered the pregnancy. Complete placenta previa was diagnosed during the sonogram. A condition occurring in 1 of every 200 pregnancies, placenta previa (Latin for "placenta first") means that the placenta is implanted abnormally, in the lower rather than upper part of the uterus so that it partially or completely covers the outlet from the uterus to the vagina. Twenty-five years ago, this complication killed both mother and child in most cases. Today, the survival rate is higher, but it still meant that the chances of my having a normal pregnancy and an uncomplicated birth were diminishing quickly. The doctors were more than certain that there was little chance that the placenta would move into a safer position because it had attached itself to a large fibroid tumor. That meant that this baby would be born early—hopefully, not too early.

With house confinement and excellent medical care, we made it to twenty-four weeks. Then I started having premature contractions, but no bleeding as yet. The doctors prescribed bed rest with limited movement, very little stair climbing, and a drug called Terbutaline, which makes you feel as if your heart is racing out of control. The medicine seemed to make the confinement and lack of mobility even worse. Simple things like relaxing and reading a book or a magazine were made virtually unenjoyable because the "quiet" only made my accelerated heartbeat seem louder and more pronounced. It was as if my heartbeat, normally a calm, silent presence that I took for granted, was now thumping so loudly that I couldn't concentrate. If I left our bedroom and went downstairs, I had to wait two hours to go back up. I can't tell you how many times I found myself downstairs only to realize that the book I was reading was back upstairs.

But Terbutaline helped us make it to the twenty-eighth week. Then, on the evening of May 9, 1991, my contractions intensified and I started hemorrhaging. After a tense ninety-mile-an-hour ride to the hospital, I was thrilled and very much relieved to see the pastel-clad nurses at the birth center doorway, but also painfully aware of the concern on everyone's face. Within seconds my shirt and slacks were cut off and megadoses of magnesium sulfate and other wonder drugs were pumped into my veins to help stop the bleeding and prevent convulsions or seizures from my plummeting blood pressure. I had arrived at the hospital at 11:15 P.M.; by 3:00 A.M., the bleeding and contractions were under control.

At 7:00 the next morning, I was wheeled into what would be my room for the next eight weeks, if all went well. I was given strict orders: Don't move, don't eat, and don't drink anything. Just relax. Bill was wonderful. Hard-working executive by day, at night he became a champion pillow plumper and my calm, steady link to all of our hopes and dreams.

Once I stabilized, my perinatologist visited to brief us on our situation. His message was simple. Birth at twenty-eight weeks was dicey, at best. "Fetuses" at this period of gestation usually weigh about 2 pounds, 6 ounces. Bill and I both knew this was very small. If our baby survived birth at this early stage, she would have countless, life-threatening medical problems. She needed to be bigger—at least by an extra pound—to survive.

Bill and I spent the rest of that day and the next cheering each other up and making plans to bring some of my books and computer to the hospital. Mentally, we were "moving in" for the duration. While we watched an NBA playoff game in the afternoon of the second day, we had no idea that this was to be Katherine's birthday. On May 11, 1991, Katherine O'Kane Tauscher was born by cesarean section twelve weeks early and at a bouncing 3 pounds, 6 ounces—50 percent bigger than other kids born that early and precisely the magic weight our doctor had told us was optimum.

The days that followed were a series of medical crises du jour—lung, heart, brain function, and eyesight roller-coaster rides. After a respirator, numerous blood transfusions, heavy shots of steroids, and countless other procedures, Katherine blessedly suffered no lasting effects from her rushed entry into the world.

Six months later, just as we were starting to breathe easier and congratulate ourselves on having dodged a bullet, we discovered that Katherine's right hip had been out of its socket since birth. Even worse, the hip socket itself, called the acetabulum, which is the cup-shaped hollow in the hipbone into which the head of the thigh bone (femur) fits and rotates, was badly damaged so that the hip couldn't just be "popped" back into its socket. Major surgery and months in a body cast were required. Bill and I felt heartsick. For the first time, we also felt over our heads. We had some serious decisions to make about Katherine's care, many concerns, and even more questions for her doctors. Because Katherine had spent so much time on a respirator as a premature baby, her lungs were weak; Respiratory Distress Syndrome, the acute lung disease in which the alveoli (tiny air sacs in the lungs) are airless and the lungs inelastic, is common to such babies. We needed to know how major surgery and anesthesia would affect her, and how the doctors could accurately assess the damage to the hip socket, and repair it in such a way that she wouldn't require a hip replacement in a few years or become arthritic at an early age. But we also needed more basic information. Who is the best surgeon for this type of problem? What does a body cast look like? How do you care for a baby in a body cast? Change her diapers? Bathe her? Sit her up in a baby carriage, car seat, or high chair? Would Katherine ever be able to walk?

Anyone who has gone through a major illness with a loved one knows that finding the best medical care is not enough. You're hungry for more information, counseling, and support from the medical professionals involved in your case. The problem is, you've got to satisfy that hunger for more information before you can get the counseling and support you need. Thoroughly educating yourself about your problem is the only way you can communicate with, manage, and most important, motivate medical professionals to give you their best. You are responsible for informing yourself to make sure that your loved one gets appropriate, high-quality care, right from the start.

What had I learned on Wall Street anyway? Didn't I know how to prioritize issues and research complex facts? Didn't I know how to use my brain to solve problems? My professional life had given me the right tools to manage this situation. For the first time, I applied business experience, sense, and smarts to a real-life situation. I "went to school" to learn everything I could about pediatric orthopedics. I visited the library and soon knew Gray's Anatomy intimately. I did a comprehensive analysis of the various medical options available to us. I compiled a list of the best surgeons and where they were located, and interviewed them, one by one. I worked through my Rolodex, calling all of my friends with medical backgrounds for contacts who could help us. Not surprisingly, the more I intellectualized the situation and put it into a framework I was comfortable with, the better I felt.

After Katherine made it through a very successful surgery, I focused my energy on a search for child care. From just under her arms to her feet, Katherine was encased in plaster. Only her head, shoulders, arms, and feet were exposed. She would be in the cast for three long months, a brace for six weeks, and then had to learn how to walk. I needed someone full time to help me care for my "baby in a vase," and I needed her immediately!

I called nanny placement agencies in San Francisco; it was no good because we lived too far out in the East Bay. I called local agencies and waited days for a returned phone call. I called everyone I knew and placed ads in the newspaper. When I found someone with a pulse who could manage to find our house—we live in the sticks—I found myself trying to find a single reason to hire her. Soon, I felt confused, paranoid, and very frustrated.

Then, the lightbulb went on. Why shouldn't I handle finding a child-care provider the same way I had found the best surgeon in the country for Katherine? Why not apply exactly the same logical, business-based principles to managing a nanny?

I started by thinking about the many, many people I had hired during my years on Wall Street. No matter the job, skill set, or salary, I had always done it the same way: I assessed the needs of the overall organization. Then I wrote a job description and circulated it to everyone who would be involved. I used all of the resources of the firm, internal and external, to identify and attract candidates. I created a list of questions for the interview and drafted a document to give candidates that described the job requirements in detail. After thoroughly interviewing a pool of qualified candidates, I narrowed down my list and did a set of second interviews. Finally, I made my choice and offer. So why couldn't I do this now when the stakes were much higher? I was convinced that I had been going about my search in entirely the wrong way.

However, I had a problem. On Wall Street, I had depended on detailed information about a job—a set of minimum skills, experience, and educational requirements that had to be met to qualify a candidate for the first interview—and a list of duties and responsibilities that I needed to carry out the day-to-day management of a chosen candidate. None of these valuable pieces of information was available to help me hire a child-care provider for Katherine. What are the baseline requirements that can be used to qualify a child-care provider? Where does one find qualified candidates? Who qualifies them? How do I establish a "professional" working relationship with the person responsible for the care of my fragile child? As I had found before Katherine's surgery, only by thoroughly educating myself about my problem could I communicate with, manage, and most important, motivate a child-care provider to give my daughter her best. The only way to obtain optimal care for my daughter was to make it my business to learn everything I could about child care.

After I hit the books, I started to remember fragments of conversations I had had with friends going through "the child-care thing" when I was single. Their biggest frustration had been the fact that it was virtually impossible to verify a child-care provider's education, experience, and job references quickly enough to meet their desperate need for help, or feel emotionally and intellectually comfortable with the person entrusted with the care of their child.

I thought about the kinds of information that could provide me with an effective solution to the problem. The list had to include verification of identity, educational history, employment history and references, and a comprehensive, multistate check of criminal, civil, and driving records.

If only parents had a service that could provide them with this information quickly, accurately, inexpensively, and legally! Pay by credit card, and the information is delivered by fax or Federal Express within a few days. Someone had to be providing this service! I looked hard all over the country, but I couldn't find it offered anywhere. Plenty of people I spoke with said things like, "Gee, I wish I knew who offered that service. It sure would have stopped me from hiring my last nanny. It took me three weeks to figure out that she didn't have the experience she said she had."

In a few short months I became a "lay" expert in child care and founder of The ChildCare Registry, a service that provides parents nationwide with comprehensive, legally released background information on child-care providers they are considering hiring. Out of my experience growing this company and carefully researching every type of child care, I have come to believe that by applying simple, time-tested business management principles to the problems parents face when finding, hiring, and managing child care, they will feel more at ease, suffer less stress, and finally feel in control of their child-care choice.

The child-care provider–parent relationship should be viewed and handled as any manager-employee relationship, or in the case of a family day-care or day-care provider, as a consumer–provider of service relationship. This perspective helps to define roles, ensures clearly articulated duties and responsibilities on each side, and makes the relationship far more resilient because it is founded on common professional courtesy and rules for behavior. This is truly the key to the success of your child-care services since most parents can trace the problems that short-circuited their previous child-care experiences to the earliest days of the relationship. Some parents admit that in their haste to find a child care "solution," whether a nanny or through services provided in a family day-care or day-care center, they took costly shortcuts by not spending the time to assess their needs adequately, do thorough research on their options, or verify the résumé of the provider (or in the case of a family or day-care center, check out the operator's facilities or reputation). I know that these are easy mistakes to make, especially when you need to fill an immediate need . . . often as immediately as the next morning so you can go to work.

I have written this book so that parents need not compromise on their optimum child-care scenario any longer. By digesting the information or theory in child care in this book and using the easy, time-saving tools on the software, there is no reason why you can't find, hire, and manage beautifully any child-care situation appropriate for you and your family. At bottom, you'll be using basic skills and life experience you already have! There is one catch, however. To apply the principles set forth in this book and software most effectively, you'll need to employ the tools we provide regularly. Once you get started, I can guarantee that it will take less than ten minutes a week. For the first time, even the busiest parent can be a success in the role of child-care provider–manager or consumer by applying theory and tools that will shrink your learning curve and increase your ability to be on top of all the critical issues— without taking you away from precious time with your children.

Below are the steps I used to find safe, appropriate, and high-quality child care for Katherine:

1. informed myself
2. personalized my options
3. chose the most appropriate option
4. assumed the role of active manager and consumer of child-care services

Before you read on, stop to consider that these are the simple but effective steps that all consumers are supposed to take before they pay for goods and services. Before buying a VCR, refrigerator, or car, or choosing a doctor or lawyer, a smart consumer goes through each of these steps. It also works for child care—it really does! Also consider that almost everyone has worked, managed, or been managed. Even if you haven't actually hired anyone in the course of your job, you've probably been through a job search, interview, and simple salary and benefits negotiations. The process and skills you used to get your job prepare you for the task of hiring a child-care provider. Applying the basic business principles you've used or experienced in the past to hiring and managing child care works. I tried it and succeeded! Now I rely on it. If you apply the principles in this book to find, manage, and motivate your child-care provider to give your child her best, whether it's in-home, family day care, day care, or another option, so will you.

What you will find in this book is factual information about how child care really works. I include all the tools you could possibly need to hire and manage a child-care provider, but only after it has gone through the

"Ellen Tauscher litmus test." I've sifted through the reams of written materials out there on child care and carefully investigated all of the agencies, services, organizations, and associations that parents can use in their search for child care. I've hired nannies, au pairs, baby-sitters, day-care centers, family day-care providers, gymnastics teachers, music teachers, swimming teachers—you name them, I've hired them! I've spent early-morning hours looking for someone to care for my sick child, and the wee hours of the night worrying about whether my nanny would show up at 6:00 A.M. so that I could catch a plane to New York at 7:00. As a result, the information in this book is practical, truthful, and at times, very critical of child care today, but it's necessary. Because I've been there, I'm hoping that this book will give you enough factual information so that, maybe, just maybe, you won't need to go through everything I have.

HOW TO USE THIS BOOK & SOFTWARE

Parents using *The ChildCare Sourcebook* will need no other resource to find, hire, and manage child-care services. *The Sourcebook* and its accompanying software apply simple yet sound business principles, tried and true common sense, and thoughtfully researched data that is married to state-of-the-art technology.

The Book

Though the book and software were developed for use together, they should be treated separately at first. I would suggest that you first read carefully Chapters One through Nine, paying special attention to Chapter Two; and then move forward to the chapter relating to the type of child care you think you need, whether it be in-home care, family day care, day-care centers, or care for an older child. Once you have a thorough grounding in your options, you are ready to pop in the diskette and start working through my specially designed tools, guided worksheets called templates, which begin in Chapter Ten. Once completed, the templates in Chapter Ten serve as a central repository for all kinds of information specific to your personal child-care requirements. The software is designed to migrate information you have entered in one template, so that you don't need to enter the same information over and over again. This can be a real time-saver!

The Software

This book can be used entirely on its own without the software. All of the templates found on the diskette can be found in Chapter Ten. However, if you have access to a computer at home or at work, I urge you to try the software. I know that you don't have unlimited amounts of time to spend searching for the "perfect" child-care situation. The software will get you organized very quickly and cut down on the time it takes you to get used to applying business principles to the task of hiring your provider. If you need child care, I'll bet you don't have time to track down the right tax, social security, and worker's compensation forms; think of every possible interview question to ask a day-care center operator; or do a comprehensive, national background check on a family day-care provider, among the myriad other tasks you must complete when you hire child care. In addition, very few of us have the money, and none of us the desire, to hire a lawyer to draft an employment contract, or deal with the INS on an illegal employee problem. The software can help you save time and plenty of unnecessary hassle.

In designing the software, I've assumed that you're not Bill Gates. My software is word processor–based, so if you know how to turn on your PC and have Windows, you can use it. By logging on to your home or office PC, you will be able to enter information quickly, edit it, save it for future use, have a spouse or friend review it, print out a finished job description, draft an advertisement, or create a contract for services, among many other tasks you will need to tackle.

Icons

Note that the book and software employ the use of simple icons to identify each type of child-care service. After you determine the type of care you need, you can use the software by pointing and clicking on the icon that represents your desired child-care type and then work through all of the templates. Similarly, if you are not using the software, you can work through all of the templates in the back of the book using the appropriate child-care icon as your guide.

In-Home Care

Family Day Care

Day Care

Older Child Care

Legal Kit

CHAPTER ONE

■ ■ ■ ■ ■ ■ ■ ■ ■ ■ ■

Why Is Child Care Such a Problem?

> | IN THIS CHAPTER: | *The Child-Care Problem* |
> | --- | --- |
> | | *Changes in Child-Care Needs* |
> | | *The ChildCare Registry* |

THE PROBLEM

Parents today need help. At The ChildCare Registry, I receive phone calls, letters, and faxes every day from parents desperate for advice that will solve, once and for all, their child-care problems. New parents usually phone me with questions about the basics—they want to know about all of their options and how to start out on the right foot in their search for child care. They ask me questions like, "What will be better for Natalie, a nanny or a day-care center?" "Should I call my local college's placement office to get a nanny?"

More experienced parents—those who have already hired and fired numerous child-care providers—ask questions born of their previous unsuccessful attempts to handle a multitude of child care–related issues. "Does a waiting list at a day-care center really mean that it's better than one without a waiting list?" "Should I drive half an hour to my mother's so that she can take care of Suzy when I go to my yoga class, or can I drop her off at the gym child-care center? How do I know that the gym child care is safe?" Having been through the whole process before, these parents are looking for specific steps they can take to make finding, interviewing, hiring, and—equally important—managing their child care easier, less stressful, and more successful than their last experience.

1

Their questions are wildly diverse, ranging from "What would you do if you came home and found your nineteen-year-old au pair in bed with the neighbor's twenty-five-year-old son?" to "Help! My nanny is threatening to leave unless I can give her a five-dollar-an-hour raise. It took me over a year to find her. What can I do?" to "I argued with the owner of my day-care center over all those sugary snacks they were giving Tommy, and she's asked me to take Tommy out of the school. Do I have any rights?"

Far worse are the parents who have experienced first hand the horrifying result of hiring an inappropriate or frankly dangerous child-care provider, or of contracting with a day-care center with lax management, irresponsible personnel, and a willful disregard of state licensing laws. At best, these unsuspecting parents were the victims of fraud or misrepresentation by their child-care providers—at worst, their precious children were killed or suffered grievous, sometimes irreparable, injuries.

Besides an abiding love for their children, these parents all share a basic frustration over what can only be perceived as *the* question in child care: "How does a parent find safe, reliable, experienced, legal, yet affordable child care?"

Judith P.

After a number of years in the child-care business, I am no longer surprised to hear stories like Judith's. A highly successful television writer, married to an equally successful sitcom producer, Judith is an extraordinarily articulate woman. Now the mother of little Rebecca, Judith still wanted to be able to take an occasional rewrite assignment and needed child care a few hours every day. Also, with her husband John's crazy taping schedule, both parents wanted a reliable caregiver to watch Rebecca so Mom and Dad could go out to dinner alone and catch up with each other every once in a while.

Armed with excellent communication and organizational skills, Judith prepared a list of requirements for her child-care provider and set about interviewing Los Angeles nanny placement agencies. She was very clear about her requirements. However, before she went to the agencies, no one told her that she might need to modify her basic requirements, salary, or hours somewhat, or that she should thoroughly screen the people sent by the agency to be sure they met her requirements.

Because no one told her these things, Judith admits she made mistakes (albeit very common mistakes for most parents hiring their first child-care provider) and assumptions that cost her valuable work time, too many Excedrin, and ultimately her trust in today's system for hiring child care.

An hour before she called me in January 1995, Judith fired a nanny she had hired three weeks before through a top-flight southern California nanny placement agency. She had carefully described her requirements to the agency, including her desire for an experienced nanny. When the agency called to urge Judith to meet with this particular nanny, they assured her that the nanny met all of her minimum requirements and "checked out beautifully." However, after a few days of work, it was quite obvious that her new nanny had literally no child-care experience. When confronted, the agency countered by insisting that, with time, the nanny would work out. "Just give it a few more days," was the agency's response. So Judith bit her tongue and stayed home from work every morning for two weeks to "train" her new nanny. The nanny's performance and demeanor failed to improve, making Judith increasingly uneasy about leaving her child alone with the nanny. When on-the-job training failed to show any positive results, Judith had had enough and told the nanny it wasn't working out. After paying her through the end of the week and saying good-bye, Judith went into the bathroom and cried. Once again, she faced the endless search for the ever-elusive "perfect" child-care provider. To make matters even worse, Judith's agency insisted that she pay their $1,000 placement fee because the nanny had worked one week over their "return policy limit"!

Judith was frustrated and felt taken advantage of by a system that preys on desperate parents needing affordable, safe, and reliable child care—today. Judith is willing to pay a fair wage. Her toddler, Rebecca, is happy and well-adjusted. Why is it so hard for her to find a child-care provider?

Dan and Karen P.

Dan phoned The ChildCare Registry in a panic the day after he and his wife, Karen, found out they were expecting twins. Dan and Karen already had two boys, Nicholas, age five, and Michael, age three. When Nicholas was born, Karen gave up her job as a flight attendant to stay at home and care for the boys full time; so in the past, they hadn't required the assistance of a nanny, or day- or family day-care center. Also,

Karen's parents lived close by and were happy to take care of Nicholas and Michael on the rare occasions when they went out for the evening.

Now, with the twins coming, things were very different for Dan and Karen. They had moved to a bigger house in the western suburbs of New Jersey, a good hour from Karen's parents. Dan's business was thriving, requiring more time and a lot more travel away from home. Also, the new house was farther away from Dan's office, doubling his commute time. To cope with all these changes and twins on the way, Dan and Karen decided they needed an in-home provider to help with the twins, plus a good day-care or family-care center for Michael that would be close to Nicholas's preschool.

I recommended that Dan begin by narrowing down his requirements for a nanny, by writing a list of his ideal nanny's qualifications. In a nutshell, the result was a description of Mahatma Gandhi, Madame Curie, Mary Poppins, and Lassie rolled into one. His ideal candidate was a triple Ph.D. in child care, nutrition, and physical education; spoke five languages; was an emergency medical technician; and on top of that, had ten or more years of experience in infant care. With some difficulty, I managed to convince Dan to scale back his expectations a bit.

Like most fathers, Dan wanted the best child-care provider on the planet for his kids. And he knew which personal qualities would work well with his kids: a high-energy, outdoorsy type who would challenge the boys physically and intellectually. However, since there is no Harvard M.B.A. degree equivalent for child-care providers, Dan was at a loss to describe the minimum qualifications he required for the job. In addition, he felt odd about the situation because Karen, not he, would be the child-care provider's primary manager.

Elizabeth C.

Elizabeth is a recently divorced, single mother working full time as a paralegal to support her three-year-old daughter, Annie. Although Elizabeth takes home a decent salary, after paying her rent, buying food and other necessities, and paying for Annie's full-time day care, very little is left over. Elizabeth isn't happy with the day-care center Annie currently attends. She has a hard time making it to the center on time every evening because it is so far away from work. Also, since Elizabeth's divorce, the center director has twice told her that Annie's occasional temper tantrums and tears are a negative result of her "newly broken" family, a diagnosis that Annie does not feel comfortable with. Inexplicably, the center handles Annie's "bad" behavior by making her spend what appears to Elizabeth to be an excessive amount of time in time-outs. Because Elizabeth is convinced that Annie is just exhibiting normal three-year-old behavior, she wants to find a new center with staff more in sync with her own parenting style. She also wants to find a center closer to her work. A less expensive center would be nice, too!

How should Elizabeth start her search? Her job gives her little time or flexibility during the week to interview prospective day-care centers in person, or even by phone. Because most day-care centers are closed on the weekend, how can she handle this task? Is day care really the right choice for Elizabeth and Annie? Elizabeth has a few friends who take their children to family day care, but she really doesn't know that much about it. Is a nanny the right choice? Elizabeth has always thought nannies were out of her price range. Are they? How can Elizabeth be sure that the person whom she chooses to care for Annie will have the same parenting style that she has? What interview questions can she ask? Can she glean information on parenting styles of child-care providers from reference checks? And, even if Elizabeth can figure out what to do with Annie this year, what happens when Annie starts kindergarten next year and needs to be picked up at noon? What will Elizabeth do with Annie every afternoon next year?

Judith, Dan and Karen, and Elizabeth are not alone. Most parents have a hard time articulating, prioritizing, and measuring the elusive qualities they want in the person responsible for caring for their child. It's a difficult task—especially if parenthood is new to you. You can start by listing the obvious: experience, common sense, warm and loving personality, clean record, safe driver, CPR training, first aid, maturity. But, just as quickly you ask yourself: How much experience is necessary? What's a reliable measure of maturity? Where can I check to see if a day-care center owner has a criminal record? How do I really know if a family day-care center is licensed? How can I accurately judge a nanny's common sense? This is where most parents stop cold. They realize that this process is not just about hiring a person for any old job. It's not just about setting minimum educational and job experience requirements. This person is going to care for your child. The stakes don't get any higher. How can you ever know enough about the person taking care of your child?

WHY IS CHILD CARE SUCH A PROBLEM?

Child care is a problem for two reasons. The first is that parents are naturally quite uneasy about leaving their child in the care of a stranger. On some primal level, a warning signal shoots through our bodies that says, "No one cares more for my child than I do." So both on a gut and intellectual level most parents find it difficult to surrender their children to the care of strangers.

The second reason is much more subtle. It is simply that we are novices at knowing and understanding child care because most of us were never cared for by child-care providers. It's no wonder that today's single parent or family struggling to make the American dream work for them is confused about how to deal with child care. We feel hesitant and insecure because we can't rely on our own experience to guide us.

A New American Phenomenon

The act of placing your child in the care of a stranger for long periods of time is very new to American society. Even up to the late sixties and early seventies, most children in this country were cared for by their mothers, other family members, or close neighbors and friends. Only the very rich used the services of nannies, and most of the time, these nannies supplemented the mother's care as "mother's helpers." They did not have primary responsibility for the care, custody, and control of children. Mothers took care of children; fathers brought home the bacon. No one questioned this because it was the American Way. Even during World War II, when Rosie the Riveter worked long hours in the armaments factory to serve her country, a grandparent, close friend, or neighbor took care of her child. When the war ended and her husband returned from overseas, Rosie was back at home taking care of the kids. Since the need for full-time child care had been generated by a major, but temporary, national crisis, child care was considered only a temporary problem. Later, the community took over that role. You knew your neighbor well, and she knew you. Your kids went to the same schools. When you mowed your lawn on a Saturday morning, you waved to your neighbor mowing his. Most families lived in close proximity to grandparents who could help with child care. Most mothers had the same daily schedules and, in a pinch, could rely on each other for child care. Or they traded child-care services. Susan watched Sally's boys on Tuesday afternoons when Sally went to her art class. Sally watched Susan's girls when Susan and her husband went to the movies on Saturday night. No one had any impetus to develop a long-term, workable system for the care of young children.

Things changed in the seventies and eighties, when opportunities for women in the workplace expanded. Coincidentally, it also became very difficult for a typical middle-class American family to survive on a single income. Women wanted to work and needed to work. Pregnancy and motherhood could not change this fact. And with full-time work for women came the need for full-time child care.

During this time, the old neighborhoods changed dramatically. Many families left for places far away in search of better opportunities. Strangers suddenly lived in the house next door. In many regions, commuting became the norm, not the exception. No one had the same work hours or the same weekly schedule. Now, when you mow your lawn late on a Tuesday afternoon, your neighbor is just waking up after spending the previous night working the swing shift. In addition, the average number of hours spent at work every week increased dramatically between 1960 and 1990.

These societal changes have made child care an enormous issue that permeates every level of our society and every institution. No one is immune. Not the hard-working couple starting a small business that requires long hours and constant supervision; or the divorced mother and father sharing custody and child-care situations across town, across the state, and across the country; or parents working in major corporate environs where long commutes and lots of out-of-town travel make finding child care even more anxiety-provoking.

Child Care Is Still a Woman's Issue

The other reason for the glacial pace of changes to our current child-care system is the fact that, at bottom, our society still considers child care to be women's responsibility. Thankfully, this situation is changing. As more women become the primary, or at least equal, breadwinners for their families, much of the responsibility for child care will be shared by their male partners. In addition, as predominantly middle-aged, white male corporate boardrooms throughout America slowly change their compositions to better reflect today's workplace, the overwhelming need for high-quality, safe, and affordable child care will finally be recognized and addressed. If the CEO is a woman, and 51 percent–plus of the board of directors, staff, and clients in the United States are women, you can bet the CEO will think that an on-site child-care center is a good investment.

The High Demand for Child Care Hasn't Made It Any Better

There are approximately 7 million women in the United States who are pregnant or have a child less than a year old. According to the 1992 U.S. Census, over half of all new mothers work, and if they take pregnancy leave, most return to work within three months after the birth of their child. By the year 2000, more than 75 percent of mothers with children under ten will be in the work force. If the demand for child care is at an all-time high, why is it still such a problem for parents everywhere? You would think that someone, somewhere, would have figured out a way to make child care better, safer, cheaper, and easier! However, our child-care system hasn't changed at all in response to the huge increase in demand. In fact, it has gotten a lot worse. Because of the huge demand for their time, child-care-service providers have had no incentive to get better. Even if they provide substandard or unsafe services, as long as they are in business they can still hook desperate parents who need someone to care for their child *today* so they can go to work!

Child care is not solved or made any better by throwing money at it. (This is obviously good news for most of us!) Child care is not like buying a car. Most people's experience in buying a car shows that for *x* dollars you can get a car with a defined list of features and functions, and for a little more, some nifty options. By spending a few hours in dealer showrooms, a good consumer can easily create a list of car makes and models that offer comparable functions, features, and options and include prices and availability. Armed with this information, a person can decide which car salesman to make happy. This is true whether you are buying an inexpensive car or some foreign sticker-shocker. It is *not* true for child care. Though you might find someone with unbelievable qualifications applying for your job offering—a registered nurse or unemployed nursery school teacher, for example—it's highly unlikely. There is no wide spectrum of talent, experience, and education offered in child care.

When most people go car shopping, they have a type of car in mind, how much they can afford, and what features they need. Within that price range, it would not be unusual to have a choice of five or six makes and models of cars from different manufacturers offering a comparative range of features. And, even if you haven't shopped for a car in a while and keel over at the prices . . . a little leg work will get you what you want for the price you can afford. Unfortunately, in child care, there is no human equivalent of the Honda Civic at the entry level or a Maserati at the high end of the pay scale. Many parents tell me that even if they wanted to pay more for child care, they can't find "better" child care to buy. Because child care is a career dominated by women, and is not known for its high salaries or golden parachutes, it attracts only the very committed (who work with children because they love it, not because it pays well) and people who "qualify" by virtue of their willingness to work for entry-level wages only slightly above minimum wage. Child care is also an industry with very small operating margins, limited licensing laws, no nationally recognized standards, and no credentialing body with any national stature.

So, if money is no object, I don't think you will have it any easier than the rest of us—you just might pay more for the pleasure of being disappointed. Regardless of what you pay for child care, if you and your child aren't truly benefiting from the experience, even "inexpensive" child care costs too much.

THE CHILDCARE REGISTRY

Although I live outside of San Francisco, where it seems that many good child-care providers could be found, it took me weeks to hire a nanny with credentials and a background I could trust with Katherine's care. I was shocked at how helpless I was, and how little information or guidance was available for interviewing, hiring, and managing child-care providers.

One of the most frustrating problems I encountered was trying to obtain reliable background information on nanny candidates without spending hundreds of dollars on private investigators and waiting many weeks for the information. Even the simplest pieces of information are impossible to verify without professional help. For example, I tried to verify that one of my nanny candidates had a home address and a valid driver's license, and at the same time find out if she had a clean driving record. When I phoned the Department of Motor Vehicles, I was told that in California and most other states, you cannot obtain or verify information through DMV records. The California law was enacted after the actress Rebecca Schafer was killed by a stalker who obtained her address through the DMV.

I didn't have any better luck when it came to researching criminal records. Even though it was possible twenty years ago for my father to threaten to call a friend of his at the police department to "check out" my sister's and my boyfriends (and could do it), local, state, and federal criminal histories are no longer available for review by the ordinary citizen. Law enforcement is now prohibited from divulging any information on a person's criminal record, to the point that the big state and federal databases require special entry codes that identify the person inquiring about the information. It seems that a few years ago, someone infiltrated the law-enforcement ranks and was invading the criminal record databases to find some former "associates" to even the score. When the federal prosecutors realized that their own data was being used to provide information about new identities and whereabouts of case-making witnesses, they shut down general access to the files. So it is virtually impossible for anyone outside the criminal justice system or other government agencies to access driving or criminal records of individuals. This information can be accessed, however, by providing a comprehensive legal release that includes the person's name and any known aliases, date of birth, social security number, and driver's license number. Armed with the correct data, legal release, and the jurisdictions one wants to search, a parent can pay for the information by contacting one of several on-line public record search firms. (While it can be done, it will no doubt be time-consuming and more expensive than using The ChildCare Registry or an investigative company like Pinkerton.)

Even more worrisome for me at the time was the thought that, by checking on someone's background, I might trample on his or her right to privacy, or even worse, expose myself to a lawsuit for breach of privacy. So in 1992, after one full year of worrying that my nanny had something in her background that I should know about, I decided to spend some time working on an idea for a new business, something that had never been tried before but was truly necessary to me and to parents everywhere.

After many hours of reading and research, I found that parents bringing child-care providers into their homes are not the only group experiencing doubts about the suitability of the caregivers they are hiring. I was astounded to find that there is no federal minimum standard for qualifications or comprehensive background checks for the child-care providers who own, manage, or work in day care and family day-care centers. Deeper research really upset me. Not only is there no single standard but each state also has its own list of licensing requirements! This means that we have fifty very different sets of laws governing child care that act more like sieves than barriers to entry for inappropriate and unqualified persons who want to care for our children.

With this disturbing piece of information as my impetus, I decided to try to create a quick and cost-effective "national registry" for child-care providers that would give parents all of the background information they need to hire and then entrust their child to the care of a nanny, day-care provider, or family day-care provider.

To get started, I held in-depth focus groups on child-care issues with friends and business associates, all experienced parents. I found that their complaints echoed mine. It was very difficult, sometimes impossible, to hire a child-care provider with a background they could rely on. Even worse, after they managed to find and then hire a provider, many discovered that their problems had just begun.

I was sure I was on the right track after my focus groups, so I solicited the help of many friends and child-care professionals and founded The ChildCare Registry (CCR), a national child-care-provider preemployment screening and résumé-verification service. CCR provides parents throughout the United States with fast, inexpensive, legally released and accurate verification of a child-care provider's identity, social security number, date of birth, residences, education, employment references, driving record, and criminal and civil records in every jurisdiction of residence for the previous seven years. Right from the start, however, I knew that CCR's services would give parents a solution to only one small part their overall problem with child care. The system itself still needs a lot of work.

But we can't just wait around for these changes to happen. As parents who want the very best for our children, we must effect change ourselves. Parents everywhere can take action to make child care better, safer, and more affordable now by providing their child-care provider with a "real job," real responsibilities, definable skills, and respect. Parents must set standards, hire legally, manage professionally, and settle for nothing less. If we parents, as consumers, set market standards and commit to them, then plenty of good, highly qualified candidates will emerge. We must resolve to change child care for the better because if we don't, no one will. No one else has as much at stake.

CHAPTER TWO

Inform Yourself about Your Options

IN THIS CHAPTER:	*A Brief Overview of:*
	Nannies
	Au pairs
	Baby-sitters
	Family Day Care
	Day Care
	Care for Your Older Child

TYPES OF CARE

This chapter gives you an overview of your child-care options by type. Even if you come to this book knowing which type of child care you need, it will serve you well to review quickly all the choices out there so you're completely aware of the advantages, disadvantages, and responsibilities involved in each choice. More importantly, you never know when you may need to switch quickly to another option: Your live-in nanny may elope and call you with her resignation from Acapulco, or your day-care center may lose its lease and be locked up by the landlords overnight, leaving you to find alternate care immediately. You'll quickly learn that getting day care on two hours' notice is nearly impossible!

After your research in this chapter, you should be able to move quickly through the legal issues presented in Chapter Three and start working through the Needs Assessment worksheets and calendars in Chapter Four. You'll get a much closer look at your child-care choice later. For now, take a hard look at our overview of each option or combination of options available to you.

You May Need a Combination of Choices

Remember that many parents find they must combine two or three different kinds of child-care services to provide for all twenty-four hours in their child's busy day, especially if their jobs require frequent travel, commuting, or nontraditional work schedules. For example, when Katherine was two, I enrolled her in a day-care center playgroup a couple of mornings a week for more socialization. Although we already had two graduate students caring for her about 30 hours a week, I thought an organized program with good supervision and lots of kids would be good for Katherine. It turned out to be a wonderful experience for both of us, but necessitated my researching day-care centers, the programs they offered, and licensing laws, not to mention much juggling of my graduate students' schedules. If you think that a combination of choices may be appropriate for your family, spend some time with this overview and expand your universe of choices.

UNIVERSAL MINIMUM REQUIREMENTS FOR ANY CHILD-CARE PROVIDER

Although it's sometimes difficult to identify which issue ranks first in the swirling mass of issues that make up the child-care problem, I believe I've found a clear leader for number one: The hundreds of parents I've asked have overwhelmingly agreed that the fact that there are no clear, universal minimum requirements for child-care providers has made hiring nannies and choosing day- and family-care centers a frightening task. Although many groups involved in child care have issued various recommendations for hiring good child-care providers, as far as I know, no one has ever issued concrete standards that parents can rely on to ensure that the child-care provider they hire is qualified and safe. This book will. Standardization of required skills, experience, and training for child-care providers is the only way to professionalize the industry and give parents the guidance they so desperately need.

Remember, these rules are universal. They can be applied to every kind of child care that is *unsupervised* by a parent. Whether working for five minutes or five hours, part-time or full-time, in home or at a center, the person caring for your child must be prepared for any eventuality.

Note that the following list is divided into two sections, "Objectively Verifiable" and "Subjective Qualities." Objectively verifiable requirements are those that you can verify by reviewing a document, or through the help of a third party, whether it's a private investigator, a service like The ChildCare Registry, or a state or federal government agency. Subjective qualities are the positive, personal characteristics that you must try to identify during interviews and when doing reference checks.

While the list of objectively verifiable qualifications may seem obvious, and while many centers and nonprofit organizations that offer child-care services do require some of them, no U.S. state agency requires all of these as a condition for licensing a day-care or family day-care center employee.

Objectively verifiable:

- certified in infant and child CPR
- trained in first aid
- previous experience as unsupervised provider or at least one year as supervised provider
- clean criminal record for at least five years
- clean driving record for DUI offenses for at least three years
- insured, licensed driver
- high school diploma or GED
- no civil judgments involving children or child-care license revocation

Subjective qualities:

- personal maturity
- responsible/dependable
- adaptable
- fun-loving
- respectful of personal life-style choices
- warm/caring
- good rapport with children
- even-tempered

Universal Minimum Standards for Parents

I'm not going to let parents off the hook. To make child care better and safer, we need to hold ourselves to a higher standard in our dealings with our child-care providers, and go one step further. We must become consumer activists and (1) require our federal, state, and local governments to create uniform licensing laws; (2) make fast, inexpensive background checks of child-care providers the law (insist that the investigations are legally released and that such information is available for review by authorized parents to protect the privacy of providers); and (3) make sure that the child-care licensing laws in all states are funded and enforced. Let our legislators know that if budget cuts threaten licensing laws, citizens must be made aware of that fact so they can take private measures to protect their children. Here are rules for parents.

- Hire legally.
- Pay legally.
- Manage professionally.
- Provide a caregiver's future employer with honest performance evaluations.
- Become a child-care consumer activist.

IN-HOME CARE

You are hiring an "in-home" child-care-service provider when you pay a nanny, au pair, or baby-sitter to come into your home specifically to care for your children.

An in-home provider is your employee, and you are his or her employer. All of the rights, duties, and responsibilities that go along with an employee-employer relationship in the business world are at play when you hire an in-home child-care provider. And, as in the business world, the most successful employee-employer relationships are those where both parties clearly understand their rights, duties, and responsibilities to each other from day one.

It's critical that you start your relationship with your child-care provider on the right foot. To do this, you need to determine exactly who and what you are looking for, and you must be able to articulate it clearly—to your spouse, to any and all candidates for the job, to a placement agency, to a resource and referral agency (R&R), and to anyone else who can help you hire the right person.

With this in mind, let's begin by taking a look at the three most common types of in-home child-care services: nanny, au pair, and baby-sitter. Remember, this chapter just provides you with an overview that will familiarize you with your child-care options. Details on each of your options and specific tools for locating, hiring, managing, and motivating the child-care provider of your choice are available in later chapters.

NANNIES

A nanny is someone whose sole responsibility while "on the job" is to provide a safe, controlled, happy, and playful environment for your children. By definition, a nanny is an experienced, paid, unsupervised employee who is meant to maintain household rules and care for your children in the manner you prescribe.

My First Nanny

The first nanny I hired lasted less than six months. She was a full-time live-in who had told me during our final interview that she was a "tax fugitive" and needed to be paid under the table. This was a candidate I had received through a local nanny placement agency, to which I would pay a fee equal to one month of the nanny's salary (about $1,500), not including room and board and perks. Becoming her tax-avoidance coconspirator was news to me, since neither the candidate nor the agency had told me of the need for a special financial arrangement. I concluded the interview with the candidate, who seemed to be qualified and had the experience with preemies I wanted, and resigned myself to initiating interviews with a new round of candidates. Unfortunately, it took my representative at the agency, who seemed miffed that I had not signed the tax fugitive, a full week to round up any new candidates.

I was ready to hire anyone who would allow me to take a nap. I hadn't slept more than three hours a night since Katherine had arrived home from the hospital. Now I knew why they use sleep deprivation to break spies. Ravenous but

continues

unable to eat more than four ounces at a time, preemies eat more often than fully mature newborns. Even with Bill's help during the night, I needed someone to help during the day. After the drugs, stress, and physical trauma of Katherine's birth, the joy of having her home was being shadowed by my inability to stay awake and enjoy it. I desperately needed help during the day so I could be available at night, at least for the next six to eight weeks. After that, Katherine would probably be on a more accommodating sleeping and eating schedule. So it was a cranky and disoriented Ellen who began her first and last interview with a new candidate I will call "Nanny De Sade."

Nanny De Sade's appearance and demeanor made me feel quite guilty even though I had managed to shower and put on clean clothes prior to our interview. My sleep deprivation had made getting out of bed a major triumph for me on that day, but somehow, once seated in my living room facing Ms. De Sade, I felt less than triumphant. I offered her some coffee, which she refused, and started rambling. Just like an utterly broken, sleep-deprived spy, I found myself going on and on about Katherine's birth; what a miracle baby she was; how cute she was; and so on. Ms. De Sade sipped the water she had requested in lieu of coffee, smiled sympathetically, and otherwise didn't move a muscle. When I finally realized that I was rambling far too much, I apologized and said, "I hope I haven't bored you, but I think it's very important that you understand our situation and how much help we need." To my surprise she replied, "That's okay, but I have another interview in forty-five minutes, so we'll need to wrap this up soon." So much for warm and fuzzy. I picked up her résumé—it was one of the few I had received, and the only one that wasn't full of cross-outs and handwritten additions—and understood immediately why it was so professional. Ms. De Sade was a personal assistant, not a nanny. She had been employed by various companies over the past six years and had no child-care experience at all, unless being the aunt of a twelve-year-old counted. I concluded the interview as nicely as I could, trying to hide my disappointment, by telling Ms. De Sade that I really needed someone with more experience in child care, especially in the care of preemies. To this she replied, "I may not know much about playing with children, but I do know how to discipline them." That was enough for me. After saying good-bye, and silently telling her to give my best to the Marquis, I called the agency, only to get their answering machine. Great. Once again back to square one.

I phoned Bill and told him that a secretary had shown up for my nanny interview. He reminded me that the job description I had written for the agency included secretarial tasks that were to be completed when the nanny was not caring for Katherine. According to my description, she was to open mail, return phone calls, arrange appointments, and make travel arrangements when Katherine was napping or with me. I thought I had made it clear that these tasks were "filler," but instead I had confused the job description so much that I was getting candidates qualified for the optional secretarial duties but not for the necessary child-care responsibilities.

That's why it's important to take time to identify your real needs. First, decide if you really do want your child-care provider to do other duties. He certainly can do other things in the hours when he is not caring for your child, but these tasks must be described to an agency and to the provider as "light"— light cleaning, light typing, light cooking—otherwise, you will end up with a housekeeper, secretary, or cook instead of a child-care provider.

I ended up calling back that first nanny—the only one with real experience—and agreed to increase her base salary to help compensate her for the wage garnishing the IRS would initiate after I notified them that she was gainfully—and legally—employed. Although she lasted only six months (she got tired of being on the up and up with the IRS after they started garnishing part of her net wages also), she turned out to be a decent nanny.

What I Learned from My First Nanny

After that experience, I felt I could recite my mistakes chronologically and alphabetically. Here are the lessons I learned:

- Be precise about your real needs with the agency and the nanny.

- Don't mix jobs. If you need a child-care provider, hire a child-care provider, not a secretary, cook, or housekeeper.

continues

- Do a comprehensive background check. If I had done one on my first nanny, I would have found out before I hired her that she owed thousands of dollars more to the IRS than she told us. I also would have found out that she had not had a legal, taxpaying job in more than four years. If I had known this, I probably would have questioned her resolve to come clean with the IRS.

- Put everything in writing. You don't know how many disagreements I had with my first nanny over what was actually said or agreed to during the interview and contract negotiation stage.

By now I had learned a lot about the process and would never make the same mistakes again.

If You Think You Need a Nanny

If you choose to hire a nanny, you are faced with a number of decisions. Depending on your family's schedule and needs, a nanny can be full-time or part-time. Full-time is generally twenty-five to forty hours a week, and part-time is generally less than twenty-five hours a week. If you have an extra bedroom and don't mind trading some of your family's private time for added flexibility, a full-time nanny can live in your house. Otherwise, she can live in another location and commute to your house for work. If you wish, your nanny can help you drive the children to and from appointments, school, or after-school activities (she'll need a driver's license and insurance, which we'll discuss later in Chapter Five) or assist with some of the household cooking and cleaning. Start thinking about your ideal nanny's job description now—you will need to make some solid decisions as you work through the Needs Assessment worksheet in Chapter Four.

Remember that, as an employer, you are responsible for setting regular work hours, a fair rate of pay, and benefits and vacation policy. You are also responsible for complying with all state and federal employment and immigration laws, and paying taxes for unemployment insurance, social security, and worker's compensation each time you pay your nanny.

Nannies, whether live-in or live-out, will be more expensive than either day-care centers or family day care by virtue of the fact that you bear the burden of the entire cost yourself. However, there can be no denying the benefits of your children having the undivided attention of a well-managed, well-trained, happily employed provider.

Prerequisites for any person you are considering employing as a nanny are the "minimum provider requirements" discussed on page 15, but you should also consider the following criteria. (Remember: This is just a brief overview. Look for more details on locating, interviewing, and reference and background checking in Chapter Five.)

Experience vs. Education. Practical experience in child care is far more important than education. Look at your child-care provider candidate as most companies now view M.B.A.'s. M.B.A.'s are great; they indicate that the person has engaged in dedicated, specialized study in a business school that is credentialed by the appropriate educational bodies. But the important thing is that the candidate has also interned at one or more businesses and has been graded and reviewed regarding his or her performance and grasp of sophisticated, real-world business issues. The M.B.A. degree is just icing on the cake. Since child care has no M.B.A. equivalent that parents can use as a guide, and since there are no tests to pass or boards of review that can accurately evaluate a provider's qualifications, experience is the key element to look for.

In order for you to entrust your child to a provider, you must be able to feel confident that she can manage all situations by herself, without your supervision. This requires two elements: First, that the provider is "qualified" by virtue of experience, maturity, and skills; and second, that you as parent and manager have fully briefed the provider on how you would like her to handle various situations. Of course, there is no way that your provider can know how you would act in every situation, especially early in her employment with you. However, as a caring parent and responsible employer you should continually assess your provider for strengths and weaknesses and spend time every week building on the strengths and working together one by one on the weaknesses. Don't overreact to weaknesses—we all have them—but work with your provider to identify them and overcome them. This is the part of managing child care that takes a significant amount of time and skill. However, it can make all the difference in the world, and can change an average provider into someone who is gaining new skills and confidence. I'll give you plenty of guidelines for positive management of your nanny in Chapter Six.

Your Nanny Needs a Warm and Loving Personality. Although experience and common sense are paramount, in the absence of warmth and love, all the experience and common sense in the world won't make your child happy with your nanny. When parents ask me what level of warmth and love is appropriate in a nanny, I always tell them to think about their first-grade teacher. First-grade teachers seem to give children just the right degree of warmth, love, and attention. Too little warmth is not what your child deserves from his caregiver. On the other hand, an excess of warmth can lead to identity and separation problems and other uncomfortable issues you don't want to deal with, including parent and provider jealousy.

The fundamental role of a child-care provider is to supplement the parents' role, not replace or contradict it. It is critical that your nanny understands your desire for appropriate warmth and closeness, and does not confuse the relationship by becoming a pseudofamily member. Although there are abuses on both sides of the parent and provider relationship, I have spoken to far too many parents who are resigned to keeping a nanny they would otherwise terminate because they are being manipulated by an inappropriately close relationship fostered by the nanny with the child. Though we all hope for continuity in our children's care, being held hostage by your nanny says more about your lack of attention to managing the nanny than it does about the nanny's relationship with your child. Don't confuse the issues. Set clear guidelines and manage the relationship.

Au Pairs

An "au pair" is typically an English-speaking European woman between eighteen and twenty-five years old who has received a one-year cultural exchange visa that allows her to trade forty-five hours of child care for room, board, modest compensation, and day-to-day life in an American family.

Although an au pair is responsible for helping you care for your children, your au pair is not your "employee," per se. To be frank, an au pair's relationship with a family is frequently closer to guest than to employee. If you are considering an au pair, remember that the term "au pair" is French for "on par"—meaning equal to members of the family. They should be treated as such.

Au pairs are significantly less expensive than nannies. However, this is because their responsibilities are supposed to be fewer. Although your au pair may be highly responsible and have plenty of child-care experience, caring for your child is not necessarily your au pair's number-one priority. Gaining insight into American culture is her number-one priority. If you don't keep this in mind, you could very easily lose your au pair and be stuck back at square one with no child-care provider at all.

My Au Pair Experience

Many parents describe their experience with an au pair as similar to "having a teenage child in the house." They say that they went through all of the angst and agony of being a teenager all over again with their au pairs. I can certainly relate to their perspective because I went through the same thing. In 1992, after Katherine's hip surgery, I contracted with a nationally known au pair agency. I requested a young woman from the U.K. because that is where my grandparents and my husband's grandparents came from at the turn of the century. I filled out what seemed to be a lot of paper work about our family and sent it off. Within a couple of weeks we were "approved," which I thought was interesting because none of the information I forwarded seemed to have been verified, but the hefty deposit check for the agency's even heftier fee had been cashed. About a week later I received a call from a local area coordinator who wanted to "see our house." We arranged a mutually agreeable time and the coordinator arrived, with her ten-year-old daughter in tow. After a house tour, I asked a few more questions, but frankly felt ill at ease asking more in-depth questions in front of the daughter. With a promise that we were to be highly recommended, the coordinator left.

Over the next two weeks I received copies of completed questionnaires on various Irish and British au pair candidates. The questionnaires had a picture and factoids about each girl, including a personal statement on why she wanted to be an au pair. Although each one mentioned child-care experience,

continues

most were vague, and since most candidates weren't over twenty-one, I figured their experience couldn't be that extensive anyway. I was encouraged to call each candidate of my choice at their home to interview them. Unfortunately, the first three I called had already accepted placements, so my calls were an expensive waste of time. And, since the next planeload of au pairs was due to leave in less than three weeks, and the information on each candidate had been circling prospective parents for the last eight weeks, I was beginning to worry about the suitability of the pool of candidates that was left. Within a day I received a new batch of candidates and quickly settled on Miss U.K., a postal worker, twenty-one years of age. U.K.'s application told of a few teenage baby-sitting assignments and of helping a very close friend who was a recent mother. Her attached photo showed a chipper face with a warm smile and an air of maturity. I called her at home, managed to reach her, and was pleasantly surprised that her picture seemed to be an accurate depiction of her personality—as far as one can tell over the phone. I told her about Katherine, our family, where we lived, what type of duties she would have, what her room in our house would be like, and what our plans for the summer would be. U.K. was thrilled to hear that we lived in California and that she would have the use of a car. She said all the right things about loving children, and we agreed to speak the next day after she had spoken to her parents. When I told my husband about her, he agreed that she was the best we had seen and that, barring any overt change in attitude or facts, and after speaking to her parents, we should extend her an offer.

I called as agreed the next day and got U.K.'s mother. As warm and pleasant as her daughter, U.K.'s mom expressed enthusiasm for her daughter's venture and spoke of her in loving terms. U.K. then got on the phone and the conversation resumed where it had left off the previous day. We agreed to sponsor her for the one-year commitment. I called the agency, gave them the go-ahead, and sent the plane fare.

U.K.'s itinerary called for her to leave England with about twenty other au pairs and travel to New York for a three-day orientation with the agency before traveling to her new "home." On the day U.K. arrived in New York, I called her at her hotel and spoke to a jet-lagged and very subdued young lady. The agency had some get-acquainted briefings and some fun excursions planned, so we didn't talk long. I told her I would be at the airport to meet her later in the week.

A few days later, I met an even more jet-lagged and subdued young lady at the San Francisco Airport. But even through her fatigue, it was apparent that U.K. had a winsome smile and dry British wit. U.K. and Katherine became quick pals. With U.K. safely ensconced in her room, I planned the next week for her, which included a shopping trip and lessons from a local driving company to acclimate her to driving on the right side of the road. And, because U.K. would only be working twenty hours a week and Katherine's other two part-time nannies would still be working, though on reduced hours, U.K. would still have plenty of time to adjust to her new position after she got used to the time change and caught up on some sleep.

I didn't begin to really worry until after the third day of red, teary eyes and a hand constantly full of tissues. "Allergies?" I asked. "Nooooo," she sniffled. "Just a little homesick." After the fifth day, the crying had not abated and a new problem emerged. Sadness. Unrelenting, morose sadness. I encouraged U.K. to call her parents and friends back in England, hoping it would make her feel better. She did, but there was no improvement. Although her exposure to Katherine was still limited and chaperoned, I became increasingly worried about how she would manage alone. I felt awful, but I knew U.K. felt worse.

At the end of the week, I called the au pair agency's local area coordinator. She called back four days later, but by then I had called the agency headquarters back East for advice. After reading me all the clauses in my contract that stated that U.K. had to stay with us, the agency representative asked to speak to U.K. After a few minutes, she was crying hysterically. Essentially, the agency read her the riot act and then told that she would forfeit her deposit (over 500 pounds or $1,000) if she didn't get her act together. Great! It doesn't take a psychiatrist to know that the cure for homesickness is not intimidation. After U.K. placed a call to her parents that made her feel a little better, she apologized profusely and promised to try harder. The poor kid. She cried and apologized for the next week.

continues

Meanwhile I was getting nothing done. I lurched from trying to shore up U.K. to patching together a work schedule for the other providers to keeping a vigilant eye on Katherine's reaction to an increasingly morose "playmate." It wasn't working. Perhaps a change of venue would help?

My original plan of leaving Katherine with Bill and three nannies for the weekend I had to go to New York was quickly becoming an Ellen, Katherine, and U.K. trip to New York. I thought that the change, a visit to my parents in New Jersey, and some time alone with Katherine and myself might perk U.K. up. I was wrong. By the middle of the second day in New York, I realized that U.K. was getting worse and that the only humane thing to do would be to send her home. My call to the agency was the same as the call two weeks before: Did I understand the terms of the contract and that the agency would replace U.K. with another au pair if she chose to go home? U.K. would lose her deposit (as if she cared by now) and she would have to pay her own way home.

Almost as distraught as U.K., I decided to call her parents from New York and advise them of my decision to fly her back. What I found out made me even more crazy. It seems that the whole au pair jaunt was her father's idea and was meant to heal a broken romance and a "dead end" job at the post office. Of course the poor kid was homesick. She wanted to fly halfway across the world for a year like she wanted a root canal with no anesthesia. Since U.K. was clearly frightened of her father's reaction, I agreed to call and talk to him to let him know that we supported her decision to return to England.

I explained the depth of his daughter's misery and had a frank discussion with him about his daughter's comparable lack of maturity for her age and what can only be called terminal shyness. He agreed, and explained that that was why he had sent her to the United States. Without knowing it, I had been the person charged with helping her gain maturity and come out of her shell.

Now I perceived the root of many misconceptions with the au pair system. Potential au pairs and their families are pitched a cultural experience or exchange along with a very romanticized view of life in America. Certainly, the concept of exchanging the experience of living in the United States for work as a child-care provider is highlighted, but like anyone who is selling something, the agencies probably paint a picture of more fun and frolic than work. Not surprisingly, U.K.'s father thought of this one year "exchange" as a kind of finishing school. I have subsequently found out that many au pairs and their families think of the year as a "travel-the-USA, go-to-school, find-a-husband adventure." U.S. parents, of course, are encouraged to think they are getting qualified, experienced, live-in child care for one year at rock-bottom wages. No wonder there are such egregious abuses of the relationships on the part of both au pairs and parents.

After having to deal with U.K.'s problems virtually alone without any support from the agency, I now believe that the agency unscrupulously "parks" au pairs with families, while betting on the parents' desperate need for child care, especially cheap child care. If a parent gets out of line, they get whacked in the head with the contract.

If You Think You Need an Au Pair

An au pair will be able to provide you with forty-five hours of child care per week for the program year, essentially full-time care. The forty-five hours a week can include some light housework associated with child care—laundry, cooking meals for your child, and straightening up your child's room and play area—but cannot include what would be considered "heavy" chores like yard work, scrubbing floors, and cleaning windows. In return, you'll need to provide your au pair with one and a half days off per week and a modest stipend—around $100 a week, a private room, preferably a private bathroom, and three meals a day, snacks, and so on. You must also give your au pair two weeks of paid vacation, to be taken at a mutually agreed-upon time. If your au pair will be driving your car, you must provide her with automobile insurance. You are not required to pay for health insurance for your au pair, although you will need to work out who pays for any medical expenses not covered by health insurance. Your au pair will not need her own private telephone line, although you may want to give her one. Again, you'll need to work out who pays the bill.

If you decide that an au pair is what you need, make sure you insist on at least the following list of prerequisite guidelines. These can be confirmed by your review of certification papers and diligent reference checking on the part of the au pair agency.

General Guidelines for Hiring an Au Pair

Remember: This is just a brief overview. Look for more details in Chapter Five.

- Check whether she is currently certified in CPR, infant CPR, and first aid.

- Interview her thoroughly by telephone to make sure she has the skills and experience you require. Does she seem to have a warm and loving personality?

- If possible, call the families she has baby-sat for in the past for references, and include direct questions about the amount of time she was unsupervised.

- Make sure you feel comfortable with her level of maturity. This is a subjective issue, and is usually dependent on first impressions. Was she able to communicate well with you during your telephone interview?

If you read magazines or watch some of the current tabloid television shows, you know about some of the other potential perils of hiring an au pair. Cases like the one where the "Swiss nanny" was accused of burning to death the child in her care bring to light the important issue of background information. Even though the jury rendered a "not guilty" verdict in that case, at the time of this writing the family is suing the au pair agency because they found out the au pair lied on her application and fabricated her references and experience. The fact that the agency didn't discover the fabrications doesn't jibe with their marketing materials that assure parents that all au pairs are "carefully screened."

As a result of this case and others like it, the United States Information Agency (USIA), the federal agency that regulates au pair programs, has issued new rules that took effect January 1, 1995, and that require au pairs to undergo more extensive reference checking and a background investigation, including a criminal records check. This is a step in the right direction, but parents please take note: Full-scale background checks are not currently available for au pairs. The agencies can and must do comprehensive reference checking, but European criminal, civil, and driving records are to date inaccessible to

American investigators. We hope that access will be facilitated in the future, but in the meantime, until background-check technology has evolved to the point where such records are fully available, I'd recommend that you spend a little more money to hire a nanny with a clean record you can rely on.

Baby-sitters

For the purposes of this book, a baby-sitter is what I was in 1965: a young, inexperienced caregiver who generally needs adult supervision and plenty of guidance. Hired on an irregular basis to provide short periods of care, a baby-sitter should work four to five hours or less. Baby-sitters are usually paid by the hour and tend to be the child of family friends or acquaintances.

In the late spring and summer of 1965, when I was twelve years old and getting ready to enter my freshman year of high school in the fall, I was Wanda and Linda Davis's baby-sitter. The Davis girls, who were five and seven at the time, lived two houses away from my house. On the nights I was to sit, Mr. and Mrs. Davis would have the girls already fed, bathed, in bed, and asleep by the time I arrived. Amply supplied with pretzels, Coke, and a *TV Guide*, I was given the phone number where I could reach them, told when they would return, and encouraged to call my mother if I needed anything. I was paid $1 an hour, but always got $5 even though the Davises were invariably home well before midnight. Except for the titillating sense that I was all alone, which I liked, I found baby-sitting boring. Once in a while, I would watch Wanda and Linda and my own little sister, Sally, in my family's fenced backyard, but that job boiled down to my ignoring them as much as I could while they played with their Barbies. In truth, I was always supervised. I was the juice fetcher, potty taker, and arbiter of small disputes. If anything went wrong, I could call for help—my own mother was 150 yards away.

Most important, I was not a child-care provider as defined by this book. I wasn't, and frankly couldn't be, an unsupervised employee who had responsibility for the care, feeding, and socialization of small children.

Except in an emergency, baby-sitters should not drive your child anywhere, and should not be given the responsibility of bathing your child and making meals, especially if they are tending more than one child. Pizza or meals that you have prepared ahead of time are sufficient. With younger children, it may be helpful to schedule your baby-sitter to arrive after your child has gone to sleep.

Because baby-sitters have limited exposure to your child, they don't know very much about your child and require very specific instructions from you: "You may reach me at 555–9276. Suzy can have one cookie and can watch the video we rented for her. She can stay up until we get home."

Because background checks cannot be performed on people under the age of eighteen, it is important that a baby-sitter under eighteen is supervised. Experience must be your guide here. Because you don't have objectively verifiable information for experience, education, and other critical issues to rely on, you can't use the same criteria for evaluating a baby-sitter as you would a nanny.

General Guidelines for Hiring a Baby-sitter

Remember: This is just a brief overview. Look for more details on locating, interviewing, and reference and background checking in Chapter Five.

- Check whether she is currently certified in CPR, infant CPR, and first aid.

- Call the families she has worked for in the past for references, and include direct questions about the amount of time she was unsupervised.

- Interview her thoroughly to make sure she has the skills and experience you require.

- Make sure you feel comfortable with her level of maturity. This is a subjective issue, and is usually dependent on first impressions. Was she on time for your first meeting? Does she seem organized, able to communicate well, able to differentiate work time from social time? Does she seem obsessed with nails and makeup? In general, try to use the same tests that you use with your own kids to decide if they are ready for responsibility.

- If the baby-sitter is over eighteen, do a comprehensive, multistate background check that includes a review of driving, criminal, and civil records in every jurisdiction where the baby-sitter has lived during the previous five years. Complete details about how to do a background check are included in Chapter Five.

Pros and Cons of In-Home Care

In-home care has the following advantages:

- It is by far the most flexible child-care option currently available. You can set a provider's schedule to fit your own schedule. Family day-care and day-care centers are open for a certain number of hours only, and these are strictly enforced.

- If you require child care on the weekends or evenings, or if you are a frequent traveler, you can schedule care.

- You can arrange to bring your nanny on your family vacation, so that both you and your kids get a chance to relax.

- If your child is sick, you will have care. Family day-care and day-care centers have strict rules to prevent parents from dropping off sick kids.

- If you have two children and the older child is too sick to go to school or is on school vacation, your in-home provider can care for that child also.

- You don't need to spend time driving your child to and from a family-care or day-care center.

- You set your child's daily meal, nap, and play schedule.

- Your child doesn't need to adjust to new faces or a new setting. He plays with his own toys and sleeps in his own bed.

- Your child may not get as many colds or other illnesses, because she won't be exposed to as many germs as she would in a family day-care or day-care center.

- If your child has any special physical or emotional requirements, in-home care may provide him with the most comfortable, secure environment and one-on-one attention.

- Your nanny may also perform household duties, such as light dusting and vacuuming, preparation of some meals, or your child's laundry.

- If you have two or more children, in-home child care may be less expensive than family day-care or day-care services.

However, in-home child care can have the following drawbacks:

- In most cases, it is the most expensive child-care option available.

- Your child may be isolated, unless you have a regular playgroup or set frequent play dates with other children.

- If the provider quits without notice, you may be left without care, and it could take you a long time to find another suitable provider.

- If the provider is sick or late, you may be left without care.
- Unlike at a family day-care or day-care center, no one is supervising your nanny when you aren't home.
- In-home child-care providers are completely unregulated by the state or federal government.
- A degree of family privacy is lost when you bring someone into your home to care for your child, especially if she or he lives with you.
- As an employer, you are required to know and comply with all applicable state and federal regulations, and pay unemployment insurance, worker's compensation, and social security taxes.

GROUP CHILD CARE

Parents have two choices if they are considering group child care: family day care or day-care centers.

Family Day Care

Family day care is child care provided in someone else's home. Family day care is based on the age-old child-care model our parents, grandparents, and great-grandparents used, that of paid or unpaid child care provided by a family member, close friend, or neighbor in the comfort of their own home. Now, however, there is one critical difference in the arrangement: Today it is more likely that you don't know the care provider very well, if at all. You probably have neither a personal history nor a business history with the person who will be caring for your child.

These days, family day care can be an ongoing business, or it can be a more temporary service provided by a parent staying home for a couple of years to care for his own child, but who would still like to bring in a little money to keep the family financially afloat.

Family day care is minimally regulated by states. The regulatory scheme that governs day-care centers is generally not applicable to family day-care centers. Most family day-care homes are not regulated at all—no FBI checks, no set child/teacher ratios, no programming requirements, no food safety requirements, no building or fire code compliance, and so on. As a parent you need to be very aware of the standards that apply in your state or you will be running a huge risk.

Also, facilities sponsored and owned by religious institutions are unregulated in most states. We'll discuss this type of family day care in more detail in Chapter Seven.

Even in those states that do regulate family day care, those regulations depend on the number of children the provider cares for. In many states, family day-care providers caring for one to three children are exempt from the regulations. A family day-care provider who takes on more than three children becomes subject to state regulations that vary widely from state to state and can include meeting certain fire and health standards, medical examinations, TB screening, child abuse index clearance, criminal records check, fingerprinting, and periodic inspections. Chapter Seven will delve into all of the complexities of family day-care regulatory schemes so that you will understand exactly what your state's regulations cover.

I strongly suggest that you require the family day-care provider, and anyone else in the provider's household over the age of eighteen, to submit to a comprehensive, national background investigation. By doing this, you can protect your child from a provider or household member with an inappropriate or downright dangerous criminal record. But remember: This does not protect your child from anyone under the age of eighteen in the household! (In most states records of any and all criminal proceedings against minors are sealed under court order and cannot be reviewed by anyone.)

Unregulated Family Day-Care Providers

You may decide that a smaller, unregulated family day-care home is more appropriate for you. These are usually quite affordable and are often offered by family members, close friends, and neighbors. However, there are two major disadvantages to unregulated child care. First, as stated above, there are no regulations to ensure safety and health-related issues. Second, it can be more difficult to manage and motivate your provider if she is a family member or close friend.

If you feel comfortable having a family member or close friend provide you with family day-care services, there are a few things you can do to avoid problems. First, be clear up front about your requirements, and second, draft a comprehensive legal agreement using the Legal Kit in Appendix 1. This way, there will be none of the false expectations, misconceptions, or misunderstandings so prevalent when people mix business with friendship or family.

The Prerequisites for Family Day-Care Homes

Remember, this is an overview. Later in the book, I'll give you more information on what to look for in family day-care homes, and a number of tools you can use to locate, hire, manage, and motivate a family day-care provider:

Personal Qualities of the Provider

- Experience. Be sure to check references.
- Good reputation. Ask neighbors or other parents that you meet at the provider's home.
- Good physical and mental health, plus lots of energy.
- Warm and loving personality.
- Organized, professional management of the center.
- Excellent communication skills.

Health/Safety of Facility

- Complies with any family day-care home regulations in your state.
- Free of accident, fire, or health hazards (presence of childproof sockets, locked drawers, high medicine chests, and so on).
- Adequate fire extinguishers and smoke detectors in all areas of home.
- First aid certification.
- Infant/child CPR certification of provider.
- Adequate controls for heating, ventilation, and lighting.
- Easy-to-reach telephone.
- Clean criminal record, child abuse record, and neglect record for every adult in home.
- Family medication out of reach.
- Home clean and pest-free.
- Family pets kept away from children.
- Good, balanced meals are prepared for children.

Child-Care Space

- Enough play space.
- Napping space for infants and older children.
- Appropriately sized children's furniture and baby furniture.

- Storage space for each child's belongings.
- Playground nearby.
- Age- and gender-appropriate toys and equipment with plenty of variety.
- Large enough area to accommodate all children during inclement weather.

Pros and Cons of Family Day Care

Family day care has the following advantages:

- In most regions of the country, it is the least expensive child-care option.
- Some family day-care care providers have more flexible hours than day-care-center providers.
- Your child may feel more comfortable in a homelike atmosphere.
- Depending on the number of children in the home, your child may receive more personal attention than he would in a day-care center.
- Some family day-care providers will care for a mildly ill child.

Family day care has the following disadvantages:

- In most states it is unregulated.
- Family day-care providers can call in sick.
- Your child may be sick more often—and as a result you may be sick more often—because of his exposure to other children.
- Other family members, whom you don't know and over whom you have virtually no control, have access to your child.
- Family day care is often a temporary business that operates on a shoestring. It may close, or go out of business, just when you most need it.
- Family day-care providers may not have set policies or procedures—you could be surprised by a sudden change in a policy or procedure you have come to rely on, like closing hours.
- Depending on the number of children the provider cares for, your child may receive less personal attention than he would in a day-care center.
- There may not be as many toys, games, and activities as you would find in a day-care center or in your own home.
- The family day-care provider's residence may not have easy access to an outside playground.
- Family day-care providers often take holidays and the summer off.

DAY-CARE CENTERS

Day-care centers are out-of-home facilities providing comprehensive child-care services, including education and age-appropriate programming, to infants, toddlers, and preschool children. Day-care centers can be owner-operated, part of a regional or national chain, owned and operated on or off site by a corporation for the use of its employees, or owned and operated on or off site by the federal government for use of its employees.

Although some day-care centers may open earlier and close later, most have regular hours, opening between 7–8 A.M. and closing between 5–6 P.M. Many day-care centers also offer half-a-day child-care services or playgroup services for parents on certain days of the week. You can choose to send your child to a center every day of the week for the entire day, or just on Mondays, Wednesdays, and Fridays from 8:00 A.M. to noon. Some centers are open year-round; others are closed during all or part of the summer and for state and federal holidays.

Day-care centers are regulated by the state and comply with any and all state requirements for child/teacher ratios and center group sizes, programming, food safety, and building and fire safety codes. Laws governing the operation of day-care centers vary dramatically from state to state. Some states require teachers to have certain minimal qualifications, and almost all states require them to be fingerprinted and checked out by the state department of justice and perhaps the FBI. However, a few states—Missouri, Kansas, Oregon, New Jersey, and New York—don't require background checks or a scan of child-abuse indexes in other states where the provider has resided. In addition, the minimal qualifications for employment vary considerably, and very few states require any experience in child care at all—just a degree in early childhood education.

After some digging, I uncovered a very disturbing fact. Even in states that require day-care workers to be checked out by the FBI, on any given day, in any given week, it is highly probable that the day-care provider taking care of your child has not been checked out by the FBI. Here are two reasons: First, most states only require an FBI fingerprint check if the provider is a relatively new resident to the state. However, the state has no independent way of verifying if providers are telling the truth when asked how long they have resided in the state. So if a provider has, for example, lived in California for less than two years, she is supposed to submit two sets of ten-tip fingerprints for the background check. One set goes to the California Department of Justice, the other to the FBI. But if the provider lies about how long she has resided in the state, only the California check is done. The second reason: It takes six to eight weeks for a day-care-center owner to receive a clean bill of health from the FBI or a state's department of justice on a new employee. Turnover in day-care centers is unbelievably high; some have an attrition rate of over 40 percent, while most day-care-center profit margins are slim. The owner of your local day-care center has no legal obligation to wait the six to eight weeks for the okay from the government before letting her employee care for your child, although she is required to supervise the employee. This is no consolation because, realistically, not every minute of this employee's time with your child will be supervised. The staff in most centers is stretched too thin. So beware: In day-care centers across the country, I estimate that over half of all the employees are still waiting for a "clean bill of safety."

The Prerequisites for Day-Care Centers

Remember, this is an overview. Later in the book, I'll give you more information on day care and a number of tools you can use to locate, choose, hire, manage, and motivate a day-care provider.

- *Hours.* Make sure that the center's hours fit your schedule.
- *Holidays and summer months.* If you need day care on holidays and during the summer, be sure your center is open. Many aren't.
- *Group size.* Day-care centers usually group children by age. Make sure that your child isn't going to get lost in a crowd.
- *Caregiver/child ratio.* Make sure that there are enough teachers to provide quality care to the group. As you've seen in the state licensing laws, the caregiver/child ratio is regulated by the state and is based on the age of the child. I would recommend a ratio that for infants is 1:2 and toddlers is 1:3.
- *Safety.* Ask to review comprehensive background checks on every person in the center. It's very likely they won't have any but will tell you that state licensing laws require thorough investigations by the FBI. Remember that it takes six to eight weeks for the okay from the FBI, so beware of any new employees!

- *Age-appropriate programming.* Make sure that there are plenty of planned activities, toys, games, art supplies, and outdoor playground equipment to keep your child stimulated, happy, and occupied.

Pros and Cons of Day Care

Day care has the following advantages:

- Most centers provide a wide range of age-appropriate toys, games, and activities.
- Day-care centers are ongoing, established companies that you can usually rely on to stay in business.
- Day-care centers are subject to state and federal regulations, although the regulations are often quite minimal.
- The cost of day-care centers varies widely. It is likely that you will be able to find a good center that fits your budget in your area.
- Your child will have the opportunity to interact with a wide variety of children and adults, and will develop the ability to get along with others faster than with in-home care.
- Day-care centers have set policies, procedures, schedules, and a management structure that you can usually rely on.

Day care has the following disadvantages:

- Center hours are usually set in stone.
- Your child may get sick more often—meaning you may get sick more often—because of his exposure to many children.
- You cannot bring a sick child to most day-care centers.
- Depending on the size of the center and child/teacher ratio, your child may not get the individual attention she needs.
- Day-care centers are not very flexible about mealtimes, naptimes, and playtimes. Your child may require a schedule that is different from a particular center's schedule.
- Day-care centers are often closed on holidays or during the summer when you need to go to work.
- Many centers have very specific guidelines for acceptance—toilet training, age, maturity, and so on. If your child doesn't meet these (even if he's close to being trained!), you'll have to begin your search again.
- A center with a good reputation often has a waiting list and can be difficult to get into.

CARE FOR YOUR OLDER CHILD

If you are the parent of a child over the age of three, you know that child care becomes even more complicated as the years go by. The issues you were dealing with when your child was a toddler don't go away, and other issues force their way into your life.

Think about it: It's the summer before your precious daughter starts first grade, and you've got to figure out your after-school child-care situation now! Your daughter gets out of school at 2:30 P.M., but you're hard at work at your office forty-five minutes away at least until 6:00. With traffic, you usually make it home by 7:00 P.M. Your husband never gets home before 8:00 P.M., so he can't pick her up. Who is going to pick her up from school? What should her afternoon look like—should you let her take the Tai Kwon Do lessons she is so interested in? How do you get her there? If you can get her to the karate studio somehow, should she be left there alone? Can you trust the instructors? Who are these instructors anyway? If not Tai Kwon Do, then what? The questions go on and on.

If you can figure out how to handle these issues, how do you handle holidays—Christmas vacation, spring break, Martin Luther King, Jr. Day, snow days, parent-teacher days, and summer vacation?

If you need help during the school year, you have several options:

Remember, this is an overview. You will get all of the information you need about each of these options in later chapters.

- in-home provider—nanny, au pair
- family day-care or day-care center for younger children
- after-school program at your child's school
- community after-school programs
- independent after-school program

In-Home Providers

The most flexible, and expensive, after-school care is obtained when you hire a nanny. A nanny can pick your child up from school and care for her until you return home from work that evening. A nanny also allows you to handle sick days, snow days, parent-teacher days, school holidays, and summer vacation with relative ease.

Family Day-Care Providers and Day-Care Centers

If your child is in kindergarten or first grade, you may be able to find a family day-care provider or day-care center to care for your child before and after school. Day-care centers and family day-care providers often provide child-care services during the summer, Christmas vacation, and spring break. Day-care centers and family day-care providers are more expensive than school-based after-school programs or programs run by community organizations, and they may not have the same range of programming, such as art and music classes, athletics, and clubs.

In-School Programs

With an in-school program, your child will have the opportunity to participate in a wide range of organized, well-supervised extracurricular activities, like music lessons, art classes, drama, sports teams, and other athletic pursuits, and clubs like Boy Scouts, Girl Scouts, Future Farmers of America, and 4-H with other children he knows. However, in-school programs are usually closed on days school is closed.

Community After-School Programs

Community organizations like the YMCA, YWCA, Jewish Community Centers, Big Brothers/Big Sisters, local churches and synagogues, and many local colleges and universities offer after-school programs at their facilities that include art and music lessons, athletics, and academic tutoring for your child.

Independent After-School Programs

If you can arrange transportation for your child from school to the program and have a little extra money to spend, you can find plenty of classes, lessons, sports teams, and other activities to fill your child's after-school hours.

If you need help during the summer, you have the following options:

- in-home provider—nanny, au pair
- family day care or day-care center for younger children
- day camp
- resident camp

If you have decided that a full-time nanny is for you, summers won't be a problem. Likewise, if your child has been going to a day-care center or family day-care provider that is open during the summer, you can increase the number of hours your child is at the center every day, and summer will be solved.

However, if your child is too old to go to a day-care center or family day-care provider, and if your child is ready, one of the best ways to handle the summer months is to find a good summer camp. Because there are so many different types of day and resident summer camps, it is very likely that you can find one that fits your child's interests and your family's budget.

Day Camps

Day camps offer a variety of programs and activities for children ages five to fifteen. More traditional day camps offer activities like swimming, boating, hiking, horseback riding, and tennis, while others offer an academically oriented day that might appeal to your child. These newer academic camps offer a wide range of studies, including painting, music, science, astronomy, or math. Other camps can offer intensive courses in an athletic pursuit of interest to your child, including softball, baseball, tennis, or sailing. You'll find day camps organized by your local parks and recreation service, private schools, churches, country clubs, tennis clubs, and yacht clubs, and many other community organizations, and most day camps offer transportation for your child to and from camp. The price of day camps varies widely depending on the organization offering the camp and the types of activities your child will be able to participate in. For example, a traditional day camp run by the city parks and recreation service could cost you $10 a day, while a sailing camp at the local yacht club might be $50 to $80 a day.

Resident Camps

Your child can attend a resident camp for a few days, a week, two weeks, or up to eight weeks. As with day camps, some resident camps offer a wide range of traditional summertime activities, while others offer the intense pursuit of an academic or athletic activity. Independent, privately run resident camps cost about $35 to $100 per day. Camps operated by nonprofit agencies, youth groups, and public agencies range in price from $15 to $55 per day. If the price of resident camp seems out of reach, some camps offer scholarships for partial or full tuition. Girl Scouts, Boy Scouts, church-affiliated camps, and city- or county-sponsored camps usually offer some sort of financial aid if you need it.

CHAPTER THREE

■ ■ ■ ■ ■ ■ ■ ■ ■ ■ ■ ■

Let's Get Legal

IN THIS CHAPTER:	*Tax Issues*
	Overtime
	Unemployment Insurance
	Immigration Requirements
	Contracts

If merely finding suitable child care is not daunting enough, then wait till you learn that inextricably interwoven into child-care arrangements are many complicated and very inconvenient legal issues that require formal compliance and formal documentation.

IN-HOME PROVIDERS

If you decide that in-home care is your best option, you have several legal issues to understand and attend to. As you've probably read in the news over the past few years, many parents find state and federal legal requirements far too cumbersome and simply employ a nanny on an informal basis, without a written contract and without following the regulations of the U.S. Internal Revenue Service, Department of Labor, or the Immigration and Naturalization Service. Perhaps a quick tour through the legal briar patch will help clear up the issues for you.

Federal Tax Issues

Although most people have at least rudimentary knowledge of the various federal laws affecting household employees, they realize that compliance with such laws can result in additional costs, and may be viewed unfavorably by the nanny, who may not want to work for anyone who insists on reporting and withholding tax from wages.

Employee vs. Independent Contractor

Your first question should be whether your provider is considered an employee or an independent contractor. The Federal Insurance Contribution Act (FICA) and the Federal Unemployment Insurance Act (FUTA) specify withholding provisions that are applicable to employees, but not to independent contractors. FICA taxes are used to fund obligations with respect to Social Security, the Disability Insurance Trust Fund, and Medicare. FUTA taxes are used to fund benefits payable under the unemployment insurance system, which is administered through the combined efforts of the federal and state governments and are paid to employees who are terminated without cause by their employers.

If you have a right to control not only what the worker does but how the worker does it, your worker will be classified as an employee even if you do not actually exercise such control. With an independent contractor, you control only the result of the work, but not the way in which the result is accomplished. Although the IRS considers at least twenty separate factors in evaluating employee status, it is more likely that you are hiring an employee when you hire someone in your home, because there you are more likely to have direct control over the provider and his or her work. When child-care services are furnished at the provider's house, it is more likely that you are hiring an independent contractor because the provider will determine not only the daily routine but also what he or she does when not working directly with your child.

Following the hue and cry over Zoe Baird's aborted nomination as attorney general, a number of changes in the requirements for withholding and payment of employment taxes relating to domestic employees were implemented. These changes were made largely through amendments in the Social Security Domestic Employment Reform Act of 1994, which is commonly called the "Nanny Tax Act." Under the Nanny Tax Act, employers must pay taxes on any employee if domestic service is the employee's primary occupation.

Keeping Records

If your provider is an employee, appropriate record keeping is the next order of business. You should start by getting an employer identification number, which can be obtained by filing form SS-4 (Application for Employer Identification Number). You should then establish and maintain a carefully organized file on the provider that will contain the employment application and all other relevant hiring materials, the results of the background check and the results of any special testing, the employee's social security number, driver's license number, insurance information, payment and tax information, and all other pertinent information relating to the employee's performance of duties. Under federal law, the records relating to employment taxes must be maintained for four years after the date that the tax return was due, or four years after the tax is paid, whichever is later. Many state laws significantly extend the period of time during which employee records must be maintained. *Phone your state tax authority to find out how long to maintain your records.*

Paying Taxes

Once the employee file has been organized, the fun really begins. Serious communication with Big Brother is now at hand. If your employee earns more than $1,000 during the year, you must deduct FICA taxes of 7.65 percent from each paycheck. You must also pay a matching amount. Under the Nanny Tax Act, commencing in 1995, the required amounts may be paid annually when you file your Form 1040, rather than quarterly, as required under prior law.

FUTA taxes are also now paid annually on Form 1040 for any employee making $1,000 or more annually at a rate of 6.2 percent on the first $7,000 in wages, although if you also pay state unemployment tax (which will generally be the case) you may subtract, in 1995, 5.4 percent from the FUTA, with the result that the effective FUTA rate is approximately 0.8 percent.

Beginning in 1998, you will be required to increase your quarterly estimated tax payments if you are self-employed, or increase your regular withholding tax payments to take into account employment taxes you owe on your domestic worker. FICA and FUTA taxes are subject to adjustment on an annual basis to reflect future inflation.

Under current law, you are not required to withhold federal income tax from your domestic worker's compensation unless your employee specifically agrees to the income tax withholding. If such an agreement is made, your employee must sign a Form W-4 and withholding payments are then made. These are based on all cash and noncash compensation, except for certain fringe benefits such as meals and lodging. The required amount of the withholding can be found in the withholding tax tables in IRS Circular E (Employers Tax Guide).

Your employee may also be entitled to an Earned Income Credit (EIC), which may be paid in advance in certain circumstances. Domestic employees who wish to receive the advance EIC must complete Form W-5. IRS Circular E also contains Earned Income Credit Tables, which specify the amount of EIC to be paid. The appropriate amount is to be deducted from FICA and withheld income taxes and must be paid to *your* employee in each paycheck. If no income tax is withheld, you should inform your employee that he or she may have the right to the EIC but not to the advance payment. If that's the case, use Form 797 (Possible Federal Tax Refund Due to the Earned Income Credit) or Form W-2.

You are required to provide your employee with Form W-2 by January 31 of each year for the prior year's compensation. A copy of that W-2 must be sent to the Social Security Administration on or before the last day of February of the same year.

You can usually get all of these forms from a local or regional IRS office or post office, and they can generally be completed without great difficulty. In addition, the Legal Kit in Appendix 1 contains current versions of most of these forms as well as instructions for their completion.

Minimum Wage and Overtime

With limited exceptions, such as casual baby-sitting, under current federal law, domestic employees are entitled to be paid the minimum wage if they are employed in a household for eight or more hours in a workweek, or if they earn wages of at least $50 in any calendar quarter. In determining whether or not you have met the minimum wage requirements, you can include noncash compensation such as meals and lodging (assuming they are provided primarily for the benefit of the employee), to the extent of its fair value or reasonable cost.

Current federal law requires that domestic employees who do not live in the household must be paid extra compensation when they work overtime. Live-in employees do not generally have to be paid overtime, although the minimum wage requirements are applicable for each hour worked. Overtime pay rate is generally one and one-half times the employee's regular hourly rate (but must be at least one and one-half times the minimum wage) for each hour worked in excess of forty hours per week. Under current federal law employers do not have to pay overtime for Saturday, Sunday, or holiday work or for hours worked in excess of a usual number of hours on any particular day (although California and some other states may, under certain circumstances, require overtime in such cases). Also, no current federal law requires employers to provide or pay for vacations or time off on holidays. Although federal law is generally controlling, some state laws provide greater benefits than those afforded by federal law—and there are a significant number of such states.

Worker's Compensation and State Taxes

Some form of worker's compensation insurance program is applicable in all states. This insurance provides payments of medical expenses and lost wages to employees who are injured at work. Covered employees receive benefits without regard to fault and are usually precluded from seeking damages separately from the employer for any work-related accidents. Many states exempt domestic employees from the worker's compensation system altogether, although the employee may often voluntarily accept coverage. If your state does require worker's compensation, you are required to obtain *liability insurance* through private insurance, an insurance company, state insurance fund, or self-insurance. The cost of such insurance is not usually prohibitive (for example, in New York, coverage for one employee is approximately $417 a year) and provides significant benefits when compared to the alternative, a potentially large damage claim by an uncovered employee.

The fact that a state does not require an employer to provide worker's compensation insurance does not relieve you from the obligation to pay for the type of job-related expenses normally covered by worker's compensation. The potential damages that may be awarded to an uncovered employee could be much greater than the payments under worker's compensation. *Consider obtaining liability insurance to protect yourself.*

Unemployment Insurance

Each state currently requires you to pay unemployment insurance taxes on domestic employees who were paid at least $1,000 in any one quarter during the current or preceding year. The actual amount of wages that are subject to the state tax varies widely. The amount of tax is also affected by the frequency of turnover among the employer's workers, with higher payments generally being applied to employers who experience frequent turnover. State filing requirements usually involve the filing of one or more tax forms, which include at least the amount of the tax due and the amount of taxable wages paid to each domestic employee.

Several states, such as New York and California, have a disability program that requires employers to pay a special tax to fund the programs or to pay for private insurance coverage that meets state requirements. These programs generally have thresholds of $1,000 or more in wages paid for domestic work in a calendar quarter of the current or preceding year.

Personal income taxes on wages paid to domestic employees are also imposed by many states and localities. The type of wages that are subject to the tax and withholding requirements generally follow the federal pattern.

Immigration and Naturalization Service Requirements

If your employee is not a U.S. citizen, you must confront yet another legal obstacle. Current law requires you to examine original documents (except for a birth certificate, which may be a certified copy) that establish legal status of your employee. It is up to the employee to choose which documents will prove his or her legal status. You should not demand to see other specific documents, as this may establish grounds for a potential unfair-immigration–related employment practices case.

Hiring unauthorized aliens is punishable by fines that increase with subsequent violations. Also, deportation of the illegal alien is possible. So you must have the domestic worker complete and sign the Immigration and Naturalization Service (INS) Form I-9 (Employment Eligibility Verification) within three business days from the date of hiring. A Form I-9 is included in the Legal Kit. You must keep the completed Form I-9 for at least three years after the date of hire or one year after employment is terminated, whichever is later. You do not need to file Form I-9 with the government.

Other Concerns

What happens if your nanny takes your child and a friend to a soccer playoff game and has an automobile accident en route, and it is later discovered that your nanny not only did not have a valid driver's license but was also subject to seizures? Are you liable? Is it possible that you may be sued by the child's friend? Unfortunately, the answer to both questions may be yes. Under emerging legal theories, there is an increasing recognition of liability of employers for the negligent hiring of employees.

Negligent hiring arises when the employer fails to investigate adequately the fitness of an employee prior to hiring. Positions involving a high degree of trust usually carry high standards. If the standards are not met, both you and your employee may be held accountable for injuries caused by the employee to another person. With this in mind, *take every step you can to ensure that the person you are hiring is fit to be employed as a child-care provider. The only way you can protect yourself from this kind of lawsuit is by taking great care during the interview, reference check, and background-check process.* The information and templates provided by this book make hiring a nanny carefully a lot easier!

Contracts

There are still more compelling reasons to "get legal." If your nanny demands a vacation, refuses to drive your child to the soccer playoffs, or demands a significant severance payment when fired for her persistent failure to show up for work, what can you do? What if there are legitimate differences of opinion over the nanny's scope of duties or the hourly work schedule? This is where a contract will help. Sure, the existence of a written contract does not mean that all controversy will be eliminated, but the likelihood of a dispute will certainly be reduced. The written contract will also provide a medium for the parties to discuss and resolve most important issues in advance of employment so that the working relationship can be clearly understood at an early date. The contract forms in the Legal Kit in Appendix 1 are designed with these concerns in mind.

DAY-CARE AND FAMILY DAY-CARE CENTERS

Obtaining child care at an employer-sponsored day-care center or at a center that is part of a well-recognized national chain poses the fewest legal problems to a parent, mainly because these day-care centers provide the physical facility and staff. Applicable licenses, permits, worker's compensation insurance, federal and state tax requirements, employee obligations, and all other legal requirements incident to a center's operation are the responsibility of the day-care-center owner/operator and not the parent. Although the legal concerns confronting a parent who uses a day-care center may be less obvious and serious than those for other types of child-care arrangements, some issues do remain. First, if this is not an employer-sponsored center, then there will probably be a contract involved. Make sure you examine this carefully to protect your interests. If the center does not provide a contract, you should arrange for a simple written agreement that covers the scope of the center's responsibility, staffing matters, hours of use (including appropriate flex hours to cover emergencies), and payment and termination provisions. This should be signed by you and the director or owner of the center. Many of the provisions contained in the sample Child-Care Contract included in the Legal Kit are also applicable to child-care arrangements with a day-care center and may be useful in reviewing a contract provided to you by a day-care center. Remember that informal oral agreements are ripe for controversy and should be avoided. In addition to an agreement, you should also make sure you get the following information, and verify it whenever practical:

- visitation policies for parents
- the nature and amount of liability insurance carried by the day-care center
- the current status of all licenses
- the type of background checks and screening used
- the policies for drug testing and physical examinations for employees
- the center's policies on physical punishment (which is prohibited under many state laws)
- the educational requirements for employees and specific training given employees
- any records or investigations of the day-care center for child abuse and maltreatment
- any other litigation or investigations, including insurance claims

Family day care raises many of the same legal issues as day-care centers. As with day care, you should arrange to have some kind of written agreement. You should also make sure to check the background and personal history, education, skill, and character of the provider. *You will, of course, need to verify all of this information independently,* rather than through materials furnished by the provider.

Without appropriate licensing standards and related regulatory safeguards, the odds are stacked heavily against parents. You have only your own diligence and persistence standing between your precious child and possible tragedy. Following the suggestions in this book, utilizing the Legal Kit in Appendix 1, and otherwise "getting legal" should not be considered as obstacles merely to be overcome, but rather should be viewed as *essential tools* for procuring and maintaining safe and suitable child-care help in a poorly regulated and highly risky environment.

CHAPTER FOUR

Determining Your Personal Child-Care Needs

Using The Templates

In this chapter, you will have your first opportunity to use the templates found on the diskette that accompanies this book. For this chapter, and the chapters that follow, I recommend that you read the chapter all of the way through before sitting down at your computer. By reading the material beforehand, you'll understand exactly how each template is to be used. This will help you immeasurably, and it is likely that you will have no problem answering all of the questions presented by the templates. If, however, you have read through a chapter completely and are still stumped by a question in a template, take a minute to refer back to the chapter on that particular issue. Remember that answering certain questions may take considerable thought and some discussion with family members. If you feel uncomfortable using a computer, you'll find all of the templates in Chapter Ten.

Now that you have a pretty good understanding of the various types of child-care services that are available, it's time to get real about your family's child-care needs. Many of these steps may seem like an analysis of the obvious. However, I've found that developing a clear and very realistic understanding of your child-care requirements, as a family, will make the job of choosing appropriate child care foolproof. It will also make hiring and managing your child care far less stressful. You will personalize your child-care options as you work through the Needs Assessment, a template that assembles all the variables regarding your decision into one easy-to-use document. If you're a single parent, the Needs Assessment will help you make sure that you've covered all your bases. If you're married, it will be helpful to review and edit the final document with your spouse, and encourage a partnership in this process, even if the ultimate responsibility for managing the child-care situation falls to one partner specifically.

I've found that for many parents, working through the steps in this chapter is the first time they have ever really taken a long, hard look at their needs and the feasibility of meeting those needs. So please do every step. We have attempted to minimize your work by using check boxes wherever possible. Include any comments or questions you may have in the margins.

STEP ONE: DO A HOUSEHOLD PROFILE

A Household Profile serves as the foundation for your search for child care. Spend a little time thinking about all of your current child-care resources, whether paid or unpaid. You may have forgotten some resources, or you may find that you have more resources than you originally thought.

View the task of completing the Household Profile as similar to listing your assets when completing a financial profile. You can't make any effective investment decisions until you know where you stand *now*. The same goes for making an investment in child care. Take a look at Dan and Karen P.'s Household Profile below before you complete your own Household Profile. As you may remember, Dan and Karen have two children and are expecting twins. With the move away from Karen's parents and Dan's added commute time, they really need someone to help Karen during the day with the twins, and to find a child-care solution for Michael.

■■■■■■■■■■■■■■■■■■■■■■■■■■■■■■■■■■■

DAN AND KAREN P.'S HOUSEHOLD PROFILE

A. _Karen_   _Daniel_
_____

    Parent Name   Parent Name

B. _Nicholas/5_   _Michael/3_   _Twin A/newborn_
_____

    Child Name/Age   Child Name/Age   Child Name/Age

    Twin B/newborn
_____

    Child Name/Age   Child Name/Age   Child Name/Age

C. List all existing household employees, their duties, and salaries.

    Marta   _housecleaning 3 × week_   _$8/hr_
_____

    Name   Duties   Salary

_____

    Name   Duties   Salary

D. List all nonsalaried child-care help you may currently use, their duties, and
hours. (For example, if Grandma or Aunt Lisa regularly sits with the kids on
Wednesday nights, or if there is a neighborhood mom who sits for you in
exchange for your sitting for her, please list it here.)

    Grandad P.   _child care_   _2 Sat. P.M. per mo. with boys_
_____

    Name   Duties   Hours

■■■■■■■■■■■■■■■■■■■■■■■■■■■■■■■■■■■

STEP TWO: CALENDARING

Calendaring allows you to assess each family member's true daily and
weekly schedule, and includes detailed information about where each
person needs to be every day and at what time; what time each person
needs to leave the house every morning; who's going to need to work
late; who needs to be picked up or dropped off; and all the other little
time-consuming extras that make life so chaotic. Once you have
completed your calendaring, you'll see very clearly any gaps in your
child-care coverage or empty spaces in your child's day that call for a
playgroup or a lesson. Detailed calendaring is also your shortcut to
scheduling an in-home provider's work hours—with one quick look you
can see where and when you most need help.

Completing Your Calendars

Complete a weekly calendar for each adult and child you included in your Household Profile. The easiest way to do this, and the most fun, is to go to your local copy shop and make a number of copies of a blank weekly calendar onto transparencies. Then, get a big box of thick, colored pens, and assign a different color pen to each person you will be calendaring. Start with your own calendar. With your color pen, X-out each of those hours when you are unavailable for child care. Be entirely realistic here. You are "unavailable" when you are at work, commuting (make sure you allow for that frequent, very frustrating traffic jam), Friday or Saturday nights out with your spouse or friends, when you are exercising, gardening, or pursuing hobbies, and so forth. Most important, include a reasonable amount of time alone. On the same calendar, have your spouse mark his or her "unavailable times" in color pen. Then, take another calendar sheet and write out your child's schedule in detail. You can include schedules for two children on each calendar. Finally, take out a third calendar and mark the hours your current paid or unpaid child-care provider works.

You can also use whatever calendar application is on your computer. Create a file for each family member. When you have added all of the information discussed above, print out the calendars onto paper or transparencies.

By overlaying your calendar with your child's, you will be able to identify quickly those hours when you most need help. Take a blank calendar and put a big X in the hours when you need child care. Compare this calendar with the calendar you made for the person who is currently helping you with child care, and take a colored pen and fill in those hours when you already have some help. After doing this, you will clearly see those "X-ed" hours when you most need additional help with child care. You now have a realistic schedule for child care that will prove very useful when you look into day care or family day-care centers or interview in-home providers.

Before you begin completing the calendar template, take a look at Dan and Karen P.'s calendars below.

Don't Be Alarmed by the Number of Hours You Need Care

After you do a realistic schedule for child care, you may be troubled or feel guilty about the number of hours of child care you really require every week, or the fact that the hours when you most need child care

YOUR FAMILY'S CALENDARS

Weekly Planner — MONTH: KAREN — YEAR:

	SUNDAY	MONDAY	TUESDAY	WEDNESDAY	THURSDAY	FRIDAY	SATURDAY
7 AM							
8		drop off Nicky, Mikey	drop off	drop off	drop off	drop off	
9							
10		errands		errands		errands	
11		pick up Nick & Mikey	pick up Nick & Mikey	pick up	pick up	pick up	
12 NOON		GYM	Lunch w/ Louise	GYM	Other Lunch dates	GYM	
1							Free Time
2							Free Time
3			drive Nick To Karate		drive Nick To Karate		Free Time
4				Drive Mikey To playgroup			
5							
							6-11 Dinner w/ Dan

Weekly Planner — MONTH: HOURS WE NEED CHILDCARE FOR TWINS — YEAR:

	SUNDAY	MONDAY	TUESDAY	WEDNESDAY	THURSDAY	FRIDAY	SATURDAY
7 AM							
8		✗	✗	✗	✗	✗	
9							
10		✗		✗		✗	✗
11					✗		
12 NOON		✗	✗	✗	✗	✗	
1						✗	
2							
3				✗	✗		
4				✗			
5							
							6-11

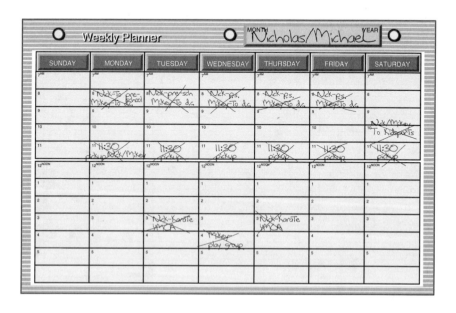

aren't regular nine-to-five-type work hours. First, remember that all your child care doesn't need to come from the same place. Your child doesn't need to spend twenty hours a day with a nanny. You can break up your child's day with a number of different options—playgroups, Grandma, Gymboree, and a nanny, if you need to!

Second, remember that your child-care schedule must truly benefit you and your children. If nine-to-five doesn't work for you, don't hire a provider or enroll your child in a day-care center that must adhere to those hours. If you choose to hire a live-in employee, cluster her work hours around those times that really help you. Feel free to schedule your nanny to work odd hours and even have some time off; you might only need her from 7:00 A.M. to 10:00 A.M., and then again at noon to pick up the children at preschool and play dates. If your in-home provider can begin work early in the morning, she may be able to help get older kids dressed and ready to go so Mom and Dad can take turns driving them to school and spending time with younger kids who don't need to run out of the house. There may even be time for Mom to take a shower!

I'll say it again: Give yourself the flexibility you need by developing a realistic schedule for you and your kids and by making the right child-care choices. I've found that there are three peak times of the day when parents need the most help. The first is early morning. The second is early afternoon (noon to 2:30 P.M.), when most preschools and playgroups end for the day and children need to be picked up, errands must be run, and nap schedules for younger children must be maintained, but when most parents are still at work. The third is late afternoon to early evening (4:30 P.M. to 7:00 P.M.), when Mom and Dad have just returned home from work exhausted after battling traffic, but dinner still needs to be prepared and eaten. For parents with children in day care or family day care, this time of day is even more complicated, because most day-care centers and family-care centers insist that parents be punctual when they pick up their children. Unfortunately, business meetings, demanding bosses and clients, traffic delays, out-of-town business trips, bad weather, and younger children with the sniffles can make it impossible for you to be there on time or be there at all.

Have a Plan B and Even a Plan C

It is really crucial to have Plan B (Plan A being your original pickup plan) and Plan C pickup plans if your child is in a day-care center. What this means is that at least two other individuals must know your child's pickup time and the center's location, and that both have been cleared by you for emergency pickup of your child. Most centers have authorization forms that parents sign at the beginning of the school year. Wisely, there are lots of blank spaces on the form, so use them! If a natural second or third option for emergency pickups doesn't pop instantly into your mind, look at your child's play friends and offer to be one or more of their mom's Plan Bs, if they will be your backups in an emergency.

STEP THREE: COMPLETE A NEEDS ASSESSMENT TEMPLATE FOR THE TYPE OF CHILD CARE YOU ARE CONSIDERING

There are four different Needs Assessment templates: in-home, family day care, day care, and care for older children. Working through the template questions that relate to the type of child care you are considering will provide you with the structure you need to conduct a rational, objective, and results-oriented analysis of your requirements. The Needs Assessment organizes your child-care requirements into blocks of information that can help you figure out whether the type of child care you think you need is really the most appropriate. Once you are certain that you have chosen the right type of care or combination of services, the Needs Assessment then organizes your requirements into blocks of information that will prove indispensable during your search for a child-care provider.

If you are considering an in-home provider, after completing the Needs Assessment you will be able to:

- decide whether an in-home provider is right for your family
- write a concise job description for a nanny
- write an ad for a nanny
- find the best nanny agency
- conduct a phone screening interview of a nanny
- conduct an in-person interview of a nanny

If you are considering family day care, after completing the Needs Assessment you will be able to:

- decide if family day care is right for your family
- conduct phone-screening interviews of family day-care providers that will eliminate inappropriate providers

If you are considering day-care centers, after completing the Needs Assessment you will be able to:

- decide if a day-care center is right for your family
- conduct phone-screening interviews of day-care-center owners or managers that will eliminate inappropriate providers

If you are considering care for your older, school-age child, after completing the Needs Assessment you will be able to:

- decide which kind of after-school care is most appropriate for your child and your family
- conduct informed phone interviews with directors of after-school programs that will eliminate inappropriate programs
- decide what kind of care is most appropriate for your child during the summer
- conduct informed phone interviews with directors of summer programs that will eliminate inappropriate programs

Take a minute to look at Dan and Karen P.'s Needs Assessments below. Remember, they needed an in-home provider for the twins and a day-care center for Michael.

■ ■ ■ ■ ■ ■ ■ ■ ■ ■ ■ ■ ■ ■ ■ ■ ■ ■ ■ ■ ■ ■ ■ ■ ■ ■ ■ ■

DAN AND KAREN P.'S IN-HOME
CARE NEEDS ASSESSMENT

Basic Requirements

1. The position is
   ☑ full-time (25 to 40 hours)
   ☐ part-time (up to 25 hours)

2. The provider will
   ☐ live in (accommodations, room, board, and salary)
   ☑ live out

3A. The provider will be required to drive and be the holder of a valid driver's license and be insured or insurable:
   ☑ yes   ☐ no

B. If the provider is required to drive, who will provide car:
   ☐ parent   ☑ provider

C. If parent's car is used, may provider use it in the provider's off-duty hours?
   ☐ yes   ☐ no

D. If provider drives own car
   ☑ proof of insurance will be required
   ☐ parents will provide insurance or add provider to family policy

E. Will the provider be compensated for gas use while on the job? (The current rate is $.29 per mile)
   ☑ yes   ☐ no

F. Will there be a policy for small cash expenditures and reimbursement for gas and other incidentals?
☑ yes   ☐ no

G. If you answered yes to question 3F, will you provide a list of "cleared" expenditures along with a simple expense form and payment policy?
☑ yes   ☐ no

Duties and Qualifications

4. The provider will report to
Karen
_____
Name of parent or parents

5. The provider will have responsibility for these children:

Child's name	Age
Nicholas	*5*
Michael	*3*
Twin A	*newborn*
Twin B	*newborn*

6. Please check the following areas of responsibility/duty:
☑ light cleaning
☑ cooking meals for children
☑ driving
☑ bathing
☐ children's laundry
☑ adhere to nap/bedtime schedule
☑ adhere to dietary restrictions
☑ reinforce family rules
☑ carry I.D., medical forms/releases at all times

7. Please check the following minimum qualifications:
☑ high school degree
☐ college/advanced degree
☐ previous child-care experience
☑ previous infant-care experience
☑ English speaking
☑ infant/child CPR certification
☑ nonsmoker
☑ 7-year, national background check including civil, criminal, and driving
☑ U.S. citizen or legal alien

Salary, Holiday, and Sick-Day Policy

8A. The salary will be based on:
☑ fixed hourly rate
☐ flat monthly rate

B. The rate amount will be:
$/0
_____

C. The salary will be paid:
☐ weekly
☑ biweekly
☐ monthly

9. Will there be any paid benefits?
☑ medical insurance
☑ dental insurance
☐ life insurance

10A. Will there be paid holidays (non-work days where the provider still receives a salary)?
☑ yes
☐ no

B. If yes, which holidays?
☑ all federal holidays
☐ all federal and bank holidays
☐ the following list of holidays:
    New Year's
    Memorial Day
    July 4
    Labor Day
    Thanksgiving
    Christmas
☐ no holidays will be paid unless by previous agreement, and each holiday will be assessed for child-care needs.

11A. Will sick days be paid?
☑ yes
☐ no

B. If yes, how many sick days per year?
☑ 1–3
☐ 3–5

C. If yes, what is paid sick-day policy?
☑ sick days paid after 90-day employment review
☐ sick days paid after_____-day employment review

12. If the provider is due one week's paid vacation scheduled at a mutually agreed-upon time, then the vacation will be after:
☐ 6 months of employment and favorable review
☑ 9 months of employment and favorable review
☐ other

Accommodations

13. If you have chosen a live-in provider, please check the following features that best describe the provider's living arrangement:
☐ private bedroom/bath
☐ separate kitchen/eat alone
☐ share kitchen/eat alone
☐ eat with family
☐ private telephone
☐ shared telephone
☐ television in room
☐ share laundry

Work Hours and Scheduling

14. The provider's regular work hours will be: 8:30 A.M. to 5:30 P.M.

15. The provider will be required to work:
☑ evenings
☑ weekends

16. If evenings and weekends are required, and are over and above regular work hours (40 hours a week), how will the provider be compensated? (Keep in mind that you are not required by law to pay overtime to a live-in employee.)
☑ at normal rate per hour
☐ at 1.5 times the normal rate
☐ other

17. Will the provider be required to travel with the family? (Remember, travel with the family is not a substitute for paid vacation.)
☐ yes
☑ no

18A. Will the live-in provider have guest privileges?
☐ yes
☐ no

B. If yes, in what areas of the home will these privileges be allowed?
☐ provider's quarters
☐ family area
☐ by mutual agreement

C. Will the live-in provider be allowed to have overnight guests?
☐ yes
☐ no
☐ by mutual agreement

Child-Care Management

19A. Will there be regularly scheduled meetings between provider and parent(s)?
☑ yes
☐ no

B. If yes, how often?
☑ weekly
☐ biweekly
☐ monthly

C. When will the provider get her weekly work schedule?
☑ at previous week's meeting
☐ as needed

D. Will there be other management/ provider communication, other than at meeting?
☑ yes
☐ no

E. If yes, please check the other types of communication you will require from the provider on a regular basis:
☑ daily diary
☐ weekly report

NOTES: _____
_____
_____
_____

DAN AND KAREN P.'S DAY-CARE NEEDS ASSESSMENT

Basic Requirements

1A. The center must open at:
☐ 6:00–7:00 A.M. ☑ 7:00–8:00 A.M.
☐ 8:00–9:00 A.M. ☐ after 9:00 A.M.

B. The center must close at:
☐ 4:00–5:00 P.M. ☐ 5:00–6:00 P.M.
☑ 6:00–7:00 P.M. ☐ after 7:00 P.M.

2. I want my child to attend:
☐ every weekday, all day
☐ three days a week, all day
☑ every weekday morning
☐ every weekday afternoon
☐ three days a week, mornings
☐ three days a week, afternoons
☐ other_____

3. The center must be near my:
☐ work   ☑ home   ☐ other

4A. The center must be open:
☑ 12 months a year
☐ 9 months a year (closed during summer)

B. The center must be open:
☑ on the following holidays
MLK Birthday
_____

5. The center must have the following features:
☑ playground
☑ separate area for napping
☐ separate area for diapering
☐ plenty of toys/activities for infants
☑ plenty of toys/activities for toddlers

6. The maximum number of children in my child's group must be:
☐ 1–3   ☑ 3–6   ☐ 6–9

7. Parents will be welcome in the center at any time: ☑ yes ☐ no

8. The center will be licensed:
☑ yes   ☐ no

9A. I can pay the following rate for day-care services:
☐ $50–$100 a week
☐ $100–$200 a week
☑ $200–$300 a week
☐ more than $300 a week

B. I can pay the center:
☐ weekly   ☑ monthly
☐ biyearly ☐ once a year

Teacher Qualifications

10A. My child's teachers will have the following minimum qualifications:
☐ high school degree
☑ college/advanced degree
☑ previous child-care experience
☐ previous infant-care experience
☑ English speaking
☑ infant/child CPR certification
☐ nonsmoker
☑ 7-year, national background check including civil, criminal and driving

Child-Care Management

11A. Will there be regularly scheduled meetings between provider and parent(s)?
☑ yes   ☐ no

B. If yes, how often?
☐ weekly ☐ biweekly ☑ monthly

C. When will the provider get your weekly work schedule?
☐ at previous week's meeting
☑ as needed

D. Will there be other provider/
parent communication, other
than at meeting?
☐ yes ☑ no

E. If yes, please check the other
types of communication you will
require from the provider on a
regular basis:
☐ daily log
☐ expense reports/weekly

F. Please check the following items
you will provide the provider and
update on a regular basis:
☑ emergency phone numbers
☑ approved transportation form
☑ medical forms/releases

NOTES: _____
_____

COMPLETING YOUR NEEDS ASSESSMENT TEMPLATE

It's time to get started! Complete the Needs Assessment template for the child-care option you think you need. If you're pretty sure you want in-home care, complete the In-Home Needs Assessment. If you are looking for a family day-care provider, complete the Family Day-Care Needs Assessment. If you know you want a day-care facility, fill out the Day-Care Needs Assessment. And, if you need care for your school-age child, complete the Older Child Needs Assessment.

Helpful Hint: Do a quick review of the options in Chapter Two if you find yourself bogged down in the middle of a set of questions wondering whether you have chosen the right type of child care. If you decide that you haven't chosen the right type of child care, try completing a Needs Assessment template for another type of child care to see if you can find a better fit. Remember, you may need a combination of care to get the full complement of coverage you need. So work with me on this—we'll figure it out!

Turn Your Completed Needs Assessment into a "Description"

Before you start searching for a child-care provider, you need to interpret the results of your Needs Assessment and organize it into concise, accessible, and portable blocks of relevant information. In this section, you'll learn how to take the findings of your completed Needs Assessment and turn it into a concise description of the child-care services you want to find. For parents in the market for an in-home provider, the resulting document will be a classic and eminently useful Job Description. For those looking for high-quality group child care, the document will be a Family Day-Care Provider Description or a Day-Care Center Description outlining everything the facility must have to warrant your consideration. And, if you are looking for a resident camp for your child, you'll be able to create a Resident Camp Description.

With your description in hand, you will be ready to start your search for your provider or program. The chapters that follow give you all the details you need to organize a well-planned, successful search, and then hire, contract, manage, and motivate the child-care provider you choose.

If you are using the software, the items you have checked in your Needs Assessment will be organized into a Description automatically. If you are not using the software, turn to Chapter Ten and complete the Description template designed for the type of care you are interested in.

Dan and Karen P.'s In-Home Provider Job Description

Once you complete the assessment, take a pad and write down each of the Needs Assesment form's major categories: Basic Requirements; Duties and Qualifications; Salary; Holiday and Sick-Day Policy; Work Hours and Scheduling; and Child-Care Management. Then list your needs within each category and leave out all of the options you've rejected. Below is what the P.'s In-Home Provider Job Description looks like. If you need to, take another look at their In-Home Child-Care Needs Assessment on pages 61–63 before moving forward.

Basic Requirements

full-time

live out

drive own car

own automobile insurance

reimbursed gas and other expenditures

bathing

maintaining nap and bedtime

dietary restrictions

reinforcing family rules

carry proper I.D. and medical releases when out of the home

Duties

report to Karen

care for Nicholas, Michael, and twins

light cleaning

light cooking

driving

Qualifications

high school degree

previous infant experience

English speaking

infant/child CPR

nonsmoker

background check

U.S. resident or legal alien

Salary, Holiday, and Sick-Day Policy

$10 an hour

Paid biweekly

Medical, dental plan

Paid holidays off: New Year's, Memorial Day, July 4th, Labor Day, Thanksgiving, Christmas Day

Paid Vacation Policy: Accrued at one work day per month beginning first month of employment. Days accrued may be taken after the first 9 months of employment, favorable review, and by mutual agreement.

Work Hours and Scheduling

8:30–5:30 weekdays

evenings and weekends

40-plus hours paid at normal rate per hour

Child-Care Management

weekly meetings

weekly schedule at previous week's meeting

daily log

Dan and Karen P.'s Day-Care Center Description

Basic Requirements

opens 7–8 A.M.

closes 6–7 P.M.

Michael will attend every weekday morning

must be near home

open 12 months/year

open on Martin Luther King Day

has playground, separate napping area, and plenty of toys and activities for toddlers

3–6 children in Michael's group

parents are welcome at all times

center is licensed

$200–$300 a week, paid monthly

Teacher Qualifications

college degree

previous child-care experience

English speaking

infant/child CPR

background check

Child-Care Management

monthly meetings with provider

schedule provided as needed

provide and update emergency phone numbers, approved pickup and transportation forms, medical authorization

HOW LONG WILL YOUR SEARCH FOR CHILD CARE TAKE?

The search for appropriate child care is anxiety-provoking, but many parents find themselves doubly anxious because circumstances often leave them without any time to find a new child-care situation. So how long will a search take? As you might expect, each type of child care has its own timeline. The scarcity of services in certain markets, among other factors, can make a search take even longer than usual and may require you to select an option that is not your first choice or the most optimal for your family.

To help you plan accordingly, here are some basic timelines:

In-Home Search Timeline

Parents launching a search for in-home care need to face the fact that while placement agencies can be expensive and may not offer the screening you need and think you are paying for, one of the main reasons that placement agencies exist is that they provide parents with candidates to interview quickly. If you choose to go it alone and submit an advertisement to the local newspaper, keep in mind that it may take at least one week even to talk to a candidate. Likely, once you place the ad you'll wait a few days until it is published, and then another week until you see responses. Then you must add time to sift through the candidates that respond. While a newspaper ad offers parents the most control over the candidate search process and is less expensive than an agency, it is far more time consuming, and can take two to three weeks if the first ad doesn't produce enough qualified candidates.

Once you start interviewing, you may find your ideal nanny in the first couple of days of interviews. If you do, add on the four to six days it takes to receive the results of your background check. If all goes very well, your search for an in-home provider will take at least two weeks, and that's assuming you can schedule interviews quickly (balancing your schedule and the candidate's available time can get tricky). If all doesn't go well, it could take far longer. Remember that a child-care search can be a full-time job, and one that you may be doing in addition to full-time parenting and/or a full-time job. So don't get discouraged if the search actually takes much longer than you anticipate.

Family Day-Care Provider Search Timeline

By using your local resource-and-referral agency (more about R&Rs in later chapters) to compile a list of all available family day-care centers, it should take only a few days of solid work for you to sift through the list, place the telephone interview calls, and cull the list down to those centers that meet your minimum requirements. The majority of your time and energy will be spent on the in-person visits and interviews. Assuming that your qualified family day-care providers have openings and can pass the phone interview and in-person visit phase, finding a family day-care provider should take a week to a week and a half. If no openings are available, your search could take days longer.

Day-Care Center Search

As with a search for family day-care providers, calling a resource-and-referral agency for a list of day-care centers will expedite your search. The most time-consuming parts of the process will be the telephone interview and visiting those centers that make the cut. Once again, a little luck goes a long way. If the center of your choice has an opening, you're in the money and your search may only take a week to a week and a half. However, be sure to keep your options open by thoroughly screening your second choice in the event that your number-one choice doesn't have an opening in your child's group or if your child doesn't meet the center's requirements.

IF YOU STILL CAN'T FIND A GOOD FIT FOR YOUR CHILD OR FAMILY

If, after reviewing your description, the child-care option you are considering isn't working for you, consider another type of child care. Go back to Chapter Two and study the various options available to you. Select another type of child care, and complete the corresponding Needs Assessment. You may find that you have discovered a better fit for your child and your family. If it still doesn't work, don't be too discouraged. Because child-care options are fairly limited, and child care is a difficult proposition no matter how appropriate a certain type of care may be, some parents find that nothing works very well. If this is your situation, rank your choices from "best" to "worst," and start searching for "best." The child care you end up with may not be perfect, but if you use the information, tools, and templates provided by this book, you'll be sure to obtain high-quality, safe, and appropriate care for your child.

CHAPTER FIVE

■ ■ ■ ■ ■ ■ ■ ■ ■ ■

Finding and Hiring Your In-Home Child-Care Provider

IN THIS CHAPTER:

Selecting an Agency

Writing and Placing an Ad

Interviewing

Background and Reference Checking

The Employment Contract

GETTING STARTED

Now that you know exactly what you require in a child-care provider, you're ready to start your search. To assemble a pool of prospects, you have two choices—you can recruit nannies yourself or you can obtain the help of a nanny placement agency.

Obviously, recruiting a nanny on your own involves a large investment of time and effort. However, it is significantly less expensive than going through a nanny placement agency. Keep in mind also that no matter what type of promises an agency makes about the safety, reliability, and training of their nannies, you cannot rely on them to do the extensive interviewing, reference checking, and background checking that is critical when you bring a stranger into your home to care for your child. If you have the resources to pay an agency, I suggest you view the transaction this way: You are paying the agency to assemble a pool of candidates, so you won't need to write an advertisement, review résumés, or schedule interviews yourself. You will still be responsible for careful interviewing, verification of certifications, and extensive reference and background checking to make sure that the nanny you choose from the agency's pool is safe, is appropriate, and meets all of your requirements.

Start by Getting Organized

Start by taking a few minutes to get organized. You'll find that by putting together everything you need for the project in one place, the whole process will be less confusing and stressful. If you have room, try to set up a permanent workspace for yourself, preferably at a desk with a phone. Add some manila files, a desktop file holder or a file cabinet, a pocket calculator, stationery, envelopes, and a few legal pads and pens, and you're done.

If you have a computer and a printer, that's even better. If you don't have access to a computer, look in the yellow pages to locate the nearest retail copy center—you will want to use their copy machines to copy forms and checklists directly out of this book.

If you live in a small home or apartment and don't have enough room for a permanent workspace, purchase a large, inexpensive "accordion" file holder that has ten or more sections, and use one of the sections to hold your supplies. The other sections can hold your forms, documents, notes, etc. During your search for a nanny, keep this file folder next to the phone.

If you don't have an answering machine, consider buying one. You definitely want to be able to get messages from prospective nannies. Or call your local phone company to ask if they provide voice mail. If they do, sign on for a few months. My guess is that this is a service that you will keep after you've hired your nanny. It is a handy, reliable, and inexpensive way to communicate with her when you are not able to speak face to face, or if you are in a meeting, on the road, or otherwise temporarily unavailable. You can have a separate voice mailbox for your nanny with a privacy code that makes it convenient for her to get messages from you but keeps your family's messages private, too. Another high-tech but relatively inexpensive solution that I rely on is a pager or beeper. I have one and Katherine's baby-sitter, Cyndy, carries one when they go out. This way we can both stay in touch and keep each other alerted to those daily changes in schedule that make most moms and dads want to pull their hair out. We have a rule in our house about keeping each other informed: "If you are going to be more than fifteen minutes late, call." This simple but concrete rule sets a good, understand-able limit on tardiness, but also is flexible enough to allow for Cyndy to have control and make decisions about what she and Katherine are doing. If they are at the playground or a friend's house and Katherine is having a great time and wants to stay, Cyndy can make that decision based on what they are meant to do next. Assuming that staying at the friend's house doesn't mean canceling something else, Cyndy has the power to make the decision. I just want to know where they are and when I can expect them home.

The least expensive pagers "beep" you and leave a phone number for you to call to get the information. Cyndy has this type. More expen-sive, but I think well worth it, are the alpha-numeric pagers, which I carry, that give you an 800 number for your caller to call and leave a sixty-character message for you like, "Cyndy and Katherine are home from Chuck E. Cheese. All OK." Usually, when I get these messages by prearrangement I don't even call back because I know that they are home safe, and that Cyndy will follow through with Katherine's bedtime routine.

Checklist of Things to Buy

- accordion file, desktop file holder, or file cabinet
- pocket calculator
- manila folders
- stationery and envelopes
- assorted pens and pencils
- answering machine or voice-mail service

SOURCES

Employee Assistance Programs

If your company has an Employee Assistance Program that offers dependent-care referrals, check in with them for a list of recommended child-care providers in your area. Be sure to find out how your company or the referral agency compiled the list. Have your company and the referral agency established certain standards for the providers they rec-ommend, or is it just a random list of local centers? If your company has standards, what are they and how far do they go? Additionally, ask if your company offers a Dependent Care Assistance Program that provides financial assistance to defray dependent-care expenses by allocating payroll funds into a special account. These funds are not subject to federal taxes, or certain state and social security taxes, but you should be aware of several thorny issues regarding the possible loss of unused funds, potential reduction in future social security benefits, and other rules. However, it is important to know about the option and give yourself the chance to weigh the benefits and problems with the program director to see if you can make it work for you.

The Nanny Placement Agency

Many parents who can afford it will opt for using the services of a nanny placement agency to expedite their search for child care. Although there are some advantages to this, remember that you cannot rely on your agency, no matter how "good" or expensive it is, to do due diligence for you. You yourself must check out your chosen nanny thoroughly before allowing her access to your child.

Contrary to what you may think, even the best nanny agencies don't have a large pool of well-trained, experienced, qualified, and background-checked nannies waiting around for their next assignment. A successful nanny placement is based more on market conditions, time of year, what you are willing to pay, and serendipitous luck of the draw because you will only be introduced to the pool of candidates available and registered with that agency over the two or three weeks of your search. Keep in mind that you will be introduced to whomever the agency believes you may hire—which is not necessarily whom you may want, need, or can afford. Agencies find nannies and place them on an as-needed basis. That means that even the best nanny agency in town will offer you the next nanny who walks in their door if she looks neat and clean, can speak tolerable English, and has a green card—even if she is untrained, unqualified, and unsafe. Because of the low pay and even lower esteem our society has given child-care providers historically, agencies often have a difficult time attracting even out-of-work, undereducated, and untrained people, much less the bright, educated, motivated, and safe nannies most parents desire.

Let me assure you that I'm not trying to bash nanny placement firms. However, parents often have unrealistic expectations about what these agencies can and will do. It's important to remember that an agency's only responsibility is to send you nanny prospects to interview. Agencies are paid a fee for every placement, so it is their job to encourage a match—but only you will know if it is an appropriate one.

Though many agencies try to match candidates' skills with a family's needs, only you can truly know what you need and can afford. An agency won't help you manage or mediate with your nanny once she is your employee. Think of a nanny placement agency just as you would anyone else selling a product with no further responsibility to you after you take delivery—and with a limited and onerous return policy. Just as you would never buy a car, refrigerator, or other high-ticket item without thoroughly researching your needs, what you can afford, and the dirty little secrets of the industry, you need to be well versed in your local nanny placement agencies' business practices, reputations, contracts or service agreements, and return policies.

Many agencies convince parents that they'll take special care in those they represent because children are involved. But you should always remember that at the heart of their business, placement agencies are paid a fee for making a placement—any placement. There are certainly reputable agencies that provide good services and build strong reputations based on this fact, but the lack of industry-wide standards for licensing and insurance has created a thriving environment for many small, unincorporated agencies that clearly care little for anything other than the transaction fee for placement. And, while many agencies, including the more reputable ones, claim to do candidate screening, most don't and frankly can't. Parents must have child-care providers checked out by an independent third party who gets no fee for placement and whose only business is to verify this type of sensitive data. Just as you wouldn't have the car salesman test-drive a car for you and report back to you about the quality of the ride, you shouldn't trust the agency to verify a nanny's credentials objectively. You'll learn how to verify credentials later in this chapter.

Hiring a nanny placement agency will provide you with a pool of willing nanny candidates quickly. You won't need to write and place an ad; nor will you necessarily need to prescreen candidates by phone. The agency will do these preliminary steps for you. I do recommend, however, that you guarantee that each candidate the agency refers to you has received your minimum requirements in writing before you waste your valuable time on an in-person interview. Ask the agency to give each candidate a written list of your requirements. Then ask the agency to have the nanny initial the list once she has reviewed it, and give it back to the agency representative. Be sure that the agency keeps each of these initialed documents in your file for future reference.

If you do opt to go with a nanny placement agency to set up a pool of nanny prospects for you, here are some general guidelines.

Selecting an Agency

Your first step is to find an agency. Try phoning your local child-care resource-and-referral service. They will be able to give you a list of agencies within your zip code. You can get the number of your local resource and referral agency by phoning Child Care Aware at (800) 424-2246. Also, look in the yellow pages under "child care" and be sure to ask your pediatrician and any friends with children.

Au Pair Agencies

If you are in the market for an au pair, find the name and phone number of the au pair agency closest to you and call them. There are only eight official au pair agencies in the United States. These agencies are regulated by the federal government. You must go through one of these agencies to hire a real au pair. Be aware that many people call their American or foreign-born nannies "au pairs." Some nannies call themselves an "au pair" to add cachet to their job title. In addition, some au pairs who have left their host family may try to market themselves to you as au pairs. However, once they are "free agents" these au pairs are just regular, foreign nannies who have no ties to the official U.S. au pair program.

A child-care provider is not a true "au pair" unless she has been allowed into the United States through the official au pair program. Do not hire an au pair through a newspaper ad, or an "au pair referral service." If you do, you will just get a foreign nanny or baby-sitter who hasn't passed the minimum standards required by the official U.S. au pair agencies and may very likely be in the United States illegally or have a visa that is about to expire.

Because there are only eight au pair agencies in the United States, your interaction with the agency will most likely be by phone and written correspondence. This means you need to factor in the potential time zone differences, costs, and a lag time in getting written information and materials. While many of the au pair agencies have local reps, they tend to deal with parents only while they are choosing an au pair from the general pool of candidates.

Because there are only a few official au pair agencies, you really don't have much of a choice when it comes to fees, services, procedures, and the terms of your agreement with the agency. However, I recommend that you go through the screening process I describe below for choosing the au pair agency that will work best for you.

Screening Agencies

Once you have a list together, make several copies of the Placement Agency Screening Questions in Chapter Ten and on the diskette in the in-home file, and start phoning the agencies to gather information about their services, policies, and pricing before you make your choice. Use one questionnaire per agency and take detailed notes. In addition, ask the agency for two recent clients in your area who have hired nannies or are currently sponsoring au pairs to provide references. In the case of the nanny placement agency, be sure to be referred to two different sets of parents—one who hired a nanny from that agency six months ago, and one hiring a nanny one year ago. This way you will speak to parents who have had enough experience with their choice to truly know if the candidate is working out—and has stayed.

When you go about choosing your agency, remember that you are the consumer, and the agency is a prospective provider of a service. Do not be afraid to politely ask as many questions as you feel you need to make your choice. You are choosing the agency; they are not choosing you. If you don't like what you hear, take your business elsewhere. One of the reasons child care is such a problem today is that parents don't feel empowered to act like consumers when dealing with agencies, nannies, or day- and family day-care providers. They need child care so badly that they tiptoe around, afraid to ask questions, get information, effect change, and so forth—all because they think the provider won't like them because of the questions and will turn them away. Let me assure you that you will find a better child-care provider for your child if you act like the smart consumer that you are.

Here is the template you should use to screen either an au pair agency or a nanny placement agency. This template is also found in the back of the book in Chapter Ten and on the software by clicking on the In-Home Child Care icon in the application.

PLACEMENT AGENCY SCREENING
QUESTIONS

1. "How long has your agency been in business?" _____

2. "Are you independently owned or part of a chain?" _____

3. "With whom will I be dealing and will it be the same person every time I call?"
   _____

4. "How do you recruit nannies?" ❏ Advertise ❏ Word of mouth
   ❏ Affiliated with child-care group or nanny school
   ❏ Other _____
   _____
   _____

5. "Do you verify the backgrounds and experience of your nannies?" [All will answer yes, so go on to the next question.] _____

6. "How extensive is the background check? Do you check criminal records, civil records, and driving records in every state that the nanny has lived in over the past 7 years?"_____
   _____

7. "Do you do background checks yourself or do you hire an independent, third party to investigate?" _____

8. "Will I see the written résumés on the nannies I am considering?" _____

9. "How do you check references? What questions do you ask former employers, and how do you really know they were former employers?" [Many people make up references. They have friends answer the calls who then tell potential employers everything they want to hear!] _____
   _____
   _____
   _____

10. "Do the nanny candidates sign with you exclusively?" _____

11. "Do they pay a fee to be represented by you?" _____

12. "Are your nannies certified in infant and child CPR and first aid?" _____

13. "Do you provide any training for your nannies? _____
    _____

14. "What is your fee?" _____

15. "What form of payment will you accept? Check or credit cards?" _____

_____

16. "Do you get paid up front or after placement?" _____

17. "Will you give me a refund if my nanny doesn't work out?" _____

18. "If my chosen nanny leaves me within a certain amount of time, do I get a refund or will you find me another nanny? What is that time frame?" _____

_____

_____

■ ■

Working With Your Agency

Once you have found an agency you like, make sure the agency knows exactly what you want. Clear communication is key. While it is very tempting to do all communication with your agency by phone, *be sure to follow up on these important things in writing*: (1) all communication regarding their fee; (2) their policy for refunds and/or help finding you a new nanny if the current hire doesn't work out. In addition, make sure you do the following: (1) Give your agency representative a copy of your completed Job Description and ask for any comments she might have. (2) Get a copy of the agency's contract to review by fax or in person and thoroughly review it.

Here are some other key tips:

- Work with only one person at the agency. Get her name and work schedule during your first call.

- Be precise about how quickly you need to fill the position.

- Ask when you will hear from them about the first candidate and give firm parameters on when and where you want to be called. Set a defined time for when you would prefer to do both telephone and in-person interviews and stick to it. Don't force your agency representative to play telephone tag with you and don't let them pressure you into conducting an interview at inconvenient times.

- If the agency uses terms you don't understand or acts in a manner inconsistent with what you have been told or is in your contract, get clarification right away.

- This is a business transaction like any other—only because it involves the care of your child, there's more at stake. Approach it with a businesslike attitude and demand the same in return. If at any time you feel that you are not being represented appropriately, look elsewhere immediately.

- Never see a candidate before your business relationship with the agency is finalized.

- Be conservative in your expectations for how long this process will take.

Once your agency has found some candidates, it's time to start preparing for an interview. Skip down to the section on the In-Person Interview now.

GOING IT ALONE

You've decided to forgo the assistance of a nanny or au pair agency. What do you do now? How do you start? Your local child-care resource and referral agency will only get you so far. They don't offer much in the way of individual nannies, but they can refer you to local nanny placement agencies. You can get the phone number of your local resource and referral agency by phoning Child Care Aware at (800) 424-2246.

Sometimes nannies advertise in local newspapers, on the bulletin board at your church or synagogue, or in the placement office at your local college or university.

Another way to try to find a nanny is by word of mouth. On those rare occasions when it works, word-of-mouth recommendations can be one of the best ways to find a nanny. You tell your friend you need a nanny, she tells a friend who tells another friend, and next thing you know, you're interviewing someone who worked for a friend of your friend's friend.

The problem with word of mouth is that while it can be much less expensive, it doesn't obviate all of the due diligence that a parent needs to complete before entrusting her children to someone, no matter how highly recommended. An introduction through a channel of friends completes only the first step in the hiring process—meeting viable candidates. All of the other steps in the process still need to be completed by you, regardless of who has made the introduction. Am I saying that an acquaintance would introduce you to a nanny candidate who is incompetent or inappropriate? You bet I am.

Writing Your Advertisement

Now that you have your completed Needs Assessment in hand, writing an effective advertisement will be easy. Take a look at the following ads for ideas. The first ad is based on Dan and Karen P.'s completed Needs Assessment. This ad, placed in a Sunday "Child Care" section of the "Help Wanted" listings on two different weekends in a large city newspaper and a local newspaper, garnered fourteen responses from qualified nannies who were each interviewed by telephone, four in-person interviews with final candidates, and one very competent, safe, and experienced nanny to care for the twins and the two older boys.

Example 1

Nanny Wanted: FT, Live-out for infant twins. Must drive own ins. car. Prev. inf. exp., inf. chd/CPR, high school degree, nonsmoker, lite clean/cook req'd. Must clear back. ck. $10/hr. Gas allow. Call Karen at (413) 555-8237.

Example 2

Nanny Wanted: FT, Live-in for toddler and infant. Must drive own ins. car. Prev. inf. exp., inf. chd/CPR, B.A. or B.S. pref. Must clear back. ck. $10/hr. Gas allow. Call Jill 10 to 3 P.M. (413) 555-9876.

Example 3

Live-in Child Care: FT for 6 and 7 yr. olds. Must drive. Prev. exp., CPR/first aid, lite clean/cook, N/S. $11/hr. Call Jim P.M. (413) 555-2347.

Example 4

Child Care Wanted: PT, Live-out for infant. Prev. inf. exp., inf. CPR/first aid, lite clean, N/S. $8.50/hr. Phone Liz. (413) 555-9876.

If you are using the software, once you have completed the Needs Assessment, you have all the information for your Newspaper Ad ready to be placed in the designated prioritized slots for the ad. Click on Newspaper Ad and take a look at the copy. It will include information from your

Needs Assessment. It may be a good idea to print out a copy to review. If you are using the templates in the book, flip to the back of the book, and fill in the blanks on the "Your Ad" template in Chapter Ten. Note that the numbers on the ad template refer to the numbered questions on the Needs Assessment. When questions in the Needs Assessment have several answers, include the qualifications that are most important to you in the ad.

YOUR NEWSPAPER ADVERTISEMENT

Nanny Wanted: _____FT_____ , _____Live-in_____ for
                  Question 1   *Question 2*

_____3 yr. old_____ , _____Own ins. car_____ , _____BA_____ ,
   Question 5   *Question 3a to 3g*   *Question 7*

_____Prev. exp._____ , _____NS_____ , _____Lite Clean_____ ,
   Question 7   *Question 7*   *Question 6*

_____$7.75/Hr_____ , Call ____Phone Monica at (415) 844-8444 eve____ .
   Question 8   *Fill in your name, area code, and*
                                   phone number and time available.

Here's your final product:

Nanny Wanted: FT, Live-in for 3 yr. old, Own ins. car, BA, prev. exp., NS, lite clean, cook, $7.75/hr. Phone Monica at (415) 884-4444 eve.

After you review your first draft, feel free to edit it if something isn't right. You may want to add additional requirements, or take something out. Adjust your ad so that you're comfortable with the wording.

For a few days prior to placing your ad it might be a good idea to get the lay of the land by checking the classified section each day, and in the Sunday paper to determine the best placement and wording of your ad. That's a good way to plan an effective placement. Does the paper have a separate child-care section in the classifieds? If so, when does it run? It's also a good way to see if the salary you're offering is competitive and if your requirements seem reasonable. Also, check the language used; you may need to modify your ad to make it locally relevant. Many newspapers will abbreviate the words in the ad for you. If they don't do abbreviations, go through your ad and abbreviate everything you can. After abbreviating, you may want to perfect your ad some more, but for the most part, it should be ready to go.

Common Classified Abbreviations

FT=full-time	back ck=background
PT=part-time	check
NS=nonsmoker	hr=hour
ins=insured	prev=previous
pref=preferred	exp=experience

How to Place Your Ad

Now that you have prepared your copy, call the classified advertising section of the local paper with the highest circulation in your area. Most papers put their circulation on the front page, but if they don't, give the paper a call and ask. By going to the paper with the largest circulation in your area, you may pay more, but a greater pool of prospective nannies will ultimately see your ad. Remember, the bigger your pool, the greater the number of choices you have in nannies, and the better off you will be.

When you call the newspaper's classified department be sure to find out how much they charge per word or per line, and whether they charge by the day or week and what kind of payment they accept. Be sure to ask when their deadline is for Sunday submissions. (You want to be sure to get your ad in the paper on Sunday because the greatest number of job-hunting nannies will see it on that day.) Then, provide the paper with your copy. If they will accept faxes, be sure to fax your ad copy to them to prevent errors. One last thing: Be sure to look for the ad on the day it starts to run and check that your phone number and all other information in the ad is correct.

THE TELEPHONE PRESCREEN

Use your telephone to find out whether a candidate has the basic qualifications you require and be sure to leave a detailed answering-machine or voice-mail message for candidates (see box). When an interested nanny first calls in response to the ad, your voice-mail message should ask her to leave a time for you to return the call, hopefully when she has a few minutes for a brief phone interview. Be sure to tailor your answering-machine message to welcome calls from potential candidates by requesting *all* the information that you will need to return the call and assess the candidate's skills. Believe me, if a candidate cannot follow the simple instructions for data that you leave on an answering machine, you don't want to hire her.

Sample Answering Machine Message

"You've reached the Smith family. We're not home right now, but welcome your call. Please leave a message and we'll return your call as soon as possible. If you are calling about the nanny position, please leave your full name, telephone number, and a time when you will be available for a brief phone interview. We look forward to speaking with you soon."

If the nanny calls in response to the ad and happens to reach you, ask if she has time for a twenty- to thirty-minute interview right then (if you also have time); if not, schedule another time to talk at length and tell the nanny to phone you then. Whenever possible, have the nanny phone you: If she phones on time, it is a good indication of her promptness, organization, and responsibility. If she phones late, or forgets to phone, a big, very bright, red flag is raised and you might reconsider going any further with her in the interview process.

Whether you're returning calls or speaking for the first time, ask each potential nanny some basic questions so you can get a good feel for the type of person you are dealing with, her personality and ability to communicate, and most importantly, a preliminary assessment of whether the nanny has all of your baseline requirements. Try to get as much information as you possibly can by telephone. To save time, you want to be able to eliminate inappropriate candidates from the running as early as you can. I would allow plenty of time for your conversation. You should try to talk for at least fifteen minutes, but allow half an hour for each phone interview.

Take a look at the Telephone Prescreen Questions below and then flip to the Telephone Prescreen Questions template in Chapter Ten. Add any extra questions you would like to ask at the bottom of the template or on an extra page. Then, make multiple copies of the questionnaire. Use one questionnaire per nanny, filling in the answers to your questions in the appropriate spaces; be sure to take detailed notes during your conversation. If you are using the software, go to the Telephone Prescreen Questions template in the In-Home file. Review and print out multiple copies of this template and put them in your accordion file near the phone so they are handy when you get calls from candidates.

After you have asked all your questions and had a few minutes to chat, decide whether the nanny fits your requirements and warrants an in-person interview. If you are certain that you want to interview her in person, schedule the interview, and use the space at the bottom of the template to enter a date, time, and place (I did the in-person interview in my home with Katherine, so that I could get a better feel for whether a nanny fit in). Ask the candidate to bring her certification papers for infant/child CPR and first aid, and at least three employment references. Personal references are fine, but don't hold much water. Invariably they are positive, but they can't give you the information you need about the nanny's work habits, attitude, maturity, and responsibility.

If, after the phone call, you're not sure whether she fits the bill, and want to talk to some other candidates before you decide to interview her in person, tell her that you will call back by a specific time, for example, "this Friday," to schedule the interview. After you have talked to every nanny who responded, try ranking the nannies you will interview by their skills and experience.

Again, this template can be found in Chapter Ten or on the software by clicking the In-Home Child Care icon.

TELEPHONE PRESCREEN QUESTIONS
FOR IN-HOME PROVIDERS

Candidate:_____

Phone Number:_____

Date of Call:_____

Start by describing the position, pay, and hours. Then ask:

1. "Would you be able to work at the proposed pay and number of hours a week?"

   ☐ yes   ☐ no

2. "Please give me an overview of your experience and qualifications for work in child care." _____

   _____

   _____

3. "Are you certified in CPR, infant CPR, and first aid?

   _____

4. "Why did you leave your most recent job?" _____

   _____

   _____

5. "Tell me why you are interested in this job." _____

   _____

   _____

   _____

6. "What are your long-term plans or career goals?" _____

   _____

7. "Would you agree to a national investigation of your background?"   ☐ yes ☐ no

8. Include any other questions you would like to ask in the following space or on another sheet. _____

   _____

   _____

   _____

IN-PERSON INTERVIEW

_____

Date: *Time:*   *Location:*

THE IN-PERSON INTERVIEW

The in-person interview is your chance to find out everything you need to know about your potential nanny. You need to make full use of it! Many parents I talk to are very experienced interviewers for their corporate jobs, but fall apart when it comes to interviewing nannies. Sometimes it's because they don't really trust their judgment as new parents. If the nanny has some experience in child care, they may feel that she is more competent than they are at taking care of children. They don't want to betray what they believe is their ignorance by asking the "wrong" questions. Other times parents are so desperate for a nanny, they spend the entire interview trying to make a good impression. They clean the house thoroughly, dress little Suzie up in her best clothes, and try to say and do all the right things so that the nanny will want them. Still others treat the interview very casually, in the hopes that the nanny will like them, and they will be "fast friends" instead of employer-employee. They believe that, ultimately, this will make their day-to-day dealings with the nanny easier.

Each of these parents is mistaken. An interview for a nanny is just like a regular corporate job interview, except the stakes are far higher. Your child's health and safety are at risk in this transaction. For this reason, you must adhere to the standards of professionalism expected and exhibited in the corporate setting, but your questions should be more probing. And your efforts to verify the background and credentials of the nanny after a successful interview should be even more energetic than in the corporate setting. If companies around the country are redoubling their efforts to investigate the credentials and backgrounds of senior executives, middle managers, and administrative assistants, shouldn't you do the same or more with the person who is responsible for the care, custody, and control of your child on a daily basis?

Preparing for the Interview

On or before the day of the interview, read through the sample In-Person Interview Questions for In-Home Providers. Then, flip to the In-Person Interview Questions template in Chapter Ten.

If you are using the software, click on the In-Home icon, scroll to the In-Person Interview Questions template, click on it, and print it out. Also print out a copy of the Job Description template you have already completed and saved and have it ready for the candidate to review.

(Make a copy for yourself if you feel you may need to refer to it, too.) Feel free to add questions to the template. Be sure to think about your life-style and your specific needs. For example, would the provider agree to prepare kosher meals for your child; not smoke on or off the job; not wear perfume, and so on? Also, consider asking the nanny additional questions related to how she would handle specific situations, especially tricky ones. For example, if she's upstairs bathing your child when the doorbell rings, what would she do? Above all, avoid yes-or-no questions. You want to elicit in-depth responses that will give you insight into the personality, experience, and maturity of the nanny. The goal is to let her talk. At this stage, your role is to listen. Remember, you don't need to sell yourself to the nanny during the interview; take the time just to listen. After you have added your own questions, make one copy of the template for each nanny you will interview.

Sample Questions to Add to Your Template

Would you be willing to prepare only vegetarian meals for my child?

Would you feel comfortable going to church with my child on the Sundays you might be required to work?

How much television do you watch every week?

How would you handle the following situation: You have a minor fender-bender while driving my child to a haircut appointment in a very dangerous part of the city. The police haven't arrived yet. What do you do?

A few minutes before the interview, put your interview questions and a pen in the room where you will hold the interview. Make sure someone is watching your child, so that you can give full attention to the interview, but have your child stay in the house, so that when and if it is appropriate the nanny and child can be introduced.

Things to Have on Hand During the Interview

Completed Job Description	pen/pencil
In-Person Interview Questions template	extra paper for notes
	candidate's file

THE INTERVIEW

The more interviews you do, the easier they will get. Try to be comfortable yourself, and try to make the nanny comfortable. You'll learn much more about her. Start by telling the nanny a little bit about yourself, the job, and how your family operates (Mom and Dad work nine to five, older sister in day care, etc.). If the nanny candidate is coming to you from an agency, she should have already reviewed the information you provided the agency. Even so, take a minute to go over the Job Description template with her. During this time you can review the documents she has brought with her—CPR and first-aid credentials, and so forth. When she has had time to look the Job Description over, ask if she has any questions and confirm that she can perform the duties. At that point, the interview can proceed.

Run through each of your questions and take notes about her answers and your impressions as the interview continues. For example, if the nanny seems decidedly uncomfortable when you ask her about the reason why she left her last job, note it. Take your time—if you don't rush the interview you'll learn far more about the nanny. When you have gone through all the questions, ask the nanny if she has any questions for you. This can be a key part of the interview. You learn a lot about a person from her questions. Remember, this is the candidate's time to convince you to hire her. The only thing you need to be convincing about is that you are a serious parent and that you expect to have a professional, cordial, responsible relationship with your employee. You are in charge.

If you like the nanny, introduce her to your child. If you don't like the nanny, or have any doubts about anything she has told you that you may need to think about or verify, don't introduce her to your child— just end the interview at this point. If you do introduce her to your child, don't try to manage the situation—just watch how the nanny relates to your child. If she is comfortable and immediately engages your child, she has charm and unbelievable luck—a definite plus. But that doesn't mean you should hire her. And if the first few minutes are awkward, watch how she approaches your child—does she wait out a reticent kid or does she try to dominate? Is she careful not to be too loud or physically intimidating? The truth is that patience, maturity, and a friendly smile will eventually win over almost any child—no matter what her mood or how sleepy she is. So put instant bonding in the "nice to have"

IN-PERSON INTERVIEW QUESTIONS
FOR IN-HOME PROVIDERS

Here's a sample set of interview questions and answers from Dan and Karen P.'s in-person interview:

Candidate: _Nellie Smith_

Date of Interview: _March 20, 1995_

Once again, describe in detail the position, pay, and hours. Hand her the job description and run through all duties and responsibilities. Then ask:

1. "Do you have any questions or concerns about the position, pay, hours?"

   _No_

2. "What about the duties and responsibilities that this position requires?"

   Concerned about cleaning; doesn't want to do too much.

3. "Tell me a little about your family background and education."

   Born in Cleveland; only child; mother was a teacher, father a maintenance worker; public school through high school; junior college—B student. Married at 18—divorced.

4. "What was your motivation for becoming a nanny?"

   Loves children.

5. "Tell me why you believe you are the right person to care for my child."

   Lots of experience; well organized, practical, and efficient; interested in educational development of children.

6. "Run through a routine for a typical day with my child." _Fixes healthy breakfast; takes children out for long walk or to park if weather is good. Games or art projects if weather bad. Healthy lunch, then naps. Outside for play. Then starts fixing simple dinner. Bathes and puts on pajamas before dinner. After meal is quiet time—reading, listening to music. Then, bedtime. Nellie reads, or does dishes and laundry when kids are napping or asleep for night. No TV._

7. "Give me some examples of age-appropriate activities you would do with my child on a regular basis." _Painting; playing with clay/playdough; swinging; swimming; sandbox sandcastles; baking cookies; etc._

90

8. "How would you discipline my child?" _Time-outs._

9. "How would you handle an emergency, for example a fire in the house?"
   Assess situation and choose safest exit from house for children and
   myself. Get children out of house. Call police/fire from neighbor's house
   only after children are out of the house and safe.

10. "How would you handle a medical emergency, for example if my child was
    choking?" _Check airway for obstruction. If obstruction can be safely_
    removed, do so quickly. If unable to remove, do Heimlich maneuver and CPR
    if required. Call for help as soon as possible.

11. "Do you have any health or medical problems that would interfere with your
    ability to work here?" _no_

12. Include any other questions you would like to ask in the following space or on
    another sheet. _____

RECORD YOUR IMPRESSIONS

Appearance:

Neat and clean. Fine.

Attitude:

Reserved. Maybe a little shy.

Enthusiasm:

Moderate. Doesn't go overboard but isn't dragging her feet.

Intelligence:

Fine.

Common Sense:

Very high level. Excellent.

Interaction with your child:

Great—Michael loved her. Nellie is much warmer and much more enthusiastic
with Michael than me.

category and settle for competency and someone who knows how children tick.

Before the nanny leaves, ask her to give you her three employment references. Remind her that you require a background check. If you are using a background investigation service, have the nanny sit down and fill out the application and sign the release forms. If you are not using a background check service that has application forms, be sure you have the correct spelling of her name and her current address and phone number so that you can reach her. As a courtesy, let the nanny know when you will get back to her with your decision.

CHOOSING YOUR NANNY

Whether you have interviewed two nannies or twenty, one nanny should stand out in your mind as the best for the job. However, if you don't have a clear favorite, don't be discouraged. Just schedule another round of interviews for the top two or three contenders. Focus in on what is bothering you about them and try to decide whether it is really important or perhaps just a superficial interpersonal issue. If you are considering compromising on any of the minimum standard requirements we have discussed just to be done with the process, think again. However, if a nanny is eminently qualified, but you just don't like her, schedule another interview to see if you can work yourself out of it. You might have been put off by a seemingly innocent comment she made, and it taints what would otherwise have been a good interview. If that's the case, step back for a moment, do something else, and then think about the situation with a clearer head. Bad days, bad commutes, and no child care can make anyone negative. Be sure the sticking point is a true "deal breaker" before you drop a qualified candidate.

In the second interview, assess the candidate's interaction with your child. Make it the central point of the interview. After this round of interviews, I guarantee that one person will stand out as a clear leader.

BACKGROUND CHECKS

Before making any offer, make sure you do a thorough background check. This will provide you with all of the objectively verifiable information you need to be sure that you are hiring a safe nanny with an appropriate background.

The idea of investigating a person's background may seem intrusive and drastic. It is. Unfortunately, the world has changed for employers in corporate environments and employers in the home. Back in the good old days, when families traditionally raised their children in the same neighborhood and town where they themselves grew up, there was little need for multistate criminal checks and reference checks. However, we are all painfully aware of how society and families have changed. It is time to be honest and intelligent about the information we use to make our decisions.

How to Secure a Background Check on a Nanny

Once you have winnowed your candidate pool down to the final one or two candidates, perform a comprehensive verification of all of the candidate's personal data, including the items in the accompanying box.

Verify Candidate's Data in These Areas for Last Five Years

identity	criminal records search
SSI Social Security Index number	civil courts search
employment history	driving record
educational background	

Because you are considering hiring a particular candidate based on the data she supplied by her outlining her previous employment experience, any relevant education pertaining to child care, and other information, you need an independent corroboration of the claims this candidate or any candidate makes. Although the personal interview(s) are important and should add a ton of credibility, we all know that some people think that telling a "little white lie" that enhances their ability to get a job "doesn't really hurt anyone." I can think of two parties it can hurt immediately. The first person is the other, honest candidate who hasn't fabricated or embellished her background, and while qualified, pales in comparison to Ms. White Lie. You and your family are the second.

Is Ms. White Lie really Lizzie Borden? Probably not. Should she be boiled in oil for claiming an education or employment background that improves her chances of getting the job? I don't think so. However, you should certainly check her claims and verify each and every one of them to adequately assess whether your minimum requirements are being met. Then you will be able to realistically compare her to other candidates.

You have only a few options if you want to do a comprehensive, identity/education/employment verification and multijurisdictional criminal, civil, and driving records check on a potential child-care provider: (1) Do it yourself. (2) Hire a private investigator you know and trust. (3) Hire The ChildCare Registry or another preemployment screening company that can provide you with a packaged service and a legal release.

How to Do Your Own Background Check

I created The ChildCare Registry to provide parents with a service that provides legally released, comprehensive, state-of-the-art preemployment screening verifications and criminal, civil, and driving records that are completed within seven days. However, for parents who want to do the background check themselves, here is what I would do:

Get permission, in writing, from your candidate to do a background check.

Identity: In order to run a Social Security Index trace with the Social Security Administration, you will need the candidate's name and social security number and your valid federal Employer Identification Number. (See the Legal Kit for information on getting a copy of the SS 4 Form, which needs to be completed and filed by mail or by fax with your regional IRS office. The turnaround time to get your number is about ten to fourteen days by mail.) Call the IRS and Social Security Administration to confirm the validity of the name and SSI number you have been provided.

Employment: Get a complete list of all employers, including names of supervisors, addresses, and phone numbers for the last five years. Have the candidate include her job position, starting and departing dates, and salary for each employer. Call each employer, indicate that you want to verify a person's previous employment, and cross your fingers, because this can be ticklish. Personal employers, like other parents, are often hard to reach because you may not have their work numbers (I'm not sure you should call there, anyway), which means you will have to call in the evening. So you may need to be persistent, but other parents are a gold mine of information, so don't get discouraged. Business employers, like day-care centers or other previous employers, need to be called during business hours, so take the information with you to work and call during lunch or a break. This gets complicated if you don't reach anyone who can help you and you need to be called back. If you can get calls at the office, great—leave that number; but if you can't and you need to leave your home number, be sure to leave an appropriate message on your home answering machine encouraging the party to leave a detailed response for you. Some previous employers may chafe at this and refuse to leave a message with sensitive employment data on a home answering machine.

Education: Have your candidate provide you with detailed information on each education claim. Get the full name, address, phone number, dates attended, and highest grade or graduation date for each institution. If you want to verify a candidate's high school graduation, you can probably do that over the telephone by calling the administrative office of the school during business hours. Colleges, universities, and other places of higher learning are trickier. Some require an authorization and release faxed to them. Others charge a small fee, and insist on everything in writing, by mail. Many require the graduate's full name (watch out for name changes, like maiden names), date of birth, or social security number to ascertain identity and make sure you are talking about the same person. You will need to have all of this information handy when you call, so be sure to have a complete file in front of you.

Driving Records: You will want to verify that your candidate has a valid driver's license, which indicates her ability to get insurance, and that your candidate's driving record is also clear of any moving violations, driving under the influence convictions, or other serious issues. Also, keep in mind that in many states, even drivers whose licenses have been suspended can drive to and from work. So it is important to understand and verify your candidate's license status. How can you get a copy of your candidate's driving record? You can't, but she can. Once again, if you can get access to a public records database company who will accept your version of an authorization and release and sells "retail," you may be able to get a copy of your candidate's driving record. However, the only sure-fire way of getting a copy is to have your candidate go to her local DMV, pay a fee (in California it's $5), and get a *dated copy* of her driving record. But be careful. It is easy to alter, fabricate, and counterfeit documents. Laser printers and high-resolution copiers have revolutionized the fine art of document manipulation, so it is critical that you can authenticate any document received by you from your candidate.

Insist that the driving record be very fresh and current—I would recommend that it be dated within one week of your examining it.

Criminal History Records: This is really a tough one. Although no one will argue the need to be aware of any type of criminal record in the background of a personal employee, especially a child-care provider, individual citizens are pretty much precluded from direct access to this information. The ChildCare Registry has access through a network of private investigators armed with sophisticated releases. Private investigators that you may hire can facilitate the same type of public-record courthouse search, but you will have to provide them with a seamless residential history, so that they can know which county courthouses to search. Statewide criminal history databases do exist, but in only a few states.

Civil Courthouse Record Searches: Though a civil courthouse rarely provides the type of inflammatory data that might preclude a candidate from working in child care, it is the one place where extremely pertinent information can hide from view. Did you know that many child molesters are often sued in civil court by the victim and their families for recovery of damages to pay for psychotherapy for the victim? Many times this is the only relief a victim and his/her family can find in the legal system, especially if the molester is not successfully prosecuted in criminal court or if the prosecutors don't go for an indictment because the facts are murky or victims too young to testify. Civil courthouse records cannot be directly accessed by private citizens. However, they can be accessed by private detectives and should be done in each county of residence for five years. These searches need to be authorized and released by the candidate and can be expensive because private detectives usually charge by the hour. Depending on how many jurisdictions your candidate has lived in, this can add up. Additionally, you can expect to pay a document fee for each courthouse search of at least $10.

Does the background check process sound discouraging, time consuming, and expensive? Still want to do this yourself? It's up to you. The whole time I spent writing this I felt like a car mechanic describing how easy it is to change your car's oil at home. Sure, you can do it, and maybe you can save money, but what a mess! Now that you know the components of a background check and some of the little dirty secrets of this industry, you can choose to go it alone. Just keep in mind that you need to protect yourself and your candidate by having complete authorization and a written legal release to do this investigation—and the time to wait until all the pieces are verified.

A ChildCare Registry information packet, which includes everything a parent needs to request a background check including the CCR application, authorization and release, parent release, and payment form can be ordered by calling (800) CCR-0033.

Private Investigators

Private investigators generally charge by the hour and can be quite expensive; but if you have enough money and know and trust an investigator, by all means, hire her. It's best to do your homework and never just hire a private investigator out of the phone book. Private investigators range widely in their business practices, experience, and specialty. In addition, since many private investigators work for law firms or groups of attorneys but can't practice law, they generally do not provide legal authorization and release forms, so you may have to produce your own. You may be tempted to do a background check on a candidate without telling her or without a legal authorization and release, but please resist the temptation. Be sure to tell your nanny candidate she is going to be investigated, and be sure to get her signed permission to verify her records. You want to be up-front with your nanny right from the start, and you want your nanny to be assured that you are not invading her privacy. A bonus is that many candidates will come clean about something in their record that makes them inappropriate for child care, if you tell them they will be investigated. If they do come clean, you've just saved yourself a substantial amount of money. Make sure that your investigator does a check that goes back at least five to seven years, and includes verification of identity, date of birth, social security number, education, employment history and references, driving record, and civil and criminal records in every jurisdiction of residence.

Calling References

A professional background investigation will verify whether the nanny was employed by the persons she gave as her references. Now you need to call each of the references to obtain critical information about the qualities you require. If you are doing the background check and the reference-checking yourself, you'll do both tasks in one call.

Remember, a nanny must have the following personal qualities:

- personal maturity
- responsible/dependable
- adaptable
- fun-loving
- warm/caring
- even-tempered

When you reach one of the nanny's references, introduce yourself and explain that you are considering hiring the nanny. Then, ask all of the questions on the Professional Reference Report, which allows you to verify all the factual issues regarding the candidate's previous employment and the softer, more subjective information also. The questions are designed to elicit as much information as possible about the nanny's personal qualities from the reference. Feel free to ask any additional questions you would like and be sure to listen carefully. Review the sample Professional Reference Report below. Then, turn to the template in Chapter Ten or in the software under the In-Home icon:

CHILD-CARE PROVIDER
PROFESSIONAL REFERENCE REPORT

Applicant: _Nellie Smith_
Company/Parent Contacted: _Jane Brown_
Address: _222 Westwind Rd._
Newark, NJ 02114
Phone Number: _(212) 222-2222_
Individual Contacted: _same_
Reported: _____

Dates of Employment _2/92 to 4/95_
Starting Position _nanny 2/92_
Ending Position _nanny 4/95_
Salary $_7.75 hr_
Reason for Leaving: _Their child was in fifth grade; didn't want nanny anymore._

Dates of Employment	☑ VER	☐ INC	☐ CNV	☐ NR
Starting Position	☑ VER	☐ INC	☐ CNV	☐ NR
Ending Position	☑ VER	☐ INC	☐ CNV	☐ NR
Salary	☑ VER	☐ INC	☐ CNV	☐ NR
Reason for Leaving	☑ VER	☐ INC	☐ CNV	☐ NR*

Results: _____
_____
_____
_____

How would you rate his/her overall job performance on a scale of 1 to 10 with 10 being excellent? _9_____
Did he/she show improvement/growth in the position? _yes_____
What were his/her strengths? _Follows directions very well, warm, capable, responsible_____
What were the areas that you would recommend improvements (weaknesses)? _a little shy with adults—hurt communications somewhat___
Would you reemploy?   ☑ Y   ☐ N
Any trouble with:
    Attendance   ☐ Y   ☑ N
    Attitude   ☐ Y   ☑ N
    Dependability   ☐ Y   ☑ N
    Teamwork   ☐ Y   ☑ N

Additional Information:_____
_____
_____

*VER=VERIFIED; INC=INCORRECT; CNV=COULD NOT VERIFY; NR=NOT REPORTED

Subjective Data

Did you enjoy having her in your home? _Yes, very much. She was like a member of our family._

Was she willing to put in extra effort or time when it was required?_____
Always.

Is she a flexible person? Can she handle the chaos of everyday life with children? _Yes, she seems to get calmer and quieter as the noise and chaos gets greater._

How did she handle constructive criticism? _That was always a little difficult. She always changed her behavior immediately, but could be somewhat grim after the criticism._

How would you rate her level of personal maturity? _Very, very high._

How did your child feel when she left? _He misses her but he doesn't think he needs a nanny anymore._

Additional Questions: _____
_____
_____

You're Hired!

■ ■

THE EMPLOYMENT CONTRACT

Too often parents feel that everything is working out fine with their nanny when out of the blue, she threatens to quit unless they give her the five-dollar-an-hour raise they promised her six months before; three weeks off they promised her in the second interview; or the day off every other week that they agreed to over the phone. Don't get caught in this trap. Make sure everything you promise is in writing.

The Legal Kit, found in the software under the Legal Kit icon and in hard copy in Appendix 1, provides you with the following:

The Legal Kit

- Contract for Child Care

- Minimum wage, overtime, and benefits laws

- Termination policy

- Worker's compensation insurance

- A list of other useful federal and state forms and their description

Employment contracts are formal, legally binding agreements that serve as the basis of your employer-employee relationship. A contract gives you one more opportunity to be very clear about what you require the nanny to do, family rules, salary, benefits, vacation policy, and your management policy. Realize that until a contract is signed by you and the nanny there is no deal, and everything is open to negotiation.

Pull out your Needs Assessment, turn to the Legal Kit in Appendix 1, find the sample employment contract, and start drafting your contract. If you are using the software, open the Legal Kit file and click on the contract template. Don't forget to complete Schedule 1: "Description Of Additional Child-Care Responsibilities and Special Instructions." This is the template that allows you to include anything that doesn't fit into the contract template. For example, under "Additional Child-Care Responsibilities" you might want to write, "Nanny will make sure that Suzy practices the alphabet and counting for at least half an hour every day." Under "Special Instructions" you could include important safety rules not covered by the contract, such as "Nanny will keep the doors to the pool area shut and locked at all times," or to protect a child from an allergic reaction, "Nanny will not allow Suzy to eat any food or food product that contains nuts."

Take a look at the sample contract Dan and Karen P. used. *Note: The completed version below is merely illustrative of the type of information that may be included in your particular contract. In the Legal Kit, you'll find a complete discussion of each paragraph of the contract and the contract schedules and, when appropriate, instructions for completing the blank spaces in the form contract and contract schedules are provided.*

CONTRACT FOR CHILD CARE

THIS CONTRACT FOR CHILD CARE (the "Contract") is made and entered into on the *1st* day of *September* , 19 *96* between *Dan and Karen P.* ("Employer") and *Nellie Smith* ("Employee") and contains the terms and conditions of Employee's engagement by Employer to provide the child-care services herein described. The following sets forth those terms and conditions:

1. Term.
This Contract shall commence on *September 1*, 19 *96*, and shall continue indefinitely thereafter until either Employee or Employer shall provide written notice to the other of such party's notice of termination. Any such notice of termination, and all rights and obligations of the parties under this Contract, shall be effective immediately upon the delivery of such notice personally by one party to the other or upon the deposit of such written notice in the United States Mail, certified mail, return receipt requested, addressed to the party to whom such notice is to be delivered at the address for such party set forth below. Employee expressly acknowledges and agrees that this Contract is a contract terminable at will by either party at any time, without notice (other than the limited notice described above) and with or without cause, and that, except as may be specifically provided for in Paragraph 10 below, upon termination, Employee shall not be entitled to receive any severance pay, vacation pay, sick pay, or any other compensation or benefits. Employee hereby releases Employer from making any such payments or providing any such benefit, to the fullest extent permitted by law.

2. Children.
Employee agrees to provide child-care services for the following children (the "Children"):

Nicholas P. _____   5-6-91 _____
        Name   Date of Birth

Michael P. _____   3-7-93 _____
        Name   Date of Birth

Twins _____   6-12-96 _____
        Name   Date of Birth

4. Location and Schedule of Hours.
The Employee will provide child care to the Children at _101 Doe Street, Anywhere, U.S.A._, except to the extent that the responsibilities of Employee as specified in this Contract require Employee to provide transportation for the Children or otherwise render child care at remote locations. The Employee shall either:
(check appropriate box)

☐ a. Provide child-care services on a live-in basis, in which event full-time lodging and regular meals will be provided to Employee by Employer; or

☑ b. Provide child-care services during the hours of _8:00 A.M._ to _5:00 P.M._ on _Monday through Friday_, with such variations thereof as Employer may from time to time reasonably request, but generally including at least the same number of hours of work as contemplated by the regular schedule specified herein.

Employee also acknowledges that Employer's child-care needs may from time to time require Employee to work on holidays or hours which may substantially exceed the hours included in the regular schedule specified above and Employee agrees to make every effort to accommodate Employer's reasonable requirements in this regard.

4. Responsibilities.
The child-care duties of Employee shall generally include the responsibility for supervising and attending to the physical and emotional health, safety, and well-being of the Children at all times during which Employee is performing the child-care services contemplated hereby. Without limiting the foregoing general overall responsibilities of Employee, Employee's specific duties shall include the following:
(check all appropriate boxes and provide details)

☑ a. Cooking and cleaning:_____
☐ b. Bathing and personal care:_____
☐ c. Health and medical care:_____
☑ d. Social and recreational: _Take Michael to park, mall, etc. as needed_
☑ e. Transportation: _Provide automobile for limited transportation of children and running errands._
☑ f. Shopping and errands: _Run errands as needed._
☐ g. Educational:_____
☐ h. Ironing and Laundry:_____
☑ i. Other Responsibilities and Special Instructions: See Schedule 1 attached hereto (Description of Additional Child-Care Responsibilities and Special Instructions).

In the event that Employee's duties shall include providing transportation for the Children, Employee shall furnish his or her own automobile and shall keep it maintained and repaired in good driving condition. Employee shall maintain automobile insurance on the automobile with such coverages and in such amounts as Employer may reasonably require and certificates shall be delivered to Employer from time to time as may be necessary to confirm the existence and effectiveness of such insurance. All costs associated with the automobile, including the insurance, shall be the responsibility of Employee without reimbursement or additional compensation to Employee, except to the extent that the parties shall specify otherwise in the Contract Addendum referred to in Paragraph 12 below.

5. Payment Terms.

Employee will be paid:

(check appropriate box)

☐ $_____ per hour

☐ $_____ per week

☑ $ _1,000.00_____ per month

☑ Other: _See Contract Addendum for automobile reimbursement._____

Employer will deduct the following from Employee's paycheck:

(check all appropriate boxes)

☑ Social Security and Medicare taxes

☐ Federal income taxes

☐ State income taxes

Other taxes:

☑ Long distance or toll phone charges:_____
Other deductions (specify):_____

The Employee acknowledges that Employer has advised Employee that Employee may be entitled to earned income credit (EIC). By checking the following box, Employee represents that Employee is eligible to receive advance payment of EIC, that Employee has provided Employer with a copy of a completed Form W-5 (Earned Income Credit Advance Payment Certificate) and Employee requests that Employer include the appropriate amount of EIC in Employee's paychecks:

☑ Employee is to receive advance payment of the EIC.

Employee will be paid at the following specified intervals and dates:

☐ Once a week on every_____

☑ Twice a month on the _15th_ and _last_ day of each month.

☐ Once a month on_____

☐ Other:_____

Employer and Employee shall review Employee's compensation payable hereunder, in the event of Employee's continued employment hereunder, not less frequently than annually, but Employee acknowledges and agrees that Employer shall have no obligation to increase such compensation at the time of any such review, or otherwise.

6. Overtime.

If Employee works more than forty hours in any single week (and is not engaged hereunder to perform child-care services on a live-in basis), Employee shall be entitled to receive overtime pay at the rate of one and one-half times Employee's then hourly rate. No overtime pay shall be paid to Employee if Employee performs the child-care services hereunder on a live-in basis, regardless of the number of hours worked. No overtime pay shall be payable solely because Employee works on any one or more holidays or on Saturday or Sunday or for working more than eight hours in any single day, unless then applicable law shall require any such payments, or unless provided for in Paragraph 7 below.

7. Benefits.

Employer will provide Employee with the following benefits:

(check all appropriate boxes)

☑ Meals:_Three meals per day_____

☐ Room and board:_____

☐ Sick leave:_____

☑ Vacations:_You will be entitled to one week of paid vacation for each full_ _year that your employment hereunder continues, the specific time of_ _which must be approved by Employer._

☑ Holidays:_You will be paid for all federal holidays, but you will not have to_ _work on those days._

☐ Health insurance:_____

☐ Transportation:_____

☐ Worker's Compensation:_____

☐ Other:_____

8. Licenses and Certificates.

In connection with the performance of Employee's duties hereunder, Employee has provided Employer with appropriate documentation to establish the following:

(check all appropriate boxes)

☑ a. Valid Driver's License

☑ b. Evidence of CPR proficiency

☑ c. Evidence of Life Saving proficiency

☑ d. Evidence of First Aid proficiency

☑ e. Evidence of Health Insurance

☑ f. Evidence of Automobile Liability and other Insurance

☑ g. INS Form I-9

☑ h. Form W-4

☑ i. Form W-5

☐ j. Other:_____

_____

_____

Employee agrees to promptly notify Employer of any change in status that would render any one or more of the foregoing (which have been checked as being applicable) inaccurate or not current.

9. Employment Application.

Employee has completed and provided to Employer an Application for Employment ("Employment Application") in connection with Employee's employment hereunder. Such Employment Application contains a variety of facts, statements, and references provided by Employee and Employer has relied upon the accuracy thereof in hiring Employee. Employee represents and warrants to Employer that all information contained in the Employment Application is true and correct in all respects and that the discovery by Employer of the falsity or inaccuracy of any such information will subject Employee to immediate termination by Employer.

10. Severance.

In the event Employee's employment is terminated at any time after Employee has worked hereunder for at least _6 months_ , and such termination of Employee is not for cause (including any termination pursuant to Paragraph 9 above), Employee shall be entitled to severance in the amount of $ _two weeks' pay_.

11. Return of Materials.

Upon termination of this Contract, regardless of how termination is effected, or whenever requested by Employer, Employee shall immediately return to Employer all of Employer's supplies, computer and other equipment, all cards, disks, tapes, and other media, all educational and entertainment materials, and all other property of Employer used by Employee in rendering the child-care services hereunder, or otherwise, and which is in Employee's possession or under Employee's control.

12. Additional Terms and Provisions.

Employer and Employee recognize that certain changes in the working relationship contemplated hereby may occur from time to time and that such changes may necessitate modification of this Contract. Schedule 2 attached hereto contains a form of Contract Addendum which may be utilized by the parties to memorialize any such changes. Each such Contract Addendum which is completed and signed by the parties hereto, together with all other schedules and agreements executed by the parties pursuant hereto, shall be deemed to be incorporated in this Contract for all purposes as if set forth in full herein. No agreement, amendment or modification of this Contract shall be effective unless it is in writing and signed by both parties hereto.

13. Governing Law.

This Contract is executed and delivered by the parties in the State of _California_ and shall be construed in accordance with and governed by the laws of such State.

Dan and Karen P. (Employer)

Employer's Address:

101 Doe Street

Anywhere, U.S.A.

Nellie Smith   (Employee)

Employee's Address:

102 Doe Street

Anywhere, U.S.A.

■ ■

In Chapter Six, you'll find everything you need to set up an organized system for dealing with your legal obligations as an employer and manage and motivate your new employee.

CHAPTER SIX

■■■■■■■■■

Managing Your In-Home Child-Care Provider

YOU'RE HIRED!

Now that you've hired your nanny, you have a few things to accomplish before her first day of work. You want to be organized and well prepared for her arrival—the better you start your relationship, the better you will be able to manage and motivate your nanny over the course of your relationship. If you are competent and professional in all your dealings with your nanny, she will have more confidence in you, and in turn, will be motivated to handle her child-care responsibilities in a competent and professional manner. Keep in mind the old maxim "How you start is how you finish" as you work through the following tasks in preparation for your nanny's arrival.

Prepare your nanny's quarters if she is a live-in. Start with a fresh coat of paint, set up a private phone line, and clear all of your family's belongings out of the closets. If your nanny doesn't live in, it's still a good idea to clear out a few drawers in the powder-room cabinet or create some space in a closet for the nanny to keep some toiletries, an extra work shirt, and some other personal items. Just as you probably have a desk or locker at your office where you can store items to keep you fresh and comfortable, it is important to remember that your private home will now become a workplace for your child-care provider. The more you extend yourself to make your child-care provider feel that you consider her a professional, the faster a strong employer-employee relationship will develop. You can do this by supplying the support and the infrastructure common to all other workplaces.

Think about and prepare a policy about receiving telephone calls, mail or packages, and visitors at your home. Because of the relaxed atmosphere of your home, keeping a businesslike environment is difficult if not impossible. However, your home is a workplace and your nanny's primary responsibility is caring for youngsters who have a nasty habit of getting into trouble if left alone for ten seconds. Set a policy that allows short, informative calls from your provider's family, friends, and so on. No gabfests will be tolerated.

If you have a live-in you may want her to use a P.O. box to receive her mail. I'm still getting mail meant for our live-in four years ago. It's a good idea to tell all personal employees, whether live-in or not, that they can't use your house as a mailing address. You don't want to be involved with lost packages, or even worse, illicit or illegal items sent through the mail. Set a policy and make your nanny abide by it.

Prepare an Emergency Medical Authorization Form that allows your new nanny to authorize emergency medical treatment for your child. Turn to Chapter Ten and complete the Emergency Medical Authorization template. If you are using the software, open up the In-Home file and click on the Emergency Medical Authorization template. Keep an extra medical authorization in a safe place in your house and tell your nanny where it is. There are two places where the medical release should be kept at all times: (1) Ask your nanny to keep a copy in her wallet, or the place where she keeps her driver's license. (2) Put a copy of the release in the glove compartment of the car(s) that your child may ride in. Put them in other obvious places, update them all every six months, and make everyone in your family aware of where they are kept.

If your child is in day care or preschool and your nanny will pick him up, be sure to update the Approved Pickup and Transportation form you gave the school at the beginning of the year. If the school doesn't have a form, review the sample below and use the Approved Pickup and Transportation template in Chapter Ten to draft your own. If you are

YOUR CHILD'S EMERGENCY
MEDICAL AUTHORIZATION

To Whom it May Concern:

As the parent of___*Michael P.*___, I hereby authorize ___*Nellie Smith*___ to approve emergency medical treatment for our child. Our child's date of birth is ___*March 7, 1993*___. He/she is allergic to ___*codeine*___. His/her pediatrician is___*Dr. Jerry Ross*___, who may be reached at ___*(413) 555-9296*___.

Our child's insurance carrier is ___*We'll Cover You Insurance Company*___, and the policy number is ___*123456789-10*___.

Our address ___*96 Mockingbird Lane, Birdville, NJ, 34526*___ and our phone number is ___*(413) 555-5643*___.

___*Dan P.*___
(parent's signature)

using the software, open up the In-Home file and click on the Approved Pickup and Transportation template.

Because the first few days of a new child-care situation are hectic and confusing, it's a good idea to schedule and pay for a few hours of orientation with your new child-care provider to get her familiar with your house, your child, your neighborhood, and her duties. Remember to keep it to a few hours and do it when it works for you, for example in the evening or the Saturday or Sunday morning before she starts. It's also the best time to get all of the time-consuming paperwork issues settled and so that you can start fresh on her first day.

Plan on staying home a few hours on your nanny's first day on the job, and for the first week spend some extra time in both the morning and evening debriefing your new employee. The first few days and weeks are your opportunity to set the tone for your relationship with your nanny—professionalism and mutual respect.

■ ■ ■ ■ ■ ■ ■ ■ ■ ■ ■ ■ ■ ■ ■ ■ ■ ■ ■ ■ ■ ■ ■ ■ ■ ■ ■ ■ ■ ■ ■

APPROVED PICKUP
AND TRANSPORTATION

FOR _Michael P._

(your child's name)

The following persons are authorized to pick up _Michael P._ and drive him home from your facility:

Dan P.

Karen P.

Nellie Smith (Nanny)

Ann Bown (grandmother)

Signed:

_____Dan P._____   _Dated: May 5, 1995_____

(Parent's Name)   *(Date)*

■ ■

When Your Nanny Arrives

When your nanny arrives for her first day on the job, find a way to keep your child occupied for a while. Then:

- Have your nanny complete all her tax forms, and then be sure to review her proof of citizenship or legal residency. Have the nanny complete her W-4 and make sure that the employment agreement is signed. (See Legal Kit in Appendix 1.)

- Show her around the house. If she's a live-in, get her settled in her quarters. If she is a live-out, show her the private space where she can store her personal items, purse, change of clothes, and toiletries. Give her a clean set of towels for her use, and maybe something special like pretty, scented soap from the child(ren).

- Go over work hours, salary, benefits, and vacation and holiday policy, and all other policy issues one more time, just to make sure you are both in agreement.

- Give her your child's emergency medical authorization. Tell her to keep it in her wallet at all times and show her where you keep the extra copies you made.

- Give your nanny her own set of car keys (if she's using your car), and show her where title and insurance cards are kept.

- It will be important for your nanny to know how your house operates, so spend a few moments showing her how the heating, air conditioning, and major appliances work. Point out where the smoke alarms are throughout the house and where the nearest fire alarm box is located if you are in an area that uses them.

- Organize all of the basic items it takes to get into your house, building, and garage, like keys, security codes, and garage door openers. Fill out the Household Inventory Items list template found in Chapter Ten and on the diskette in the In-Home file as you give her the items. Have her check each item off and sign it. Put the executed copy in her Provider's Personal File.

- Give her an updated copy of your weekly schedule and other family members' weekly schedules (see Chapter Four).

- Give her an updated copy of your child's schedule (see Chapter Four).

- If she will drive your child to and from school, classes, playgroups, and so on, plan on taking her with you the first day or ask a friend who has a child going the same places to pitch in a few mornings by letting the nanny follow her as she drives to school or errands. Most communities and large cities are now mapped in a pretty sophisticated way, so buy a Thomas Guide or other similar cross-referencing map and ask your nanny to keep it in the car.

- Make a copy of classmate addresses and phone numbers and ask your nanny to leave them in a folder in the car so that she can always stop and call if she is lost or late to pick up your child(ren) from a playmate's house.

- If you have time that day or that week, try to introduce your nanny to your child's teachers.

- Give her expense forms to use to keep track of any of your money she spends, or to get reimbursement for any of her own money she spends while taking care of your child. Ask her to complete an expense form at the end of every work day; otherwise she may lose her receipts, forget her mileage, or forget to record miscellaneous expenses that didn't have receipts.

CHILD-CARE MANAGEMENT

During the In-Person Interview you not only explained the various duties you would require of your child-care provider, but (I hope) you

■ ■ ■ ■ ■ ■ ■ ■ ■ ■ ■ ■ ■ ■ ■ ■ ■ ■ ■ ■ ■ ■ ■ ■ ■ ■ ■ ■ ■ ■ ■

HOUSEHOLD INVENTORY ITEMS

I, _Nellie Smith_ , acknowledge that on, _June 17, 1995_ , I have received the following items that are the property of _Dan and Karen P._.

Key to front door

Key to back door

Key to garage

Key to pool area

garage door opener

Visa card

Telephone credit card

These items are to be used by me in my capacity as an employee of _Dan and Karen P._ and are to be returned upon request, upon my voluntarily leaving their employ, or at termination. Additionally, I agree not to duplicate any keys or to give any other party access to _any security codes   garage door openers   and the P. family's unlisted telephone numbers._

Nellie Smith   _243-9936_

Provider Name   Phone Number

■ ■

discussed child-care management and your use of it. Perhaps you showed your candidate, now your employee, copies of the various templates she would be required to complete on a daily and weekly basis; the work schedules; your child's schedule; and the weekly meeting agenda. Your nanny's first day on the job is "where the rubber meets the road." The daily interaction between a parent and child-care provider is fundamental to the success and longevity of the employer/employee relationship. Therefore, it is incumbent upon both parties to be cooperative, communicative, and responsible. However, as we have stressed throughout this book, no one has a bigger stake in this relationship than the parent—so it is you who must maintain the diligence required to achieve this success.

PROVIDER DAILY EXPENSE REPORT

Name: _Nellie Smith_   Date: _November 15, 1996_

Expense Detail

Breakfast:

Lunch: _McDonalds—$7.75_

Dinner:

Snacks: _Jellybeans—$1.50_

Parking: _At mall—$5.00_

Entertainment: _Movies—$12.00_

Auto Mileage @ $.29/mile: _32 miles = $9.28_

Telephone:

Other: _Paint set—$6.50_

TOTAL EXPENSES: _$42.03_

Less Advance: _$30.00_

Balance Due Me: _$12.03_

The above is a true accounting of the costs I have incurred.

_____ _Nellie Smith_ _____
(provider signature)

PLEASE ATTACH RECEIPTS

(For Parent—Date paid: _November 17, 1996_   Amount _$12.03_)

Because we have all been in situations where lack of enforcement of simple rules has created a chaotic and ultimately unsuccessful venture, it is important to view the first few weeks of your new child-care-provider's employment as a strictly "by the book" time period. Until this endeavor finds its rhythm, as all prosperous relationships do, you will need to (1) print out a comprehensive schedule for your child-care provider, your child, and you; (2) set your weekly meeting date and agenda and keep to it; (3) Try out all the management templates at least once. My guess is that within a month, you will be able to pick and choose the ones that work for you and your provider.

How Does Child-Care Management Work?

As you now know, I have spent my professional career, both on Wall Street and at CCR, motivating clients and coworkers to perform in certain ways. For clients, my role was simply to convince them to use my firm's services or to buy, use, and recommend my product. For my coworkers and the people who reported to me, my role was to motivate them to substantially enhance the productivity of our business unit—and the profitability of our company. Your relationship with your child-care provider is no different. That is why I believe that using the same techniques I developed over a twenty-five-year career in business will work! Additionally, child-care management is the final component of the step-by-step process we have developed in this book. You have done fine work in analyzing your situation and attracting, interviewing, choosing, and hiring your candidate. However, the truth is that all of this good work is for naught if you don't appropriately manage and motivate this new employee to provide the best care for your child(ren). Like well-assembled chocolate cake ingredients left too little or too long to bake, all of the effort expended so far to find the right child-care provider for you will be wasted if you and she don't maximize every opportunity to provide the best care. And while it would be nice to think that because a person is getting paid a fair wage, the employer will get optimum performance, we all know that this is not what we can or should expect.

The Daily Log

Whether you leave your child alone with your nanny for an hour, a day, or a week, you want to know what happens while you are gone. However, your nanny is not going to remember everything or even know what to tell you unless you give her some sort of fast and easy written record for her to keep while you are gone. The Daily Log template is a simple form that allows your provider to make quick notes throughout the day about incidents and facts that are important to you, from what and how much your child ate to how long she napped to what toys she played with and whether she was agitated, happy, sad, sleepy, cranky, and so on. You'll be glad you have this information because at some point you are really going to need it! For example, if you can't get your child to go to sleep at her regular hour one night, you'll be able to figure out the reason why by looking at the nanny's notes for that day—maybe your daughter took a very long nap too late in the afternoon. If your child has a bad stomachache one night, you'll be able to tell your pediatrician exactly what your child ate for the last twelve hours. And, if your child happens to say a new word or learn to crawl up and down the stairs while you are gone, at least you'll know it happened. You won't have to rely on your nanny to remember to tell you.

To make sure that the log is accurate, ask your provider to include as many details as possible and use the "misc. notes" space. Remind her to make notes in the log throughout her day; otherwise she may forget to include important details. (The daily log form may also be used by day-care and family-care providers.) Make multiple copies of the Daily Log template in Chapter Ten, or if you are using the software, print out multiple copies of the Daily Log found in the In-Home file, put them in a manila file, and give them to your nanny.

Weekly Meetings

Weekly meetings with your nanny are critical. With your busy schedule, it probably will be the only time that you and your nanny really communicate every week. To manage your nanny well, you've got to make sure that the lines of communication are always wide open. The weekly meeting is a regular opportunity to air, discuss, and solve any problems, change schedules, review the activities of the previous week, organize activities and meals for the coming week, and develop a solid, positive relationship with your nanny. Not only can the weekly meetings strengthen your personal relationship with your nanny—by giving you a regular opportunity to think about, discuss, and plan your child's daily care—the weekly meeting will also improve the care both you and your nanny give your child. And finally, if you want your nanny to care for your child in a competent and professional manner, you've got to treat your nanny like a professional—the weekly meeting is your prime place and opportunity to do this.

As you can see from the sample Meeting Agenda on page 118, the agenda is designed to keep you on track in your meetings with your nanny, and make sure you cover everything that must be covered for the coming week. It also helps you keep a written record of what was decided, said, or promised by you and your nanny.

The Meeting Agenda template is found in Chapter Ten and in the In-Home file if you are using the software.

DAILY LOG

FOR _Michael P._

DATE: _June 17, 1995_

Breakfast Time: _7:30 A.M._

Foods Eaten: _Cream of Wheat, 3 strawberries, milk_

Lunch Time: _11:30 A.M._

Foods Eaten: _1/2 slice cheese pizza, apple, o.j._

Dinner Time: _5:00 P.M._

Foods Eaten: _macaroni & cheese, milk_

Snacks Time: _10:00 A.M._

Foods Eaten: _Yogurt_

Time: _3:00 P.M._

Foods Eaten: _5 oreos_

Naps Time: _10:30 A.M._

Length of Nap (min/hrs): _50 min._

Time: _2:00 P.M._

Length of Nap (min/hrs): _60 min._

Potty Time: _8:30 A.M._   Type: _2_

Time: _11:20 A.M._   Type: _1_

Time: _1:45 P.M._   Type: _1_

Time: _4:15 A.M._   Type: _2_

Medication Time: _N/A_   Type: _____

Activities (please list)

  alphabet—can go up to m

  numbers—up to 10

  went swimming

  played in sandbox

  played with dog

MISC. NOTES:

  Michael was cranky today—doesn't seem to be sleeping very well.

■■

MANAGEMENT WEEK BY WEEK

The First Week

The first week is your opportunity to familiarize your nanny with the way you and your family do things. It also is your opportunity to observe the new nanny's interaction with your child, and to make sure that all of the impressions you received during the interview process were correct. For example, your nanny may have been a great communicator during the interviews, but do you feel any resistance from her when you delve a little deeper into some of the events of her day with your child? Your new nanny may have been slightly anxious and shy during the interview and on her first day. Has she loosened up a bit as the week goes on, or is she still edgy? If your child didn't take to the new nanny immediately, have things improved a week later? Does your nanny seem overwhelmed by her duties and responsibilities after a week, or is she handling everything just fine? These are the types of things you need to look for during your nanny's first week, and then consider. If your nanny is still edgy, maybe that's okay. If you feel fine about it, then you may want to give her a little more time to adjust. However, if she makes *you* edgy, you may need to reconsider whether she is working out. You may decide to terminate her and hire your second choice. It's up to you. You need to use your own good judgment here. Remember, one parent may be fine with something that would drive another parent crazy.

MEETING AGENDA

Meeting Date: _September 12, 1996_
Meeting Time: _4:00 P.M._

ITEM 1: _Scheduling—next week's/next month's_

meeting notes: _____
_____
_____

ITEM 2: _Can Nellie go with us to Wally World in June?_

meeting notes: _____
_____
_____

ITEM 3: _Michael needs to eat less sugar and more vegetables._

meeting notes: _____
_____
_____

ITEM 4: _Work on alphabet at least 3x a week._

meeting notes: _____
_____
_____

ITEM 5: _Michael's antibiotics schedule—2x a day for the next_
two weeks

meeting notes: _____
_____
_____

ITEM 6: _Nellie was late two times last week. The first time—_
25 minutes, the second time—15 minutes. This constitutes the first
warning.

meeting notes: _Nellie was very apologetic—said she's been having car trouble,_
but the car goes to the mechanic this weekend, so it shouldn't happen
again.

NEXT MEETING: Date _September 24, 1996_   Time _4:00 P.M._

(Make two copies of this form—one for parent and one for provider)

118

Tips for Managing the First Week

- Communicate, communicate, communicate. Let your new nanny know exactly how you want things handled, show her where everything is, and ask her if she has any questions. Do this several times. Make sure she knows that with you, no question is a dumb question.
- Stay home as much as possible to observe and train.
- Don't criticize or correct the nanny in front of your child and other family members. You want your child to respect the nanny's authority. If something she says or does requires correction but doesn't threaten the health and safety of your child, make a note to yourself and bring it up in a private conversation later that day or in your weekly meeting, if it can wait.
- At the end of the first week, make a realistic assessment of the nanny. If everything's fine, great. If some things aren't so good, do you want to discuss them and give the nanny more time to adjust? If things are not working out, is it time to terminate the nanny and try out your second choice?

The First Month

Continue to carefully observe your nanny throughout the first month. As with the first week, use the first month of the nanny's employment as an opportunity to determine whether she is going to work out in the long run. At the end of the first month, you should feel confidence in your nanny—you should trust her to do things the way you would. If you don't trust your nanny at the end of the first month, you need to determine why, and then decide how you are going to handle it. Is it a training issue that you can solve with a little more time? Is it an issue related to age, experience, or education? Or is it personality? Can you fix the problem or is it a lost cause? If it's a lost cause, you need to turn your attention to the issues surrounding termination discussed in the following section.

Tips for Handling the First Month

- Communicate, communicate, communicate. Have weekly meetings, or more if needed. Articulate what you expect in a clear and concise manner. Encourage your nanny to ask questions. Keep lines of communication wide open.
- Come home at unexpected times. The best way to feel confident that everything is as it should be at home is to return home when

your nanny doesn't expect it—you'll find out firsthand what is going on at home.

- Call home often to check in with your nanny. Let your nanny know that you are thinking about your child and her.

- Make sure your nanny feels that she can phone you whenever she needs to when you are out of the home. Assure her that she is not bothering you when she does call.

- Observe your child carefully. Is she happy with the nanny, calm and confident, and does she look forward to the nanny's arrival? If, after a month, your child is not adjusting to the nanny, it may be time to reconsider whether this is the best caregiver for your child.

- At the end of the first month, carefully assess whether the nanny is working out. At this point, you shouldn't need to give her more time to adjust—she should be adjusted by now. If it's not working out, it may be time to terminate her and start your search for another nanny.

WHAT IF THERE IS A PROBLEM?

There are times when things just don't work out. Even if we have exhausted every opportunity, interviewed every candidate, done a thorough background check, and hired and managed effectively, something can still be wrong. Because this is a relationship, you can only control your half of it. So if the worst happens and, after repeated tries, you find that you can't fix the situation, here are some ways to fairly, quickly, and legally extricate yourself.

If this employee is a relatively new hire, say within the last six months, my guess is that the problem(s) stem from one of two areas: personality or performance. While it is certainly not necessary for an employer and employee to get along, it is more than reasonable to expect it, especially in this most intimate type of employment situation (your kid, your house). As the employer and manager you need to take the initiative and follow the Problem-Solving Steps described in the box.

Keep in mind that personality problems always affect performance. So be on your toes. Listen to your gut and stay faithful to your weekly meetings, and you may be able to manage your way out of a new nanny search.

Because most of us miss the first sign of trouble, and probably the second, we are often shocked and angry when we finally notice something is wrong. A real sign of trouble is if your child-care provider is acting out or exhibiting strange behavior. This could be because she has not come to you and expressed the need to talk about an issue that has grown very bothersome to her. One of the reasons the weekly meetings are so important is to facilitate open lines of communication. And, frankly, as in any relationship, if one is paying attention, the little stuff can't float by.

In the problem-solving box I have given you some steps to take if the problem is strictly a performance problem stemming from a policy, procedure, or lack of one. For example: One or both of you have slipped into the nasty little habit of being five to ten minutes late. It's now the rule, not the exception. Maybe you didn't say anything the first few times because your schedule allowed it and you tend to be late, too. This isn't cause for great alarm, but it needs to be fixed before it gets even more out of hand. You, the parent/manager, are effectively giving your okay to her inappropriate employee behavior. Chronic lateness ruins friendships and marriages. It is probably the most abused but tolerated part of life, but is totally inexcusable in professional relationships. So make the rules and keep them. At your next weekly meeting start off by apologizing for the last time you were late. Tell your provider that you both

Problem-Solving Steps

1. Identify problem.

2. Assess its seriousness and the effect it's having on the child(ren).

3. Review provider's weekly meeting notes and the last quarterly review for clues to underlying causes.

4. Look for other causes of problem.

5. Meet with provider as soon as possible armed with your assessment of issues and proposed remedy.

6. Listen to your provider's point of view.

7. Jointly enact new policy, procedure, or solution. Agree to review its effectiveness at next week's meeting.

need to be more thoughtful and considerate. Put a smile on, then ask for her comments and listen. Ask again if there are any other issues bothering her and make it clear that you want to hear what she has to say. In closing, be sure to tell your provider that you both need to move on and work to reestablish the trust and rhythm you had before.

The tips in the box will work when applied to a situation involving a generally happy, functioning employee with whom you have developed trust and who is performing in the A–/B+ range. But there is always the chance that the situation is more serious. For example, you have a standing policy that your son, Kevin, can never go to the playground in winter without his heavy coat, hat, and mittens. Two weeks ago, you ran into Debbie from the third floor, whom you hadn't seen in a few weeks. Mark, her son, is Kevin's school- and playmate. Mark has had tubes in his ears since the beginning of school to combat chronic and painful ear infections. You ask Debbie how Mark is, hear he is doing well, and are stunned when she comments on how "healthy" Kevin must be not to need a hat in such cold weather. As you attempt to maintain your composure, you make sure that she really saw Kevin without his hat. "Oh, yes, he never has his hat on at the playground," she says. "And where is Donna, the nanny?" you ask. "Sitting talking to the other moms and nannies." It wouldn't be so bad except that this has happened before and you have made yourself perfectly clear that it is very important to you that your son wear his hat. Question: Is this a big deal or a little deal? That depends on two things. One is how you handle it and the other is how Donna the nanny handles it. What should you do, once you calm down?

1. Wait until you can discuss the matter unemotionally. This may take a few moments, or you may need to sleep on it and wait until the next morning.

2. Take a look at Donna's Personnel File and review copies of previous weekly meetings. Also, get out a copy of Kevin's schedule and look for where you wrote "HAT AND GLOVES AT PARK" in big letters.

3. After Donna is off duty and out of earshot, talk to Kevin. Ask him if he has forgotten to bring his hat to the park. It could be that Kevin is a normal six-year-old and forgets. Just as likely, Kevin may wear the hat and gloves and then take them off when he thinks Donna isn't looking. In either case, you still have a nanny performance problem. Donna is responsible for

reminding Kevin to bring his hat and gloves. If he does bring them and takes them off, that means that Donna isn't as diligent as she should be in enforcing the rules, or she just plain isn't watching what he is doing. You will need to get the facts from Kevin before you speak to Donna to be sure you will use the correct approach.

4. Once you have calmed down and talked to Kevin, tell Donna you need to talk to her. Make sure you have enough uninterrupted time to deal with this, at least fifteen minutes. Frankly tell her about your conversations with Debbie and Kevin. If your assessment is that she is just out to lunch about the hat, tell her that you consider this to be a performance problem. Tell her that you now know that Kevin brings the hat to the park but takes it off after a few minutes when he thinks he can get away with it. You have spoken to Kevin and laid down the law. The hat stays on, or no roller hockey. But you consider the problem only half solved. Donna's lack of enforcement of the rules is not only sending Kevin a bad message but has shaken your trust in her. You need to feel confident that Donna, as your surrogate, is maintaining the household rules while you are not there to do it yourself. You don't want Kevin getting the impression that there are rules when Mom and Dad are around, but Donna is a pushover. Even more importantly, tell her your concerns about Kevin's safety. Sure, not wearing a hat isn't like forgetting to fasten a seat belt, but it is below freezing out there. And if your nanny can rationalize no hat, is a pain-in-the-neck seat belt far behind?

How can this problem be resolved so that Kevin knows what to expect and Donna performs as she should? Here are some ideas on how to tackle this type of problem:

1. Assess the seriousness of the problem.
2. Thoroughly review your existing rules and procedures and decide if they are adequate.
3. Review the provider's Personnel File and look for parallel issues or similar performance problems exhibited in the past.
4. Decide if this is a problem with the policy itself, or if it stems from the provider's lack of understanding the policy, inability to enforce the policy, or lack of focus.
5. If you decide that the problem is the policy itself, either by your own analysis or during your meeting with your provider, ask

for her input in developing a new policy so that you both have ownership. Make sure that your intent is very clear. The more you make it a collaborative effort, the more likely your provider will buy into the policy and wholeheartedly embrace it.

6. If you decide that your problem is not in the policy itself but in your provider's lack of enforcement, you will need to go a few steps further.

    a. Decide if the policy is important and put together a list of your reasons.

    b. Evaluate your provider's skills and personality and decide where the weakness is.

    c. If it is a weakness with a skill, training and support should help.

Say she's a fair but unimaginative cook. Your kid won't eat anything she makes. She burns the macaroni and cheese and puts mayonnaise on all the sandwiches, even though your kids don't eat it. Discuss it with her. Remember not to make it personal, so praise her other strong qualities while you make it clear she'll never win the Betty Crocker Bake-Off. Ask her if she likes to cook. Ask her if some new cookbooks would help. Gauge her level of enthusiasm for trying harder (it's only lunch, anyway). The key here is to let her know that burning grilled cheese is a problem that can be fixed if you apply yourself. And it's part of the job and a requirement. If you are patient and supportive (cut out simple recipes from the major women's magazines), she should improve. If she doesn't, this may not be a skill problem but a personality or attitude problem. If your evaluation indicates that personality is all or part of a performance problem, here are some ways to evaluate and deal with it.

Let's go back to Kevin, the kid without the hat, and Donna, the nanny. Here's what Kevin's mom should do:

1. Evaluate the depth of the personality/attitude problem. A Ph.D. may be helpful here, but not necessary. Personality issues that negatively affect productivity can be passive in that they are ingrained habits or traits that affect a person's ability to work with others. Attitude problems, on the other hand, rarely are passive and sometimes have an in-your-face, belligerent effect. As an employer you need and want a provider who has the maturity and patience to deal with small children; a bad attitude flies in the face of what you need in a child-care provider. Does

mom think Donna is just blatantly ignoring her wishes and rules? Is Donna angry about something else?

2. Does your provider really understand what you want? Are your instructions clear and precise? In this case, it is hard to make a case that Donna didn't understand what Mom has written on Kevin's weekly schedule ("HAT AND GLOVES AT PARK"). She may not intentionally be disregarding the rule, but if she is allowing Kevin to take off his hat she may be saying that she thinks it's a dumb rule. By not discussing her problem with you (maybe she's uncomfortable making Kevin do what is expected of him) and suggesting an alternative, Donna is deliberately ignoring your instructions and creating a coconspirator in your child.

3. If you believe your instructions are clear and your provider has been given sufficient notice of your requirements, is she being insubordinate? While the jury isn't in yet, it certainly appears that Donna is willfully ignoring your explicit instructions. An employee who willfully (and in this case, repeatedly) ignores your policies and procedures is guilty of insubordination. And, while every ignored policy doesn't doom the relationship, you as manager need to act quickly and decisively to stop this behavior.

As a manager, it is your responsibility to lay out rules and policies clearly, and to stop problems early. These are the points you need to make, in person, calmly but seriously:

- Explain once and for all why this rule or procedure is important.

- Make clear that it is unacceptable for the provider to substitute her judgment for yours without discussing the issues with you. (Donna had ample opportunity to discuss the hat issue with you.)

- If the provider considers some policy, procedure, or rule to be capricious and unenforceable, she needs to continue abiding by it, but she should speak with you about it as soon as possible. Make it clear that her suggestions and changes are more than welcome, are in fact expected, but that no rules can be changed until you have been consulted and have made your determination as to how to proceed.

- During your next weekly meeting, ask your provider how the amended policy is working out. At this time, inquire if there are any other issues that she feels similarly about and how you can work together to resolve problems in the future.

- Put the incident behind you.

By dealing with every incident—no matter how minor it seems—in this way, you'll likely avoid any major conflicts. Your nanny will know firsthand that rules are important to you, but that so is her input and communication.

What If You Suspect Alcohol or Substance Abuse?

You may have observed some aberrant behavior, or worse, had it reported to you by either a friend or even your child. Unfortunately, as a personal employer you are not immune to the human problems that spill over into work and create productivity problems that affect businesses large and small. If you work, nothing I say in this section is going to shock you. But it will depress and scare you. Alcohol and substance abuse has become the number-one cause of poor employee productivity in businesses nationwide. If legions of professional managers at companies all over the country have a tough time diagnosing and managing this problem, what can you do? It would be nice if you had the time and resources to deal with an alcohol or substance-abuse problem

■ ■

IS THERE A PROBLEM?

1. Is there any mention of this type of behavior from any previous employer?

   ☐ yes   ☑ no

   If yes, add notes: _____

   _____

   _____

   (This is why it is critical to go back at least five years. If alcohol or substance abuse is the problem, it could be an old one and may have not been experienced by the last employer.)

2. Were there any issues regarding the provider's driving record?

   ☐ yes   ☑ no

   If yes, when, where, and how did provider explain to your satisfaction during interview? _____

   _____

   _____

   (Another reason why a review of driving records is critical. No DUI's or DWI's is a good indication of sobriety but is only good until the date of the last record check.)

3. Any criminal convictions for alcohol- or substance-abuse–related issues?
   ☐ yes   ☑ no

   If yes, when, where, and how did provider explain to your satisfaction during interview? _____

   _____

   _____

4. When did you notice a decline in work behavior or performance? _last month_

   _____

5. Was there a specific incident that precipitated your concern? ☑ yes ☐ no

   Describe: _I came home from work and Nellie was asleep in Michael's bedroom with Michael on the bed next to her. I couldn't wake her up for at least 10 minutes, even after turning on the lights, speaking loudly, and then shaking her. Finally she woke up. What if there was a fire, or if Michael was ill? This same thing has happened three times now._

6. Have you previously discussed issues with the provider that now appear to be a precursor of the current behavior?   ☐ yes ☑ no

   If so, what does your Provider's Personal File reflect? _____

   _____

   _____

7. How is your provider's behavior affecting your child(ren)? _____

   _____

   _____

   Are you worried about their safety?   ☑ yes ☐ no

   Do they know or notice something is wrong?   ☑ yes ☐ no

   Is/Are your child(ren) reticent or anxious about being with the provider alone?
   ☐ yes ☑ no

   Are your child(ren) acting or speaking out because they sense something about the provider has changed?   ☐ yes ☑ no

■ ■

in your child-care provider, but you don't. You will need some help to accurately assess the problem, intervene for the safety of your children, and terminate the employment relationship. On page 129 are some steps for you to use to assess whether alcohol or substance abuse could be a factor in your nanny's poor performance:

Please keep in mind that the information in the boxes is meant to be used by you to assess the situation, and then go on red alert—but do not make accusations. Not one of the symptoms listed, in and of itself, constitutes a reason to hit the panic button. I, for example, like both breath mints and perfume. So be sure to look at everything in context. The list may indicate a problem if two or more items are observed as new components in your nanny's behavior. Armed with your observations, you can then make a decision about the safety of your child(ren) and if and when you may need to intervene. This is where review of your weekly meeting notes and notes during your in-person interview, the results of the background check, and your quarterly performance review can be of enormous help to you. Pull out and then quickly review your provider's Personnel File. Then, take a look at the sample "Is There a Problem?" template. You can find the template in Chapter Ten or in the In-Home file on the diskette.

If any of the answers to the above questions are yes, or even a strong maybe, you should be evaluating a permanent change. One of the disadvantages of being a personal employer is that you have no personnel department or employee-assistance program office full of professionals to help you or offer counseling programs to your employee. And this isn't just about a change in employee personality or performance that may affect the production of widgets. There are safety, socialization, and interpersonal developmental issues relating to your child that must be protected and secured. So you will need to act swiftly, judiciously, and fairly. If you know or strongly believe that your provider is abusing alcohol or controlled substances and you need to terminate the relationship, follow the plan outlined in the next few pages using templates from Chapter Ten and on the software in the In-Home file.

Notes to the Provider Personnel File

After an incident, it is important that you take a couple of minutes to jot down some notes in your provider's Personnel File. Although you and your provider have distinctly different roles to play as manager and employee, it would be silly to deny the true essence of the relationship. You are collaborators in giving the best care for your child(ren). So without the bureaucratic infrastructure available to most businesses where written warnings naturally exist to "build the file" in case of future termination, verbal discussions of performance during the weekly meetings between parent and provider, and more formally at the quarterly review, are the most effective means of dealing with problems. You will, however, want to keep your own notes on what happened during the meetings so that you have a fair representation of the facts for your employee's quarterly review.

The Quarterly Review

As you review the sample Quarterly Review template below, keep in mind that the purpose of this exercise is to bring together all of the data from your weekly meetings with your provider; distill the progress made; and follow up with your provider on those issues that still need improvement. It is also a time to set out your goals and plans for the next three months and to get your provider's input on future plans. Take a few moments to prepare for the Quarterly Review meeting by scanning your weekly Meeting Agendas, paying close attention to the meeting notes at the end of the document. Make copies of specific issues from the notes that you want to discuss. If you are using the software, copy those passages from the saved weekly Meeting Agenda files and paste them onto the Quarterly Review document in the "Issues" section. Be sure to choose both positive and negative issues to highlight during the Quarterly

---

What to Look For If You Suspect Alcohol or Substance Abuse

- overall change in behavior

- tardiness or absenteeism

- aberrant behavior such as temper tantrums, crying, or melancholy

- abrupt changes in relationships with others

- change in physical appearance and cleanliness

- slurred speech

- dilated pupils

- disorientation and lack of focus

- overuse of perfume or breath mints to disguise odor of alcohol

QUARTERLY REVIEW

Date _December 15, 1996_ Provider's name _Nellie Smith_

How would you rate his/her overall job performance on a scale of 1 to 10 with 10
   being excellent? ___7___
   last quarter's rating __8__

Issues: ___Communication___
   ___Tardiness in getting to work___

(This is where you copy and paste your "issues notes" from the weekly
agenda and the "needs improvement" section of last quarter's review.)

Is he/she showing improvement/growth in the position? ___Yes___

Any trouble with:

   attendance   ☐ yes ☑ no
   dependability   ☐ yes ☑ no
   teamwork   ☐ yes ☑ no

Needs improvement: _____

Future plans: _Seems as if Nellie is happy and plans on being here for a while._

Provider's comments for future growth: _Nellie says she will work on communication skills by making a list of issues to bring up at every weekly meeting. She will also leave for work 1/2 hour earlier every day so that traffic doesn't make her late._

Review. You will want to positively reinforce those things where you have noted improvement before you begin discussing any negatives.

IF TERMINATION BECOMES NECESSARY

You have thoroughly evaluated your child-care provider's performance and behavior and found that a change is needed. This decision should not come as a surprise to the provider because there should have been a suitable airing of the issues bothering you during your last few weekly meetings. Additionally, during her last Quarterly Review, when these issues were initially discussed, you asked that she work on modifying the behavioral issues and fix the performance ones by the next review, which is very soon. Even with all these precautions, termination may still come as a surprise to your nanny, so be prepared. (I have known of some insubordinate and underperforming employees with thick employment files stuffed with warnings who were shocked when the boss finally had had enough and they were terminated!) Below I've given you a list of documents to retrieve and issues to consider before the termination meeting so you can be organized. You should have a hard copy of each in your provider's Personnel File, or if you are using the software, print out what you will need.

To Prepare For The Termination/Exit Interview:

1. Get out a copy of your contract in case you need to refresh your provider's memory on various issues that come up during the meeting.

2. If your provider is a live-in, decide how you will deal with her living with you until she can move. How much time will you give her? What date does she have to be moved by?

3. If she is a live-out, be sure to have her take all of her belongings with her when she leaves on her final day.

4. Have a copy of the House Inventory Items template on hand during the meeting to expedite the return of keys, garage door openers, beepers, credit cards, and other items, and to remind you to change the house alarm security code. Collect any School Pickup Authorization forms with her name on them.

5. Have a copy of the Provider Exit Interview template at hand so that you can take notes during the meeting.

■ ■ ■ ■ ■ ■ ■ ■ ■ ■ ■ ■ ■ ■ ■ ■ ■ ■ ■ ■ ■ ■ ■ ■ ■ ■ ■ ■ ■ ■ ■ ■ ■ ■ ■ ■

PROVIDER TERMINATION CONTRACT

Mr. and Mrs. Dan P.
127 Roundabout Road
Anywhere, ST 01234

Date
Ms. Live-In Nanny
Same address as Nanny's

Dear (_____ date _____):   employer

Effective (_____ date), your employment with (_____)
is terminated. Your final paycheck for services rendered will be given to you on
(_____). (This paycheck will also include any severance payments which
we have agreed to pay under the terms of your employment.) We will provide you
with a separate notice advising you in connection with any continuing health
benefits or other employee benefits programs which may be available to you
after termination, if any.

We will meet you at _____o'clock today to discuss exit arrangements
connected with your termination. At that time you should return the items listed
on the attached Household Inventory Items list.

If you have any questions regarding the above or other aspects of your separation from employment, please be prepared to discuss them with us at your
exit interview.

We wish you the best of luck in your future endeavors.

Very truly yours,

_____
Parent(s) signature(s)

*If parents are supplying health or other benefits, they should consult each
specific program for instructions regarding terminated employees' options for
maintaining coverage subsequently.

■ ■

The Exit Interview

Whether your nanny's decision to leave your employ is voluntary or not, she deserves an exit review to set the record straight; air any feelings she may have, pro or con; and finalize the payroll issues that may need to be discussed. If you are the only one at the meeting who knows that this is your nanny's last day, be prepared for the gamut of emotions that may be forthcoming. You may want to provide your nanny with a complete copy of the Provider Termination Contract, especially if the nanny knows that this is her final day on the job. Here are twelve tips to keeping your powder dry and remaining professional:

1. Be prepared. Have all of your paperwork with you, including your provider's final wages.

2. Be cordial. Regardless how you may feel, your nanny deserves her dignity. Let her have hers—and you'll manage to keep yours.

3. Be decisive. Don't beat around the bush. Get to the point and be frank but firm.

4. Listen. After you have presented your decision, give the provider a fair airing of her issues.

5. Ask for constructive criticism of your management style. This is a learning experience for you, too.

6. Offer her constructive criticism. Honestly appraise her skills, behavior, and so on.

7. Discuss the child(ren)'s progress. Ask for input that may help future caregivers and you.

8. Keep it professional. Although this may be your last chance to tell her how you really feel about her pathetic tuna casserole or bubble-gum chewing . . . don't. This is your last meeting, so don't let it get personal or deal in "you said, I said." It's too late to rehash all of that.

9. Openly discuss what your future job reference attitude will be. Let her know what she can expect when future employers call.

10. Set a policy about future contact with the child(ren). If it is acceptable to you, does she want the child(ren) to write or phone her? Will she keep the family updated as to her home address and phone number? If this isn't a friendly situation, ponder whether you want her sending birthday cards or other communications. Be honest and firm.

11. Fill out the Provider Exit Interview template carefully and completely. I strongly suggest that you complete it during or as soon as possible after the meeting. You will want to record your impressions while they are fresh on your mind. The Provider Exit Interview template will allow you to handle reference calls from the nanny's future employers with ease. Remember, keep to the facts; be objective and fair, but honest to all parties involved. That means you, your provider, and any future potential employers.

12. Check the Legal Kit to refresh your memory on your obligations regarding the timely disbursement of your soon-to-be-former employee's payroll. In most states, you need to have a check ready at the end of the last day. Severance is also a state-by-state issue, so brush up on your obligations and be ready to deal with it during the Provider Exit Interview.

PROVIDER EXIT INTERVIEW

Date: _February 19, 1996_   **Provider's Name:** _Nellie Smith_

Dates of Employment _6/15/95_   to _2/19/96_

Starting Position _nanny_

Ending Position _nanny_

Salary _$7.75/hr_

Reason for Leaving _getting married and moving to Bahamas_

How would you rate his/her overall job performance on a scale of 1 to 10 with 10 being excellent? _8_

Did he/she show improvement/growth in the position? _yes_

What were his/her strengths? _responsible, experienced, calm, good humor even when under stress_

What were the area's in which you would recommend improvements (weaknesses)? _needs to work on communication skills_

Would you reemploy?   ☑ Y   ☐ N

Any trouble with:

attendance	☐ Y	☑ N
attitude	☐ Y	☑ N
dependabilty	☐ Y	☑ N
teamwork	☐ Y	☑ N

Additional information:_____

CHAPTER SEVEN

Finding and Hiring Family Day Care

IN THIS CHAPTER:	*Getting Organized*
	Regulated vs. Unregulated Care
	Evaluating Providers
	Contracting with a Provider
	Managing Your Provider

WHAT ARE YOUR OPTIONS?

There are a total of 287,949 regulated family day-care homes in the fifty states and the District of Columbia, making family day care by far the largest sector of child-care services offered in the United States. Out of this massive number, 23,484 are group homes caring for seven to twelve children; and 264,465 are small homes caring for six or fewer children, including children of the provider. And, though these numbers are stunning, it's surprising to learn that family day care is the child-care service category that is still the least uniformly regulated by the states, although it is improving steadily.

Depending on the part of the country and state where you live, family day care may take a different name and will be governed by regulations with different degrees of stringency. Family day-care homes, family child-care homes, and family day homes are broadly described as a child-care arrangement in which generally up to six children all under the age of six (including those of the provider) are cared for in the home of the provider for compensation. In a larger version, large family day-care homes or group homes, a provider and one or more assistants generally care for seven to twelve children, including those of the provider and any assistants, in the home of that provider for compensation. In all cases, laws vary from state to state in determining the maximum number of children allowed in the home, with the age of the children being a prevalent determining factor.

Large family day-care homes or group homes are the family day care of choice of Kay Hollestelle, Director of The Children's Foundation, a nonprofit child-care advocacy association in Washington, D.C. According to Ms. Hollestelle, "Over the years we have tracked the growing numbers of individuals joining the ranks of regulated providers, the various changes being made in regulations, and the emergence of group or large family child-care homes. Our 1977 study indicated ten states had regulations for group or large homes, with approximately 3,700 providers. In 1983, there were sixteen states and approximately seven thousand providers. By 1990, the number of states with separate regulations for group or large family child care had grown to thirty-nine with more than thirteen thousand providers. In our 1994 Family Day-Care Licensing study, we list forty-three states with approximately 23,000 providers offering such care.

"This is one trend in child care we support. We believe that group or large family child care is a win-win situation for all involved. Group or large family child care offers more child-care slots in a specific geographic area. It offers parents a better opportunity to find affordable, regulated child care. It still offers a small group size in a homelike setting for children. It also helps providers alleviate the sense of isolation often found in family child care because a second and often third caregiver is required by law, depending upon the ages and number of children in care."

There is one quality that clearly differentiates family day-care homes from day-care centers: With family day care, the "center" is someone else's home. Unlike a facility specially designed and maintained for child care, an operator's private home, no matter how much the operator/owner has attempted to segregate the children's area from the family's living area, is still really a family's living area. For this reason, parents must be more stringent, diligent, and constant in their review of the situation.

It also adds a major change in the dynamics of the relationship between the parent and operator. Unlike day-care centers, in family day care, the fact that the site is the operator's home and that an overwhelming number of operators remain unregulated, puts parents in an uncomfortable position. Many parents admit that they were charmed initially by the informal, cottage-industry attitude of their operator, but later this same attitude made them uneasy. For example, it's probably much easier to be critical of an ongoing maintenance problem when an operator is sitting in an office, not in her own kitchen. Because many family day-care businesses are still operating outside of the state regulatory scheme, parents have no real leverage, and if something goes wrong, all they can do is look for another operator.

Because of the casual and homey quality of their businesses, many family day-care operators do not provide written schedules, programming, or payment contracts (which may seem too "businesslike"). This can make a parent who is dependent on child care in order to work very vulnerable to the whimsy of the operator. You may have no clear idea of your child's day. In addition, you may feel quite insecure about handling any disputes or misunderstandings.

If you do choose to use family day care, here are some pointers for finding the best care for your child.

Start by Getting Organized

Before you start your search for family day care, take a few minutes to get organized. You'll find that by putting together everything you need for the project in one place, the whole process will be less confusing and stressful. If you have room, try to set up a permanent workspace for yourself, preferably at a desk with a phone and answering machine. Add some manila files, a desktop file holder or a file cabinet, a pocket calculator, stationery, envelopes, and a few legal pads and pens, and you're done. If you have a computer and a printer, that's even better; you can refer to the icons along the side of these pages to direct you to the appropriate templates on the enclosed diskette. If you don't have access to a computer, look in the yellow pages to locate the nearest retail copy center—you will want to use their copy machines to copy templates and checklists directly out of this book.

If you live in a small home or apartment and don't have enough room for a permanent workspace, purchase a large, inexpensive accordion file holder that has ten or more sections, and use one of the sections to hold your supplies. The other sections can hold your forms, documents, notes, and so on. During your search for a provider, keep this file holder next to the phone.

LOOKING FOR FAMILY
DAY-CARE CENTERS IN YOUR AREA

Start by calling your local child-care resource-and-referral (R&R) agency. You can obtain the number of the resource-and-referral agency closest to you by phoning Child Care Aware at (800) 424-2246. Your local R&R should be able to give you several family day-care operators in your zip code.

If you do not have a resource-and-referral agency in your area, start networking like crazy! Try asking your pediatrician and family doctor if they know of any good family day-care operators. Ask your friends with children, friends who don't have children, friends of friends, and coworkers. If you have older children who are in school, ask other parents, teachers, even the principal. Try asking around at your church or synagogue and be sure to check any bulletin boards there. Check local newspapers, *Pennysavers*, and flyers. Or try looking in the phone book—some family day-care facilities will be listed. If a family day-care operator is listed, he or she is most likely running a business enterprise that's been around for a while and plans to stay around. This is good; it may mean that you run less of a risk that the home will close down when you most need it! Finally, check to see if your company or your spouse's company has any information on various types of child care in the area. The human resources department may have a staff member dedicated to providing employees with information on many child-care services offered locally. Most large companies have gone one step further by contracting with a company that offers information on a diverse list of services, including rehab programs, elder care, after-school tutoring for children, and hospice programs. These companies can provide you with lists of family day-care operators close to home or work. Companies that help employees with their dependent-care issues are noticing a significant reduction in the number of employee sick days (including those days that you call in sick to care for your sick child) and increased employee loyalty and productivity. If you are lucky enough to work for one of these organizations, by all means make as much use of the services as you can. While there is usually no fee to access the information, the final choice of the type of service you use—and the bill—will be yours.

Regulated or Unregulated—Narrowing It Down

There are two broad categories of family day-care homes: those that are regulated by the state and federal government, and those that are not. Unfortunately, there are as many definitions of the word *regulated* as there are states in the union. "Regulated" in one state can mean licensed; in another state it can mean certified; and in another registered. And, each of these words means different things in different states. Following are The Children's Foundation's definitions of *licensed, registration,* and *certification* for family day-care homes.

Licensed

This means that a designated state or local agency has granted formal permission to an individual or legal entity to operate a child-care facility. The agency has the authority to ensure that standards are being met; set procedures for revoking a license; and provide appeal mechanisms. In addition to the inspections carried out by the licensing agency, local fire and health departments also carry out on-site inspections of family day-care homes. Generally, a license is issued and renewed as long as all of the applicable regulations are being met. The purpose, then, is to protect vulnerable consumers by setting a minimum floor for reasonably safe service.

Type 1 Registration

Registration is a form of regulation that stresses caregiver self-inspection and parent awareness. It is intended to identify service providers that the government cannot or chooses not to license because of taxpayer cost involved in inspections or because of intense lobbying efforts by family day-care providers against licensing. The registration process works in the following way: Registration standards are usually determined by the state's health and human services department or another state regulatory agency dealing with child welfare (each state has its own name for the agency), and these are generally the same standards used in licensing. When the provider receives information detailing these standards, he does a self-study to determine whether his home center is meeting those standards. This study usually includes self-certification that the provider has met certain fire and health standards. Self-certification does not require the provider to show proof that he or she meets the standards; it merely requires the provider to sign a document saying that she meets the standards. Self-certification may or may not also include other requirements such as a medical examination, TB screening, child-abuse clearance, criminal records check, and/or fingerprinting. On receipt of this information by the state regulating agency, the home is considered to be registered and has permission to operate. Inspection visits are usually done by random sample or are only made when a complaint is lodged.

Type 2 Registration

In some states, registration is a simple sign-up procedure where operating family day-care homes are listed with the regulatory agency. These homes are only required to sign a health and safety checklist agreeing to meet minimum standards of health and safety.

Certification

For all practical purposes, certification and registration are the same but can be used to differentiate providers receiving public funds.

Here are some examples of the many complexities, variations, and quirks of the state regulations for family day-care operators:

Eighteen states, 35 percent, use licensing exclusively: AL, AK, CA, CO, DC, IL, IN, MA, MN, ND, NH, NM, NV, OK, UT, WA, and WY.

Thirteen states, 25 percent, use a combination of registration and licensing: GA, FL, KS, ME, MI, NC, NY, PA, SC, SD, TN, TX, and VT.

Five states, 10 percent, use registration exclusively: CT, HI, MD, MT, and WV.

Three states, 6 percent, use a combination of certification and licensing: OH, RI, and WI.

Two states, 4 percent, use self-certification only: DE and NE.

One state, 2 percent, uses certification: AZ.

One state, 2 percent, uses a combination of certification, licensing, and voluntary certification: KY.

All other states use a combination of voluntary registration, mandatory registration, and mandatory licensing, which are other variations on registration types 1 and 2 and certification as described above.

The family day-care regulatory schemes found in The Children's Foundation report shows just how much the regulations vary from state by state. Remember that some states have no regulations at all. If family day care is regulated by your state, you will want to be sure to check whether your preferred operator is in full compliance with all state and local licensing laws. To do this, you need to understand your state's family day-care regulations. Call the regulatory agency in your state responsible for child-care regulations, and ask them for a list of their requirements. A family day-care home's compliance with certain standards will be obvious. For example, you can make sure there is the correct number of providers caring for the children in the family day-care home. Ask to see your provider's registration or certification documents. Don't worry about offending a provider. Remember, you are the consumer and a family day-care provider is offering you a critical service for compensation. If a provider is in full compliance, she should have no problem satisfying your curiosity. If she is upset by your request, you may have a problem. To be a truly informed and proactive consumer of family day-care services, you also need to go a step further. Try to make complete sense of the language used in the regulations and some of the subtle differences among the states, and stay informed about what regulations the child-care watchdog groups say are best for children. It's hard to believe that with all the stress on education and training in most professions today, ten states, including California and Illinois (two large population centers), do not require family day-care providers to have any training at all. And while twenty-six states require training in first aid and/or CPR, the others don't. The regulations that differentiate small family day-care homes from large ones vary just as much.

Evaluating Operators

Step 1: The Telephone Prescreen

Use your telephone to narrow a list down to only the most appropriate family day-care homes. You don't want to waste your time visiting a home that doesn't have an outdoor play area if you've already determined that your child needs an outdoor play area, or spend time with a family day-care operator who is way out of your price range or at the licensing limit for the number of children in her care. Additionally, because demand is so high, a telephone call can give you invaluable information on which homes have openings.

The telephone interview can give you a good feel for the type of operator you are dealing with, his or her personality and ability to communicate, and most important, a preliminary assessment of whether the home has all of your baseline requirements. Try to get as much information as you possibly can and be sure to ask for two references: a current client and a former client. By checking with former and existing clients, you should be able to get a true account of the reliability and safety of the operator and a sense for how other children have fared in her care. Since the operator is providing the names of the references herself, don't be surprised to hear superlative praise. Concentrate instead on eliciting information about how the parents have interacted with the operator. Were the children happy and content? Did the children resist or fret about going to the operator's house? Did the operator make any sudden changes in their original agreement? Did she change prices or hours often or without suitable notice?

Perhaps the most important issue, aside from the obvious questions of safety, regulation, reputation, and price, is that your child fits into the age and sex demographics already existing at the home. This is especially critical in the family day-care home scenario because these centers are small by nature and you won't have a number of age-appropriate groups to choose from, as you would in a day-care center. This is a critical litmus test for success with a particular operator. If the children are too old or too young, or your child is the only boy or girl to attend, my guess is that the overall dynamic is wrong. Look for a place where you know your child will have fun and where there is another child or better yet, other children, who are comparable in age and sex. We all know it can be very difficult to care for children of varied ages and schedules at the same time. In addition, for all of us, an atmosphere where we feel lonely or "out of it" because we don't fit in has limited appeal. The true test of this or any other type of care where the provider must care for more than one child is that the children can interact and co-exist happily because they are well matched in age, skills, and group size. This is even more true for infants and babies under the age of two than for older children. If you are placing your infant in child care, you will want to know that the center and provider(s) are technically skilled and oriented to care for our littlest loved ones. Because infants and babies that are bottle- and diaper-dependent need so much individual care, you will want to assure yourself that the provider isn't going to be distracted by the demands of too many active older children, or that the environment is going to be too noisy and over-stimulating for a very small child. Look for a home or provider that sets appropriate limits on the number of children or caters to a specific age group.

Take a look at the Family Day-Care Telephone Prescreen Questions that follow and then turn to the Family Day-Care Prescreen Questions template in Chapter Ten. If you are using the software, open the Family Day Care file and click on the Telephone Prescreen Questions template. Once you've thoroughly reviewed the questions, add any extra questions you would like to ask in the space at the bottom of the template or on an extra page. Then, make multiple copies of the template. Use one copy for each family day-care operator you speak with, fill in the answers to your questions in the appropriate spaces, and be sure to take detailed notes during your conversation.

I would allow plenty of time for your conversation. You should try to talk at least fifteen minutes, but allow half an hour for each phone interview. Be aware of the fact that most family day-care operators will be too busy to talk to you for any length of time during the weekday—they've got children to attend to and are usually without a staff to take over for them! I would make a brief call during the day to set a time to speak later in the evening or on the weekend.

When you near the end of the phone interview, decide whether the provider fits your requirements and warrants a visit to the home. If so, schedule the visit, and use the space at the bottom of the template to enter a date and time. Work with the operator to pick a time when you can observe the children at play, and then interview her during naptime. I would suggest you arrive at a home about half an hour before naptime, spend that half-hour observing, and then use the next half-hour during naptime for the interview. Also, tell the operator that you are not bringing your child to this initial visit. It's best to bring your child to a family day-care home only after you have determined that it might be a good place for your child. Visiting a family day-care home can be a traumatic event for even the most even-tempered children. They don't know any of the children there; they don't know the provider; they are not familiar with the surroundings. And they may never see the place again! Also, if you are watching your child or trying to deal with your child's shyness around a group of new faces, you probably won't be totally focused on the list of things you need to look for in the home. You will miss a lot. Leave your child at home for this first visit.

Finally, if you're not sure whether the operator fits the bill, and you want to talk to some other providers before you decide to interview her in person, tell her that you will call her back by a specific time, for example, "this Friday," to schedule the interview.

■ ■

FAMILY DAY-CARE TELEPHONE PRESCREEN QUESTIONS

Family Day-Care Operator Name: _Karen Smith_

Location: _1214 Bay Street_

Phone Number: _381-9543_   Date of Call: _June 3_

Start by telling the operator a little about your child—name, age, sex, etc., and describe what you are looking for, especially the days and number of hours a week you require care. Then ask:

1. "What days are you open and for what hours?" _weekdays, 7 A.M._
   _to 7 P.M._

2. "How much do you charge?" _$200 a week_

3. "Do you have any openings now, or in the near future?" _yes_

4. (If your state requires licensing) "Is your center licensed?"
   yes

5. "Please give me an overview of your experience and qualifications for work in child care." _Retired 3rd-grade teacher who worked for 25 years_
   in San Francisco. Two children—ages 30 and 24.

6. "Are you certified in CPR, infant CPR, and first aid?" _yes_

7. "How many children do you care for and what are their ages?"
   3—an infant, an 18-month-old, and a 3-year-old.

8. "How many children do you care for at any given time?" _5—but only 1_
   infant at a time.

9. "Do you have any assistants?" _No_

10. "Would you agree to an investigation of your background?" _yes_

11. (If the provider has assistants) "Would you agree to an investigation of your staff?" _N/A_

12. "Would you agree to an investigation of everyone who lives in your house and has access to my child?" _Yes_

13. "Could you please describe your facility?" _1 room for sleeping with 5 cots   one play room with toys, books, games, art supplies   big backyard with swingset and sandbox._

14. "Approximately how many square feet is the indoor space?" _The indoor space consists of two connecting rooms, one about 10 x 12 (120 square feet) and the other, set up for naps is 9 x 14 (126 square feet)._

"And the outdoor play area?" _The outdoor area is a fenced 1/2 acre with play equipment that is 2 years old._

15. "Describe a typical day my child would have in your center." _The morning starts with a hot breakfast (included in fee), then if the weather is good, they take a short walk to the park down the block and swing, play, and build things in the sandbox. Back to the house for a one-hour nap, then lunch. After lunch they head out to the backyard for some games and playtime. Then, they have some quiet time where the children read or listen to music to prepare for a nap. After naps, the children get a snack— sometimes homemade cookies and milk, sometimes fruit or juice. Then, they do an organized art project until parents arrive._

16. "Is there a secure outdoor area for the children to play?" _Yes, see above._

17. "Is there a napping space for infants and older children?" _Yes_

18. "Is there storage space to keep my child's belongings?" _Yes_

Include any other questions you would like to ask in the following space or on another sheet._____

■ ■

The On-Site Visit

Once you identify a few homes that appear to have all your baseline requirements, it's time to visit. Remember, don't take your child to this visit. Wait until you find a home you feel really good about.

Review the Family Day-Care On-Site Visit Checklist below.

FAMILY DAY-CARE ON-SITE VISIT CHECKLIST

Date: _____   Time: _____

Safety

Is the neighborhood safe?	☑ yes	☐ no
House/apartment secure?	☑ yes	☐ no
House/apartment well maintained?	☑ yes	☐ no
Smoke detectors working (check to see if light indicating charged battery is on)?	☑ yes	☐ no
Fire extinguishers current (check date on canister or attached card)?	☑ yes	☐ no
Medicines locked up?	☑ yes	☐ no
Household/cleaning products locked up?	☑ yes	☐ no
Electrical outlets covered?	☑ yes	☐ no
Adequate first-aid kit?	☑ yes	☐ no
Screened windows?	☑ yes	☐ no
Secured electrical cords?	☑ yes	☐ no
Evacuation plan/emergency drills?	☑ yes	☐ no
Kitchen equipment inaccessible?	☑ yes	☐ no
Stairs gated and inaccessible?	☑ yes	☐ no

Sanitation/Cleanliness

Passes the "Sniff Test"?	☑ yes	☐ no
House appears clean/organized?	☑ yes	☐ no
Play area clean/organized?	☑ yes	☐ no
Are sheets/blankets in nap room clean?	☑ yes	☐ no
Surfaces clean?	☑ yes	☐ no
Toys/games clean?	☑ yes	☐ no
Food preparation areas clean?	☑ yes	☐ no
Bathroom clean/sanitized?	☑ yes	☐ no

Indoor Play Area

Is it cheerful/engaging?	☑ yes	☐ no
Are toys in good repair?	☑ yes	☐ no
Enough age-appropriate toys/games?	☑ yes	☐ no
Enough crafts/art supplies?	☑ yes	☐ no
Art work is displayed?	☑ yes	☐ no
Can adults see the entire room at once?	☑ yes	☐ no
Water available?	☑ yes	☐ no
Easy access to bathrooms?	☑ yes	☐ no
Cubbyholes for each child?	☑ yes	☐ no
Adequate light/ventilation?	☑ yes	☐ no

Nap Area

Quiet/restful location?	☑ yes	☐ no
Adequate ventilation?	☑ yes	☐ no
Individual cots and cribs?	☑ yes	☐ no
Cots/cribs away from curtains with pull cords?	☑ yes	☐ no
Cots/cribs new and in good condition?	☑ yes	☐ no
Cot/crib bolts and screws secure?	☑ yes	☐ no
Cot/crib mattresses in good condition?	☑ yes	☐ no
Crib side slats no farther that 2 3/8" apart?	☑ yes	☐ no
Distance from crib mattress to top of railing at least 22"?	☑ yes	☐ no
Crib corner posts less than 1" high?	☑ yes	☐ no

Outside Play Area (if any)

Enough space?	☑ yes	☐ no
Grass/plants/flowers?	☑ yes	☐ no
Enclosed and secure?	☑ yes	☐ no
Adult can see entire play area at once?	☑ yes	☐ no
Sandboxes covered?	☑ yes	☐ no
Thick pads under play equipment?	☑ yes	☐ no
Play equipment in good repair?	☑ yes	☐ no
Garden tools inaccessible?	☑ yes	☐ no

If No Outside Play Area

Is outside time scheduled every day?	☐ yes	☐ no
Is a park nearby?	☐ yes	☐ no
Is the park safe?	☐ yes	☐ no

Operator

Warm/friendly?	☑ yes	☐ no
Smiles?	☑ yes	☐ no
Positive and open?	☑ yes	☐ no
Pleasant tone of voice?	☑ yes	☐ no
Made you feel at home?	☑ yes	☐ no
Good communicator?	☑ yes	☐ no
Clean?	☑ yes	☐ no
Organized/under control?	☑ yes	☐ no
Truly likes children?	☑ yes	☐ no

Program

Set daily schedule?	☑ yes	☐ no
Posted for parents?	☑ yes	☐ no
Adequate play time?	☑ yes	☐ no
Adequate nap time?	☑ yes	☐ no
Nutritious meals/snacks?	☑ yes	☐ no
Television allowed?	☑ yes	☐ no
Access to pets?	☐ yes	☑ no

continued

Administration

Written pricing/policies?	☑ yes	☐ no
Additional staff?	☐ yes	☑ no
Family member access to children?	☐ yes	☑ no
Licensing documents in order?	☑ yes	☐ no
Fully insured (ask to see documentation)?	☑ yes	☐ no
Parents welcome at all times?	☑ yes	☐ no
Daily log?	☐ yes	☑ no
Authorized persons only may pick up children?	☑ yes	☐ no
Regular meetings with parents?	☑ yes	☐ no

Additional Comments: *The pool makes me nervous—the fence around it doesn't look secure enough. Miss Karen is a little strange—it's hard for me to relate to her.*

■■■■■■■■■■■■■■■■■■■■■■■■■■■■■■■■■■■■■■

The On-Site Interview

When you get a few moments of quiet time with the provider, ask the following questions, and be sure to write down the provider's answers. Also, feel free to ask any questions or mention any concerns that came up while you were watching her interactions with the children. You want to find out whether this provider can communicate with you. You also want to get some critical background on her child-care practices and philosophy in general, and on very specific items.

The sample answers for the visit and interview described below are ideal. You will rarely find a family day-care home and operator that manages to satisfy you on every issue. I would suggest that you view the visit and interview the following way: Issues related to the health and safety of your child are the most critical. Make sure that you feel entirely comfortable with the measures taken by the provider to keep your child healthy and safe. Of secondary importance are the programming and actvities your child will participate in while at the home. Make sure you receive a level of programming that you feel is challenging and stimulating for your child. Equally important are the organization and management of the home. Be sure that your provider considers herself to be a professional child-care provider and runs her business in a highly professional manner—then, it is far more likely that your child's care will be of high quality. Finally, subjective issues related to the provider's attitude and enthusiasm for her work (questions 9 and 10 in the interview) are important indicators of whether the provider is motivated to provide you and your child with quality service.

FAMILY DAY-CARE ON-SITE VISIT
INTERVIEW QUESTIONS

1. "How would you discipline my child?" _Short time-outs_

2. "What indoor activities do you generally encourage?" _Painting, crafts, storytelling and reading, blocks, listening to music, singing._

3. "What outdoor activities do you encourage?" _Swinging, climbing the jungle gym, planting flowers, playing in the sandbox._

4. "How do you handle mealtimes?" _Feeds infants and cooks meals while toddlers are napping, then feeds toddlers_

5. "What would you do if my child became ill at your house?" _Call me or my spouse and ask us to pick up Michael immediately._

6. "How do you handle situations where one child needs special attention, such as one child needing to go potty, or a child who has hurt himself and needs medical attention? What do you do with the other children?"

    Our bathroom is accessible from the children's play area. We have installed a Dutch door to the bathroom which has a top part that we leave open during operating hours. I can help the child going potty and supervise the other children at the same time.

7. "Do you have any regular visitors to your home during child-care operating hours? Who are they and what is their relationship to you?" _All of my friends and nonresident family members know that I am unavailable during my home's child-care operating hours. I've asked them all to call before they drop by. The only people allowed to interact with the children I care for are the parents of the children currently in our program._

8. "What is the average length of time you provide child care for your families?" _Of the 3 families that currently use my services, 1 child, who is now 3, has been with me since she was 10 weeks old. Another child, also 3 years old, has been with me a few months short of 2 years, and our most recent addition, a 2 1/2-year-old, has been with me 5 months._

9. "What is the biggest challenge you face every day?" _I love being with these kids. But I admit it is hard to keep them interested and cooperative all at the same time. It's important for me to be organized and innovative._

continued

10. "How do you keep yourself refreshed and enthusiastic about this type of work?" *I don't work on the weekends, so I look for weekend continuing education programs that offer me the opportunity to keep current on child-care issues and programming that I can offer. I also scout the TV Listings during the weekend and program my VCR for shows that are not only of interest and help to me, but fun things to show the kids. This comes in handy for rainy days and during the parts of the day when there is little or no children's programming available.*

11. "How do you handle days when you are too ill to care for the children?" *I try to phone parents the night before, or earlier, if I think I'm going to be too sick to work. Most of my parents are able to make other arrangements.*

Additional questions specific to your child's age: _____
_____
_____
_____
_____
_____

■ ■

Now, turn to Chapter Ten for the Family Day-Care On-Site Visit Checklist and Family Day-Care On-Site Interview Questions templates, or click on these templates in the Family Day-Care file on the diskette. Be sure to include any additional questions you would like to ask in the space on the bottom of the Family Day-Care On-Site Interview Questions template. Consider questions relating to age-specific issues, for example, "When do you think a toddler should begin toilet training and how would you handle it?" "How often do you change an infant's diapers?" "How often do you hold infants?" "My schedule seems to change daily. How flexible are you in terms of drop-off and pickup time, and what is your policy for handling parents who are late to pick up their child?" and so on. Then, make a copy of the two templates for every family day-care home you plan to visit.

The Visit with Your Child

Bring your child to visit a center only after you have identified your number-one choice. Because you used your first visit to make sure that the operator and the home meet all of your baseline requirements, during the second visit you can focus solely on the interaction between the operator and your child. Look for the following things:

The Operator

- When you enter the home, greets you and your child by name and immediately tries to make your child feel at home.
- Pays more attention to your child than to you.
- Introduces your child to the other children.
- Immediately makes an effort to integrate your child into the other children's activities.
- Speaks directly to your child.
- Warm and friendly, but not overbearing with your child.
- Acts comfortable with your child and with having you in the room observing.
- Uses an appropriate and encouraging tone of voice at all times, even if your child isn't responding to her overtures very well.

Your Child

- May not be completely at ease, but is not unusually anxious or scared.
- Warms up to the provider over the course of your time in the home.
- Is excited by the toys, games, and art supplies in the room.
- Understands that this is a home that is used for child care and that you like this option for her.
- Finds someone to play with because there is a good match as far as age and sex of the other children.

If all goes well during the visit to the family day-care home with your child, you need to take one more step before you entrust your child to a family day-care operator: background checks.

BACKGROUND CHECKS

It is vitally important that you know everything you can about the family day-care operator you will trust with your child. Because there are no airtight government checks and balances regulating or qualifying family day-care operators, proactive steps on your part to obtain as much information about the operator, before you drop your child off, are essential. Anyone can start a family day-care business anywhere in the fifty states anytime she wants.

I can guarantee that if a felon running a family day-care home finds out that you want to do a background check on her, she'll refuse to be investigated or she'll find a good reason not to take your kid. So don't be disappointed if your favorite family day-care operator says she can't take your child after you tell her you require a background check. It's very likely that you've just dodged a bullet and saved your child from exposure to an inappropriate or dangerous person.

Once you inform your operator that you want to do a background check on her and she agrees, it doesn't end there. Because family day care operates out of a provider's home, any family members over the age of eighteen need to be investigated. You don't know how many horror stories I've heard about wonderful family day-care providers who, unbeknownst to them, had husbands, brothers, sisters, or adult children who had access to the children and used that access to injure and abuse them. Insist on having all adults in the home investigated.

Once you have narrowed your options down to a final two homes, perform a comprehensive verification of the family day-care-center operator and employees/family members' personal data, including the following items:

Verify Operator's Data in These Areas for the Last Five Years

identity
SSI (Social Security Index number)
employment history
educational background
driving record
criminal records search
civil courts search

Because you are considering this home based on data supplied by the operator such as the home's operating record; licensing, registration or certification status; any relevant education pertaining to child care; and other information, you need to independently corroborate the claims of this operator, or any employee of the operator. And, though the personal interview(s) are important and should add a ton of credibility, we all know that some people think that telling a "little white lie" that enhances their ability to get a job "doesn't really hurt anyone." Just as in in-home child care, where a white lie can move someone with less experience and no background in child care to the front of the queue, a fabrication of a family-care-center operator's background or experience puts you at the same disadvantage. So you need to be sure the facts you are using to evaluate the home are true.

You have only a few options if you want to do a comprehensive, identity/education/employment verification and multijurisdictional criminal, civil, and driving check on a potential child-care provider: (1) Do it yourself. (2) Hire a private investigator you know and trust. (3) Hire The ChildCare Registry, or another preemployment screening company that can provide you with a packaged service and a legal release.

How to Do Your Own Background Check

I created The ChildCare Registry to provide parents with a service that provides legally released, comprehensive, state-of-the-art preemployment screening verifications and criminal, civil, and driving records that are completed within seven days. However, for parents who want to do the background check themselves, here is what I would do:

Get permission, in writing, from your family-care-center operator to do a background check.

Identity: Run a Social Security Index trace using the candidate's name and social security number. This will provide you with corroboration of the name and matching social security number. This will be very difficult for an individual to do since most public record databases don't sell this information "retail" and will want a copy of a legal release and payment up front. If you can get this information, it will probably cost $10 to $15, not including your time and phone call charges.

Employment: If this is a new home, or has been in operation only a short time, say a few years, but the operator has previous job experience in child care, you will need to verify the employment and complete a Professional Reference Report. Get a complete list of all child-care employers, including names of supervisors, with addresses and phone numbers for the last five years. Have the candidate include on the list her job position, starting and departing dates, and salary for each employer. Call each employer, indicate that you want to verify a person's previous employment, and cross your fingers because this can be ticklish. You'll also want to call other clients. Personal employers, like other parents, are often hard to reach since you may not have their work numbers (I'm not sure you should call there, anyway), which means you will have to call in the evening. So you may need to be persistent, but other parents are a gold mine of information, so don't get discouraged. Business employers need to be called during business hours, so take the information with you to work and call during lunch or a break. This gets complicated if you don't reach anyone who can help you and you need to be called back. If you can get calls at the office, great—leave that number; but if you can't and you need to leave your home number, be sure to leave an appropriate message on your home answering machine encouraging the party to leave a detailed response for you. Some previous employers may chafe at this and refuse to leave a message with sensitive employment data on a home answering machine.

Education: Have your candidate provide you with detailed information on each education claim. Get the full name, address, phone number, dates attended, and highest grade or graduation date for each institution. If you want to verify a candidate's high school graduation, you can probably do that over the telephone by calling the administrative office of the school during business hours. Colleges, universities, and other places of higher learning are trickier. Some require an authorization and release faxed to them. Others charge a fee, like $3, and insist on everything in writing, by mail. Many require the graduate's full name (watch out for name changes, like maiden names), date of birth, or Social Security number to ascertain identity and make sure you are talking about the same person. You will need to have all of this information handy when you call, so be sure to have a complete file in front of you.

Driving Records: You will want to verify that your candidate has a valid driver's license, insurance, and that your candidate's driving record is also clear of any moving violations, driving under the influence convictions, or other serious issues. How can you get a copy of your candidate's driving record? You can't, but she can. Once again, if you can get access to a public records database company who will accept your version of an authorization and release and sells "retail," you may be able to get a copy of your provider's driving record. However, the only sure-fire way of getting a copy is to have your provider go to her local DMV, pay a fee (in California it's $5), and get a *dated copy* of her DMV record. But be careful. It is easy to alter, fabricate, and counterfeit documents. Laser printers and high-resolution copiers have revolutionized the fine art of document manipulation, so it is critical that you can authenticate any document received by you from the provider. Insist that the driving record be very fresh and current—I would recommend that it be dated within one week of your examining it.

Criminal History Records: This is really a tough one. Though no one will argue the need to be aware of any type of criminal record in the background of a child-care provider, individual citizens are pretty much precluded from direct access to this information. The ChildCare Registry has access through a network of private investigators armed with sophisticated releases. Private investigators that you may hire can facilitate the same type of public-record courthouse search, but you will need to provide them with a seamless residential history, so that they can know which county courthouses to search. Statewide criminal history databases do exist, but in only a few states. California offers parents an option called Trustline, which is a database that lists child-care provider applicants whose backgrounds have been verified against the California Department of Justice criminal-histories records and the state's substantiated child-abuse files. The search is of California records only, so if your provider lived outside of California four years ago, the record will not reflect the other jurisdiction's data. The process takes 4 to 6 weeks and costs $85.

Civil Courthouse Record Searches: While a civil courthouse record rarely provides the type of inflammatory data that might preclude someone from working in child care, it is the one place where extremely pertinent information can hide from view. Did you know that many child molesters are often sued in civil court by the victim and their families for recovery of damages to pay for psychotherapy for the victim? Many times this is the only relief a victim and his/her family can find in the legal system, especially if the molester is not successfully prosecuted in criminal court or if the prosecutors don't go for an indictment because the facts are murky or victims are too young to testify. Civil courthouse records cannot be directly accessed by private citizens. However, they can be accessed by private detectives and should be done in each county of residence for five years. These searches need to be authorized and released by the provider and can be expensive because the private detectives will more than likely charge you by the hour. Depending on how many jurisdictions your provider has lived in, this can add up. Additionally, you can expect a document fee for each courthouse of at least $10.

Does the background check process sound discouraging, time consuming, and expensive? Still want to do this yourself? It's up to you. The whole time I spent writing this I felt like a car mechanic describing how easy it is to change your car's oil at home. Sure, you can do it, and maybe you can save money, but what a mess! Now that you know the components of a background check and some of the little dirty secrets of this industry, you can choose to go it alone. Just keep in mind that you need to protect yourself and your family day-care-center operator by having complete authorization and a written legal release to do this investigation—and the time to wait until all the pieces are verified.

A ChildCare Registry information packet, which includes everything a parent needs to request a background check including the CCR application, authorization and release, parent release, and payment form can be ordered by calling (800) CCR-0033.

Private Investigators

Private investigators generally charge by the hour and can be quite expensive; but if you have enough money, and know and trust an investigator, by all means, hire him. Never just hire a private investigator out of the phone book. Private investigators range widely in their business practices, experience, and specialty. In addition, because many private investi-gators work for law firms or groups of attorneys, but can't practice law, they generally do not provide legal authorization and release forms, so you may have to draft your own. You may be tempted to do a background check on a family day-care-center operator without telling her or without a legal authorization and release, but please resist the temptation. Be sure to tell your potential child-care provider that she is going to be investigated, and be sure to get her signed permission to verify her records. You want to be up-front right from the start, and you want to be clear that you are not invading her privacy. A bonus is that many people will come clean about something in their record that makes them inappropriate for child care, if you tell them they will be investigated. If they do come clean, you've just saved yourself a substantial amount of money. Make sure that your investigator does a check that goes back at least five to seven years, and includes verification of identity, date of birth, Social Security number, education, employment history and references, driving record, and civil and criminal records in every jurisdiction of residence.

Calling References

A professional background investigation will verify whether the provider was employed by the persons she gave as her references. Now, you need to call each of the references to obtain critical information about the qualities you require. If you are doing the background check and the reference checking yourself, you'll do both tasks in one call.

Remember, a family day-care provider must have the following personal qualities:

- personal maturity
- responsible/dependable
- adaptable
- fun-loving
- warm/caring
- even-tempered

When you reach one of the provider's references, introduce yourself and explain that you are considering using the provider's family day-care home. Then, ask all of the questions on the Professional Reference Report, which allows you to verify factual issues regarding the candidate's previous employment and the softer, more subjective information also. The questions are designed to elicit as much information as possible about the provider's personal qualities from the reference. Feel free to ask any additional questions you would like and be sure to listen carefully. Review the sample Professional Reference Report below. Then, turn to the template in Chapter Ten or in the software under the In-Home icon.

CONTRACTING WITH A FAMILY DAY-CARE PROVIDER

Once you've settled on a family day-care home, it's time to put it in writing. You should always insist on a written contract with your family day-care operator.

Turn to the Legal Kit in Appendix 1, or open the Legal Kit file on the diskette. There you'll find a list of issues that you should be thinking about before you sign a contract for child care. Because this contract is not coauthored by you, it is only fair to expect that it will

CHILD-CARE PROVIDER PROFESSIONAL
REFERENCE REPORT

Applicant: _Nikki Benson_

Company/Parent Contacted: _Little Brown House Day Care_

Address: _ZZZ Westwind Rd._

Newark, NJ 0Z114

Phone Number: _(201) 783-5555_

Employment _2/92 to 8/93_

Starting Position _Three-year old group leader_

Ending Position _Three-year old group leader and toddler program_

co-ordinator

Salary _$750 an hour_

Reason for Leaving _Wanted to open own business._

Results: _____

Dates of Employment	☑ VER	☐ INC	☐ CNV	☐ NR
Starting Position	☑ VER	☐ INC	☐ CNV	☐ NR
Ending Position	☑ VER	☐ INC	☐ CNV	☐ NR
Salary	☑ VER	☐ INC	☐ CNV	☐ NR
Reason for Leaving	☑ VER	☐ INC	☐ CNV	☐ NR*

How would you rate his/her overall job performance on a scale from 1 to 10 with
10 being excellent? _9_

Did he/she show improvement/growth in the position? _yes_

What were his/her strengths? _follows directions very well, warm, capable,_
responsible   .

_____

What were the areas that you would recommend improvements (weaknesses)?

a little shy with adults—hurt communications somewhat

Would you reemploy?   ☑ Y   ☐ N

Any trouble with:

    Attendance   ☐ Y   ☑ N

    Attitude   ☐ Y   ☑ N

    Dependability   ☐ Y   ☑ N

    Teamwork   ☐ Y   ☑ N

Additional information:

*VER=VERIFIED; INC=INCORRECT; CNV=COULD NOT VERIFY; NR=NOT REPORTED

Subjective Data

"Did you enjoy having her in your home?" _Yes._

"Was she willing to put in extra effort or time when it was required?" _Always._

"Is she a flexible person? Can she handle the chaos of everyday life with children?" _Yes, she seems to get calmer and quieter as the noise and chaos gets greater._

"How did she handle constructive criticism?" _That was always a little difficult. She always changed her behavior immediately, but could be somewhat grim after the criticism._

"How would you rate her level of personal maturity?" _Very, very high._

"How did the children react when she left?" _Parents still ask about her. The older kids compare our new teachers to her in a favorable way._

Additional Questions:

■ ■

represent the family day-care-operator's point of view. The operator has no legal obligation to ensure that the issues important to you are put forward in the contract—that is your obligation. So take a look at the sample contract in the Legal Kit (or in the software) and if there is something in the contract that you want to change, add, or delete, discuss it with the operator, with your suggestions in writing, before you consider signing.

MANAGING YOUR PROVIDER

The child-care-management templates discussed in Chapter Ten and in the Family Day Care file on the diskette will ease your mind and make life far easier for you and your family day-care provider. Family day-care operators are not always equipped with the word processors, printers, and copiers needed to provide documentation for parents, so those parents who use our templates can actually generate all the schedules, meeting agendas, daily logs, and other documents necessary for achieving and maintaining a highly professional, cooperative relationship with their operator.

Meeting Agenda

Use our Meeting Agenda to keep you on track in your regular meetings with your family day-care provider. Review the Meeting Agenda below to see how it is used. Then, turn to the Meeting Agenda template in Chapter Ten and in the Family Day Care file on the diskette and make multiple copies of the form. Before your meeting, fill in the items you want to discuss, and take it with you. During the meeting, you can take detailed notes and keep a copy of the agenda in your files. You never know when you may need to refer back to it.

Emergency Medical Authorization

Make sure your new family day-care operator has a copy of your child's current emergency medical authorization form. Review Your Child's Emergency Medical Authorization on page 164 and then turn to Chapter Ten and make a copy and fill out the Your Child's Emergency Medical Authorization template, or print one out after filling in the blanks on this template in the Family Day Care file on the diskette. Give it to your operator. Make a note in your calendar to check the form every three months to make sure it is current.

Meeting Agenda

Meeting Date: _April 12, 1996_

Meeting Time: _4:00 P.M._

ITEM 1: _Next week's schedule changes_

meeting notes: _____

ITEM 2: _Michael needs longer naps—he's been too tired and cranky lately._

meeting notes: _____

ITEM 3: _Michael needs to eat less sugar and more vegetables._

meeting notes: _____

ITEM 4: _Work on alphabet at least 3x a week._

meeting notes: _____

ITEM 5: _Michael's antibiotics schedule—2x a day for the next two weeks._

meeting notes: _____

ITEM 6: _Why did Oscar bite Michael last week?_

meeting notes: _____

NEXT MEETING: Date: _April 24, 1996_ Time: _4:00 P.M._

The Daily Log

If your provider doesn't have a daily log system already set up, ask him if he will keep a daily log for your child. If your child wakes up in the middle of the night with a bad tummyache, it's important for you to know how she felt earlier in the day, what she ate, and so on. The daily log provides critical information for parents who need accurate information about their child's eating, napping, activities, and bumps and bruises. Not only is the information handy for those middle-of-the-night troubles, but it also provides you with a day-to-day, week-to-week snapshot of your child's progress and changes. You can use the information to make key decisions, but more important, you don't miss anything!

To make it easy for the operator, review the Daily Log on page 165 and then make a packet of copies of the Daily Log template in Chapter Ten or in the Family Day Care file on the diskette. To maintain the

YOUR CHILD'S EMERGENCY
MEDICAL AUTHORIZATION

To Whom it May Concern:

As the parent of _____Michael P._____, I hereby authorize
_____Louise Chasen_____ to approve emergency medical treatment
for our child. Our child's date of birth is_____June 17, 1993_____.
He/she is allergic to _____Codeine_____. His/her
pediatrician is _____Dr. Jerry Ross_____, who may be reached at
(4/3) 555-9296 .
Our child's insurance carrier is__We'll Cover You Insurance Company
and the policy number is____123456789-10___.
Our address is _____96 Mockingbird Lane, Birdville, AL, 34526_____,
and our phone number is (4/3) 555-5643 .

_____Karen P._____
(parent's signature)

accuracy of the record (and keep it from being an onerous "end of the
day" task for your operator), ask her to try to fill it in as the day
progresses rather than all at once at the end of the day.

Approved Pickup and Transportation Form

Most family day-care operators are very careful about getting written
parental authorization before letting anyone other than you or your
spouse pick up your child. If your operator does not have a form that
she already uses, review the Approved Pickup and Transportation form
below, and turn to Chapter Ten for the Approved Pickup and Transportation template and make a copy of it. Fill it out, making sure
that you include everyone who will be picking up your child from the
family day-care-operator's home—for example, yourself, your spouse or
partner, your mother and sisters, your nanny, among others. If you are
using the software, open up the Family Day Care file and click on this
template.

DAILY LOG

FOR: _____Michael P._____

(your child's name)

DATE: _____June 17, 1996_____

Breakfast Time: 7:30 A.M. _____

Foods Eaten: *Cream of Wheat, 3 Strawberries, milk* _____

Lunch Time: 11:30 A.M. _____

Foods Eaten: *½ slice cheese pizza, apple, o.j.* _____

Dinner Time: 5:00 P.M. _____

Foods Eaten: *macaroni & cheese, milk* _____

Snacks Time: 10:00 A.M. _____

Foods Eaten: *Yogurt* _____

Time: 3:00 P.M. _____

Foods Eaten: *5 oreos* _____

Naps Time: 10:30 A.M. _____ Length of nap (min/hrs): *50 min* _____

Time: 2:00 A.M. _____ Length of nap (min/hrs): *60 min* _____

Potty Time: 8:30 A.M. _____ Type: *2* _____

Time: 11:20 A.M. _____ Type: *1* _____

Time: 1:45 P.M. _____ Type: *1* _____

Time: 4:15 P.M. _____ Type: *2* _____

Medication Time: *n/a* _____ Type: _____

Activities (please list): *alphabet—can go up to m* _____

numbers—up to 10 _____

played in sandbox _____

MISC. NOTES: *Michael was cranky today—doesn't seem to be sleeping very well.* _____

APPROVED PICK-UP
AND TRANSPORTATION

FOR _____ _Michael P._____

(your child's name)

The following persons are authorized to pick up_____
and drive her home from your facility: *(your child's name)*

_____ _Dan P._____

_____ _Karen P._____

_____ _Nellie Smith (nanny)_____

_____ _Ann Brown (grandmother)_____

Signed:

_____ _Karen P._____   _May 5, 1996_____
(Parent's Name)   *(Date)*

WHAT IF THERE IS A PROBLEM?

There are times when things just don't work out. Even if we have exhausted every opportunity, evaluated every option, done thorough background checks, and listened to references . . . something can still be
wrong. Because this is a relationship, you can only be responsible for
and can only control your half of it. So, if you have tried repeatedly to
fix the situation to no avail, here are some ways to fairly, quickly, and
legally extricate yourself.

This is a very different situation from one a parent might face if a
performance or personality problem arises with an employee, like a
nanny. When it's your house and your child(ren), it is hard to question
who is in charge. In the case of family child-care homes—and day-care
centers, for that matter—you are not an employer/manager but a

Problem-Solving Steps

1. Identify problem.
2. Assess seriousness of it and its effect on child(ren).
3. Look for causes of problem.
4. Meet with provider as soon as possible armed with your assessment of issues and proposed remedy.
5. Listen to your provider's point of view.
6. Jointly enact new policy, procedure, or solution. Agree to review its effectiveness at next week's meeting.

consumer, and the operator is not your employee but an owner running a business. While it is not necessary for a parent and family-care operator to get along, it is more than reasonable to expect it, especially when you are paying for a service. But if it would take more than a saint to make this work, as the parent and consumer you need to take the initiative and follow the steps listed above to ferret out the underlying issues of the problem, evaluate the options for solving it, and then weigh the options for ease of execution and opportunity for success. Keep in mind that personality problems always affect performance. So be on your toes. At the first whiff of a change in attitude or if services that you have contracted for are not performed with appropriate good will, or other parents are removing their children from the home without any apparent notice, head for the templates. You will have an opportunity to work things out, and if you listen to your gut and have remained faithful to meetings with the provider, you may be able to manage your way out of a new family-care home search.

Since most of us miss the first sign of trouble, and probably the second, we are often shocked and angry when we finally notice something is wrong. A real sign of trouble is if your child-care provider has not come to you and expressed the need to talk about an issue that is now obviously so bothersome to her that you are feeling a strain in the relationship. One of the reasons regular meetings are so important is to facilitate open lines of communication. And, frankly, as in any relationship, if one is paying attention the little stuff can't float by.

In the problem-solving box, I have given you some hints for what to do if the problem is strictly a performance problem stemming from a policy, procedure, or lack of one. For example: You have slipped into the nasty little habit of being five to ten minutes late. It's now the rule, not the exception. The first few times you had some really good excuses, but now even you think they are old. Now when you pick Abby up in the evening, Claire, the family day-care owner, doesn't cordially greet you as she once did. Abby is sitting near the door with her coat on and backpack at her feet. She seems a little uncomfortable, too. With regular meetings that provide both sides with a chance to air issues, this passive/aggressive act would hopefully happen only once. More than likely your provider is feeling put upon (she has been) but feels she can't confront you because she needs the business. You have broken the easiest rule, "Treat the other as you expect to be treated." By being late, you have been disrespectful of her as both a business owner and professional. Chronic lateness ruins friendships and marriages. It is probably the most abused but tolerated part of life, but totally inexcusable in professional relationships. At your next meeting start off by apologizing for the last time you were late. Tell the provider that you will endeavor to be on time or offer to compensate her for those times when you cannot avoid being a little late. Smile and then ask for her comments and *listen*. Ask again if there are any other issues bothering her and make it clear that you want to hear what she has to say. In closing, be sure to tell her that you need to both move on and work to reestablish the trust and rhythm you had before.

The tips in the box will work when applied to a situation where both parties are basically content with the relationship. Sometimes, however, a change will be needed.

IF A CHANGE BECOMES NECESSARY

You have thoroughly evaluated your child-care situation and you have found that a change is needed. This decision may not be a surprise to the family day-care provider if there has been a suitable airing of the issues bothering you during your last three regular meetings. But your decision to move on may still come as a surprise, so be prepared.

What You Will Need to Evaluate When Making a Change

1. Get out a copy of your contract and review it for the type of notice, if any, you need to give and in what form (verbal or in writing).
2. Settle the financial aspects as soon as possible.
3. Retrieve your child's extra clothing, blankets, toys, and other belongings.
4. If your child is old enough, let your child say good-bye to his playmates and other personnel at the center.
5. End the business relationship in a cordial, friendly manner.

CHAPTER EIGHT

Finding and Hiring Day-Care Centers

> **IN THIS CHAPTER:**
>
> *Getting Organized*
> *Compiling a List of Centers*
> *Evaluating Centers*
> *Contracting with a Center*
> *Managing a Center*

CHOOSING A CENTER

Regulated day-care centers are universally defined as facilities designed and operated by child-care professionals to care for children of various ages for compensation, for less than twenty-four hours at a time, in groups as specified by each state's regulations.

There are 92,005 regulated day-care centers in the fifty states and the District of Columbia, Puerto Rico, and the Virgin Islands. Of these centers, all are regulated through their state by the use of a licensing system, except for Pennsylvania, which uses a certification system (see Glossary for definition of terms). Day-care centers have long been recognized as offering children the safest care. In most cases, more than one adult is on the premises during peak hours; supervision and training are required by many states; and a combination of high market demand and state regulation gives day-care-center operators the impetus to offer high-quality programming, reasonable fees, and convenient hours. In addition, each state's minimum licensing requirements and on-site inspections increase your child's protection against shoddy, unsafe facilities.

Still, those requirements are pretty limited, and as a parent you must be vigilant. Although day-care centers are businesses that must provide a good, consistent service at a reasonable cost in order to survive, the lack of options for many parents and the lack of understanding of just what other options might be available provide fertile ground for parents to be without much bargaining power when it comes to upgrading service or offering constructive criticism to an operator with a waiting list of families looking for care.

The Children's Foundation's 1995 Child Day-Care Center Licensing Study has found that by far the most serious issue for parents searching for child care is the lack of any uniform state regulations for day-care centers, preschools, nursery schools, prekindergartens and/or religiously affiliated centers. It is a complex problem because although virtually all states have day-care-center regulations, every state has a different set of regulations. For this reason alone, all parents need to be educated consumers when shopping for day care, especially if you are new to your area. Study the regulations that apply to your state. And remember, because of pressure from parents and child-care advocates, day-care center regulations are changing all the time. Be sure to get timely updates on any changes your state makes. Also, remember that day-care center managers choose which type of services they offer. They also set their own requirements—some insist that children must be potty trained, or off a bottle—and operating hours. The Telephone Prescreen will cover many of these requirements, so don't be surprised if you may need to search longer than you thought for a center that will accept your child.

To be an educated consumer, you must clearly understand the terms and definitions used by your state in day-care-center regulations; they can get very confusing. Here are some examples of the terms, definitions, and mystifying menu options that states use to regulate day care as reported by The Children's Foundation Child Day-Care Study, 1995:

- 34 states or territories (64 percent) include nursery schools, preschools, prekindergartens, and religiously affiliated centers in their definition of child day-care center: AR, AZ, CA, CO, CT, DC, DE, FL, HI, KY, KS, LA, MA, MD, MI, MN, MS, NC, NH, NJ, NM, NV, NY, OH, PR, SC, SD, VI, VT, and WY.

- Illinois exempts public/private school programs serving children three years of age and older.

- Iowa exempts programs operated by public schools.

- Wisconsin exempts centers regulated through their local public school departments/private education system.

- Tennessee exempts some of the religiously affiliated programs regulated by the department of education.

- In three states (5 percent) the documented number of regulated child day-care centers excludes nursery schools, preschools, prekindergartens, and religiously affiliated centers: IN, MO, and WV.

- In two states (4 percent) the documented number of regulated child day-care centers includes nursery schools, preschools, and prekindergartens, but excludes religiously affiliated centers: VA (religiously affiliated schools may choose to be regulated) and AL.

- In twelve states (23 percent) the documented number of regulated child day-care centers includes religiously affiliated centers but excludes nursery schools, preschools, and prekindergartens: GA, ID, ME, MT, NE, ND, OK, OR, PA, RI, TX, and WA.

- Two states (4 percent) have other variations in the definitions: Alaska excludes preschools and provides no data about religiously affiliated centers; and UT excludes religiously affiliated centers and those regulated by the department of education.

Just trying to figure out how your state regulates child day-care centers is no easy matter. When you delve deeper and try to understand specific regulations—even the most obvious ones—you can run into trouble. It is very difficult to figure out just where your state stands on issues related to license renewal, general liability insurance, and unannounced inspections; prescribed standards for staff-child ratios; infant/child CPR and first aid training; or staff measles and/or HIB immunizations. The system makes it very hard for you to just "qualify" a center, long before you get to the point where it is appropriate to inquire about cost and programming, never mind whether they have an opening for your child.

Unfortunately, there isn't one state that has it all or does it all. A few states seem to have put a lot of thought, time, and money into formulating child-care legislation, but even in those states, an in-depth review of the regulations in just a few key areas makes you wonder how legislators could have made the decisions they did. But despite all this, it is possible to find a safe, reliable, and enjoyable day-care facility.

As you consider day-care centers, be sure to check whether the center you choose is in full compliance with state and local licensing laws. A day-care center's compliance with certain standards will be obvious when you visit the center. For example, you can make sure there is the correct number of providers caring for the children in the day-care center. During your visit, I would also politely ask to see a center's licensing documents. Don't worry about offending the day-care-center operator. Remember, you are the consumer and a day-care provider is offering you a critical service for compensation. If a day-care center is in full compliance with the law, the operator should have no problem satisfying your curiosity. If she is upset by your request, you may have a problem.

GETTING ORGANIZED

Before you start your search for a day-care center, take a few minutes to get organized. You'll find that by putting together everything you need for the project in one place, the whole process will be less confusing and stressful. If you have room, try to set up a permanent workspace for yourself, preferably at a desk with a phone and answering machine or voice-mail service. Add some manila files, a desktop file holder or a file cabinet, a pocket calculator, stationery and envelopes, and a few legal pads and pens, and you're done. If you have a computer and a printer, that's even better. If you don't have access to a computer, look in the yellow pages to locate the nearest retail copy center—you will want to use their copy machines to copy forms and checklists directly out of this book.

If you live in a small home or apartment and don't have enough room for a permanent workspace, purchase a large, inexpensive, "accordion" file holder that has ten or more sections, and use one of the sections to hold your supplies. The other sections can hold your forms, documents, notes, and so on. During your search for a provider, keep this file holder next to the phone.

Checklist of Things to Buy

- accordion file, desktop file holder, or file cabinet
- pocket calculator
- manila folders
- stationery and envelopes
- assorted pens and pencils
- answering machine or voice-mail service

LOOKING FOR DAY-CARE CENTERS IN YOUR AREA

Networking is one of the best ways you can put together a list of day-care centers. Talk to as many people as you can! Ask your friends with children, friends who don't have children, friends of friends, and coworkers about day-care centers in your area. If you have older children in school, ask other parents, teachers, even the principal. Try asking around at your church or synagogue and be sure to check any bulletin boards there. Ask your pediatrician and family doctor if they can recommend a center. Phone local colleges and universities to ask if they have day-care centers on campus. These centers can be quite good, and are often staffed by bright and educated students studying child development and psychology. Check your local newspaper or *Pennysaver*. Finally, phone your local resource-and-referral agency. You can get their number by phoning Child Care Aware at (800) 424-2246. They should be able to give you a list of several centers in your zip code. And, don't forget to look in the phone book—day-care centers are listed. Remember, though, that all of these resources can only give you a list of names—there's still a lot of work for you to do.

Corporate Day-Care Services and Facilities

If your company has dependent-care resource staff in the human resources department, check in with them for a list of recommended day-care centers in your area. Be sure to find out how your company compiled the list. Has your company established certain standards for the day-care centers it recommends, or is it just a random list of local centers? If your company has standards, what are they and how far do they go? This is important information for you since you will have to evaluate whether you need to verify any of the facts to see if they are still correct. Additionally, ask if your company offers a dependent-care assistance program that provides financial assistance to defray dependent-care expenses by allocating payroll funds into a special account. These funds are not subject to federal taxes, or certain state and social security taxes, but you should be aware of several thorny issues regarding the possible loss of unused funds, potential reduction in future social security benefits, and other rules that may limit your ability to choose services. However, it is important to know about your options and give yourself the chance to weigh the benefits and problems with the program director to see if you can make it work for you.

Even better, many companies are offering their employees day-care centers that are on-site or in another location. Some employers have their own centers; others run day-care facilities jointly with other area employers. While almost all employers partially or fully subsidize the cost of the services, corporate day-care options that are successful are often oversubscribed and fill up or remain at capacity for a long time. Obviously, employees with children who travel a great deal on their jobs or who work a shift schedule that isn't compatible with the center's hours are left to find their own child-care solutions. But it's something you should look into.

The Telephone Prescreen

Use your telephone to narrow your list down to only the most appropriate day-care centers. Don't waste your time visiting a center that has a two-year waiting list, a teacher-child ratio that isn't appropriate for your infant, or a fee you just can't afford.

The telephone interview can give you a good feel for the type of center you're dealing with and the professionalism of its management, and a preliminary assessment of whether the center has all of your baseline requirements. Don't be shy; make sure you get as much information as you possibly can.

Now, take a look at the Day-Care Telephone Prescreen Questions on page 178 and the Day-Care Telephone Prescreen Questions template in Chapter Ten and on the diskette in the Day Care file. Once you've reviewed the questions and sample answers, add any extra questions you would like to ask at the bottom of the template or on an extra page. Then, make multiple copies of the template. Use one copy for each center operator you speak with, fill in the answers to your questions in the appropriate spaces, and be sure to take detailed notes during your conversation.

I would allow plenty of time for your conversation. You should try to talk at least fifteen minutes, but allow half an hour for each phone interview. Remember that the center operator or the person you speak with by phone is probably not the person who will be actually caring for your child.

When you near the end of the phone interview, decide whether the center fits your requirements and warrants a visit. If so, schedule the visit, and use the space at the bottom of the template to enter the date and time. Work with the center operator to pick a time when you can observe the children at play, and during naptime make sure you'll be able to interview the particular provider who would take care of your child. I would suggest you arrive at a center about half an hour before naptime, spend that time observing, and then use the next half-hour during naptime to interview the provider. Tell the center operator that you are not bringing your child to this initial visit. It's best to bring your child to a day-care center only after you have determined that it might be a good place for your child. Visiting a center can be a traumatic event for even the most even-tempered children. They don't know any of the children there; they don't know the providers; they are not familiar with the surroundings. And they may never see the place again! Also, if you are watching your child or trying to deal with your child's shyness around a group of new faces, you probably won't be totally focused on the list of things you need to look for in the center. You will miss a lot. Leave your child at home for this first visit.

The On-Site Visit

The on-site visit is your opportunity to find out everything you can about the center you are considering. Make the most of it! The checklist found on page 180 is your assurance that you are seeing everything you should, while the interview of the provider who will care for your child covers everything else. When you get a few moments of quiet time with the provider, ask the questions from the Day-Care On-Site Visit Interview Questions template and be sure to write down the provider's answers. Also, feel free to ask any questions that came up while you were watching her interact with the children, and bring up any of your concerns. You want to find out whether the provider can communicate with you. You

DAY-CARE TELEPHONE
PRESCREEN QUESTIONS

Name of center: _Smiling Puppies Day Care Center_

Name of person you spoke with: _Karen Smith_

Title: _Center Owner_

Location: _12/7 Bay Street_

Phone number: _385-9543_   Date of call: _June 13_

Start by telling the operator a little about your child—name, age, sex, etc., and describe what you are looking for, especially the days and number of hours a week you require care. Then ask:

1. "What days are you open and for what hours?" _Weekdays, 7 A.M. to 7 P.M._

2. "How much do you charge?" _$200 a week_

3. "Do you have any openings now, or in the near future?" _Yes_

4. "Does your center comply with all state regulations? Can I review your licensing documents?" _Yes_

5. "What type of experience, training, and qualifications are your providers required to have?" _B.A. at least three years' experience in child care._

6. "Are all of your providers certified in CPR, infant CPR, and first aid?" _Yes_

7. "What is the teacher–child ratio for children my child's age?" _1:4 or 5 for all toddlers_

8. "How many children are enrolled in your center and what are their ages?" _25 toddlers, 15 infants._

9. "Can parents drop in at any time?" _Yes_

10. If your state requires it, ask: "Do all of your employees meet the state's requirements on in-service training?" _Yes_

11. "Have all of your providers been background-checked by the state or by an independent investigative service, and if so, could I review the dossiers of providers who would care for my child?" _no_

12. If your state requires it, ask: "Are all of your employees properly immunized?" _yes_

13. "Could you please describe your facility?" _5000 square-foot building divided into four large open rooms with a small, 300-square-foot office/ storage area. Each area is carpeted and furnished with young child-size chairs and desks. Each room has toilet facilities (the older children's rooms have two toilets) and Dutch doors for limited privacy and to aid supervision. Each room is designated for a particular age group and is complete with age- and gender-appropriate toys and learning activities. The building has parking for 16 cars and meets the ADA requirement with ramp access. The outdoor play facility is 3000 square feet and again is complete with swing sets, sandboxes, jungle gym, and plenty of balls and other activities._

14. "Describe a typical day my child would have in your center." _The morning starts with a hot breakfast (included in fee), then if the weather is good, they take a short walk to the park down the block and swing, play, and build things in the sandbox. Back to the center for a one-hour nap, then lunch. After lunch they have some quiet time where the children read or listen to music. Then, they head out to the play area for some games and playtime. Then, back into the center for a nap. After naps, the children get a snack—sometimes cookies and milk, sometimes fruit or juice. Then, they do an organized art project until parents arrive._

15. Include any other questions you would like to ask in the following space or on another sheet: _____

Center Visit

Date: _June 15_ _____ Time: _10:30 A.M._ _____

■■

also want to get some critical background on her child-care practices and philosophy, in general and on very specific items. Ask away! The more information you can get the better!

Carefully review the Day-Care On-Site Visit Checklist and Day-Care On-Site Visit Interview Questions. Then, turn to Chapter Ten or open the Day-Care file on the diskette for the templates. When you are thinking of additional questions to ask the provider who will care for your child, focus on issues specific to the particular age of your child, for example, "When do you think a toddler should begin toilet training and how would you handle it?" "How often do you change an infant's diapers?" "How often do you hold infants?" and so on. Once you've added your own questions, make one copy of the templates per center you are visiting. You are ready to go!

DAY-CARE ON-SITE VISIT CHECKLIST

Safety

Building secure?	☑ yes	☐ no
Building well maintained?	☑ yes	☐ no
Smoke detectors working (check to see if light indicating charge battery is on)?	☑ yes	☐ no
Fire extinguishers current (check date on canister or attached card)?	☑ yes	☐ no
Electrical outlets covered?	☑ yes	☐ no
Adequate first-aid kit?	☑ yes	☐ no
Dangerous supplies inaccessible?	☑ yes	☐ no
Screened windows?	☑ yes	☐ no
Secured electrical cords?	☑ yes	☐ no
Evacuation plan/emergency drills?	☑ yes	☐ no
Stairs gated and inaccessible?	☑ yes	☐ no

Sanitation/Cleanliness

Passes the "Sniff Test"?	☑ yes	☐ no
Does center appear clean/well organized?	☑ yes	☐ no
Play area clean/organized?	☑ yes	☐ no
Are sheets/blankets in nap room clean?	☑ yes	☐ no
Surfaces clean?	☑ yes	☐ no
Toys/games clean?	☑ yes	☐ no
Food preparation areas clean?	☑ yes	☐ no
Bathroom clean/sanitized?	☑ yes	☐ no

Indoor Play Area

Is it cheerful/engaging?	☑ yes	☐ no
Are toys in good repair?	☑ yes	☐ no
Enough age-appropriate toys/games?	☑ yes	☐ no
Enough crafts/art supplies?	☑ yes	☐ no
Art work is displayed?	☑ yes	☐ no
Can adults see the entire room at once?	☑ yes	☐ no

Water available?	☑ yes	☐ no
Easy access to bathrooms?	☑ yes	☐ no
Cubbyholes for each child?	☑ yes	☐ no
Adequate light/ventilation?	☑ yes	☐ no

Nap Area

Quiet/restful location?	☑ yes	☐ no
Adequate ventilation?	☑ yes	☐ no
Individual cots and cribs?	☑ yes	☐ no
Cots/cribs away from curtains with pull cords?	☑ yes	☐ no
Cots/cribs new and in good condition?	☑ yes	☐ no
Cot/crib bolts and screws secure?	☑ yes	☐ no
Cot/crib mattresses in good condition?	☑ yes	☐ no
Crib side slats no farther that $2^3/_8$" apart?	☑ yes	☐ no
Distance from crib mattress to top of railing at least 22"?	☑ yes	☐ no
Crib corner posts less than 1" high?	☑ yes	☐ no

Outside Play Area

Enough space?	☑ yes	☐ no
Grass/plants/flowers?	☑ yes	☐ no
Enclosed and secure?	☑ yes	☐ no
Adult can see entire play area at once?	☑ yes	☐ no
Sandboxes covered?	☑ yes	☐ no
Thick pads under play equipment?	☑ yes	☐ no
Play equipment in good repair?	☑ yes	☐ no

Center Operator

Good communicator?	☑ yes	☐ no
Accessible?	☑ yes	☐ no
Professional?	☑ yes	☐ no
Organized?	☑ yes	☐ no
Does center appear to be well managed?	☑ yes	☐ no

Provider Who Will Care for Your Child

Warm/friendly?	☑ yes	☐ no
Smiles?	☑ yes	☐ no
Positive and open?	☑ yes	☐ no
Pleasant tone of voice?	☑ yes	☐ no
Made you feel at home?	☑ yes	☐ no
Good communicator?	☑ yes	☐ no
Clean?	☑ yes	☐ no
Organized/under control?	☑ yes	☐ no
Truly likes children?	☑ yes	☐ no

continued

Program

Set daily schedule?	☑ yes	☐ no
Posted for parents?	☑ yes	☐ no
Adequate play time?	☑ yes	☐ no
Adequate nap time?	☑ yes	☐ no
Nutritious meals/snacks?	☑ yes	☐ no

Administration

Written pricing/policies?	☑ yes	☐ no
Provider background checks available for review?	☑ yes	☐ no
Regulatory documents in order?	☑ yes	☐ no
Fully insured (*ask to see documentation*)?	☑ yes	☐ no
Parents welcome at all times?	☑ yes	☐ no
Daily log?	☑ yes	☐ no
Authorized persons only may pick up children?	☑ yes	☐ no
Regular meetings with parents?	☑ yes	☐ no

Additional Comments: _Bright and cheery facility. Very clean. Loved Ms. Beamis, but didn't like the other teacher, Ms. Condor. Seems too stressed and impatient with the toddlers. Not a good sign. Next center ..._

■ ■ ■ ■ ■ ■ ■ ■ ■ ■ ■ ■ ■ ■ ■ ■ ■ ■ ■ ■ ■ ■ ■ ■ ■ ■ ■ ■ ■ ■ ■ ■ ■ ■

DAY-CARE ON-SITE VISIT
INTERVIEW QUESTIONS

1. "How would you discipline my child?" _Short time-outs_

2. "What indoor activities would you engage in with my child?" _Painting, crafts, storytelling and reading, blocks, listening to music, singing_

3. "What outdoor activities would you engage in with my child?" _Swinging, climbing the jungle gym, planting flowers, playing in the sandbox_

4. "What kind of background and experience do you bring to your job here?" _I have a degree in early childhood education from Yale, and have worked here for three years. I also had a successful baby-sitting business in college that helped me pay my tuition._

5. "What is the biggest challenge you face every day?" _I love being with these kids. But I admit it is hard to keep them interested and cooperative all at the same time. It's important for me to be organized and innovative._

6. "How do you keep yourself refreshed and enthusiastic about this type of work?"

I don't work on the weekends, so I look for weekend continuing education programs that offer me the opportunity to keep current on child-care issues and programming that I can offer.

Additional questions specific to your child's age: _____

_____

_____

_____

_____

_____

■ ■

The Visit with Your Child

Once you are satisfied that you have a first-choice day-care center and a backup choice, schedule a visit for you and your child. If this is your child's first child-care experience, it can be helpful to prepare him by reading him a book like *My Mom Made Me Go to School* by Judy Denton or *Going to School* by Anne Civari. These stories recount preparation for and first few days at school with the requisite trauma and tears. Soon, the kids in the stories grow to like school and even begin to look forward to it, and all ends well. It should be easy for you to modify "school" with "day care" instead. It's also a good idea to give your child, especially if he is older than two, enough information to answer those questions that all children ask when they start group care, including, "When is Mommy or Daddy coming back?" (There's a great little book called *Mommies at Work* by Eve Merriam that details all of the jobs that mommies do, including tightrope walkers, telephone repair, and television directing. But Mommy's best job is being a mom and coming home to her child[ren].) As all parents know, it is often very difficult to explain to a fretful child who is too young to understand the concept of time— let alone to know how to tell time—that we will return at a certain time. I found the best thing to do with Katherine was to get to know the schedule at the center, then tell her I would return after their outdoor playtime, or after their lunch break. Another trick, and believe me it is just that, is to tie her expectation of seeing me to something we will do after day care, perhaps with another mother and daughter from her class. This way Katherine knows she will see me and Sarah's mother at the same time, and that she and Sarah will be leaving together. This trick seems to allay her fear of being left alone. I was crushed when I realized that this was what she was thinking, but the "buddy" system worked and allowed Katherine to look forward to things, too.

During your visit, look for your child's level of apprehension and gauge her interest in the other children, the space, and the range of playthings and activities offered. If you can, try to plan your visit around a time of day when you can overlap more than one group activity. For example, if the plan is for a group singing or book activity at 10:30 A.M. and the outdoor play time is at 11:00 A.M., try to schedule your visit at 10:45 so your child gets a view of more than one type of activity. Even better, your child may warm up by the outdoor play time and make some new friends. This type of visit is good for you and your child since it optimizes your exposure to the center and gives your child a much more varied view of the opportunities offered to him.

Look for the following things during the visit with your child:

The Operator or Provider

- When you enter the center, greets you and your child by name and immediately tries to make your child feel at home.
- Pays more attention to your child than to you.
- Introduces your child to the other children.
- Immediately makes an effort to integrate your child into the children's activities.
- Speaks directly to your child.
- Warm and friendly, but not overbearing with your child.
- Acts comfortable with your child and with having you in the room observing.
- Uses an appropriate and encouraging tone of voice at all times, even if your child isn't responding to overtures very well.

Your Child

- May not be completely at ease, but is not unusually anxious or scared.
- Warms up to the provider(s) over the course of your time in the center.

- Is excited by the toys, games, and art supplies in the center.
- Finds someone to play with because there is a good match as far as age and sex of the other children.

If all goes well during the visit to the day-care center with your child, you need to take one more step before you entrust your child to a day-care center: background checks.

BACKGROUND CHECKS

One of the primary benefits of using regulated day care is that it provides parents with professional managers and owners that shoulder the burden that parents bear when they hire a nanny they must motivate and manage in the in-home situation. This fundamental change in roles is an intrinsic benefit to using day care, but it also weakens a parent's ability to require certain types of information—like background data on day-care-center employees.

As we have discussed, there is no state that requires the kind of comprehensive preemployment verifications of education, employment, driving, or civil court record checks as we have described. But, because many states do require criminal history record searches for all day-care workers, it is critical that you ascertain if your day-care center choice must do these types of criminal checks—and if they have been completed on everyone. Completion is a key factor for every parent to consider since in virtually every state that requires criminal checks, a new emplyee is allowed to work while the center is awaiting the results of the search. In some states, these types of searches take four to six weeks; some take months. I don't know about you, but I don't consider the requirement much comfort if the new employee is still allowed to work for weeks before clearance. So every parent must be cognizant of their state's licensing laws and even more diligent in requiring confirmation of all employee background checks.

Asking Your Day-Care-Center Owner/Operator To Do Background Checks

Because a number of day-care-center employees have access to your child, the only cost-effective way to make sure that everyone with access to your child is safe is to convince the day-care-center owner/operator that comprehensive background checks on all employees are necessary. As a parent who hasn't enrolled her child in the center and is merely considering the center, it is unlikely that you will be able to convince the owner/operator that background checks are necessary. Until parents start asking for this service from day-care centers on a regular basis, owner/operators won't provide parents with comprehensive information on their employees. Once your child is enrolled in the center, however, you may have better luck, especially if you can get other parents to join you when you ask the owner/operator to provide this service.

CONTRACTING WITH A DAY-CARE CENTER

Once you choose a day-care center, the center operator will most likely hand you a written agreement that you will be required to sign. Before you sign anything, turn to the Legal Kit in Appendix 1 and make a copy or click on the Legal Kit file on the diskette. There, you'll find an analysis of the types of issues you should be satisfied with before you sign any contract for day care. Read it carefully. Then, read your own day-care center's contract carefully. Ask the operator as many questions as you need to. You must understand and feel comfortable with every clause in the contract. Don't sign it until you do! Here are some of the issues covered in the analysis:

1. fees
2. emergency arrangements for pickups if you are not available
3. documentation of all required licenses, permits, safety and other inspection reports
4. insurance
5. background checks
6. parental visits at will
7. training and education minimum standards for all employees

MANAGING YOUR DAY-CARE-CENTER PROVIDER

Unlike the relationship a parent has with an in-home provider who is a direct employee, most day-care centers tend to have multilayered management and staff who have different roles and levels of responsibility. Although smaller centers may have a director or supervisor who also has full responsibility for a group of children, larger centers usually have a strict hierarchy, with a number of staff members caring for the children and one or more directors or supervisors performing administrative tasks, billing, and the like. Certainly, in busy and successful day-care operations, the director is also a quasi–sales manager who arranges appointments for parents seeking to place their children in the center.

It is important to maintain a professional and supportive relationship with the director of your center to make sure that lines of communication are clearly open and you have a name and face to deal with on thorny business issues like contracts and billing. Even more important is your relationship with the provider who actually cares for your child. This second person is pivotal, to say the least. Since this provider is not your employee, you can exert very little overt influence over how she does things. However, you can exert some influence by dealing with that provider with respect and cordiality. Be sure to always greet her with enthusiasm, ask how she's doing, get to know the names and ages of her own children, even bring her a little gift on her birthday. While this won't guarantee that your child will get the best care, it can be very helpful!

As you will see in the first few days that you drop off your child, the rush of parents and kids—put the coat in the cubby, lunch in the refrigerator, get out the door, and not be late for work—leaves little time for an in-depth chat with the provider about your child. Be sure to let the provider know that, whatever the center's policy may be for semiannual parent-staff meetings, you may want and need more than that, perhaps just initially. See how she responds. If she indicates that she welcomes all parents to stay a few minutes after pickup, or will even make arrangements to talk on the phone in the evening or on the weekend—great! However, if the provider seems determined to limit your access to her by spouting center rules on closing times, and makes no other offers, speak with the center manager as soon as possible. Make it clear that you intend to meet with your child(ren)'s provider(s) every couple of weeks at a minimum, and ask for her help. Be persistent. If it's important to you, it should be important to her.

Meeting Agenda

Use the meeting agenda form to keep you on track in your regular meetings with your day-care provider. Review the Meeting Agenda below to see how it is used. Then, turn to Chapter Ten or click on the template in the day-care file on the diskette and make multiple copies of the Meeting Agenda template for future reference. Before your meeting, fill in the items you want to discuss, and take it with you. Take detailed notes and keep a copy of the agenda in your files. You never know when you may need to refer back to it.

■ ■ ■ ■ ■ ■ ■ ■ ■ ■ ■ ■ ■ ■ ■ ■ ■ ■ ■ ■ ■ ■ ■ ■ ■ ■ ■ ■ ■ ■ ■ ■

MEETING AGENDA

Meeting Date: _April 12, 1996_   Meeting Time: _4:00 P.M_

ITEM 1: _Why did Conrad bite Michael last week? Who was supervising them?_

meeting notes: _____

ITEM 2: _Where is Michael's new down jacket?_

meeting notes: _____

ITEM 3: _Michael needs to eat less sugar and more vegetables._

meeting notes: _____

ITEM 4: _Work on alphabet at least 3x a week._

meeting notes: _____

ITEM 5: _Michael's antibiotics schedule—2x a day for the next two weeks_

meeting notes: _____

ITEM 6: _____

meeting notes: _____

_____

NEXT MEETING: Date: _April 24, 1996_   Time: _4:00 p.m._

■ ■

Emergency Medical Authorization

Make sure your day-care provider has a copy of your child's current emergency medical authorization form. Review Your Child's Medical Authorization below. Then, turn to Chapter Ten and fill out the Medical

Authorization template or click on the template in the day-care file on the diskette. Give it to your day-care provider. Many centers keep a master file with all medical authorizations in it for ease of access. Make a note in your calendar to check the form every three months to make sure it is current.

YOUR CHILD'S EMERGENCY MEDICAL AUTHORIZATION

To Whom It May Concern:

As the parent of _Michael P.,_ I hereby authorize _Alison Smith of the Smiling Puppies Day-Care Center_ to approve emergency medical treatment for our child. Our child's date of birth is _June 17, 1993_. He/she is allergic to _codeine_. His/her pediatrician is _Dr. Jerry Ross_, who may be reached at _(413) 555-9296_. Our child's blood type is_____.

Our child's insurance carrier is _We'll Cover You Insurance Company_ and the policy number is _123456789-10_.

Our address is _96 Mockingbird Lane, Birdville, AL, 34526_, and our phone number is _(413) 555-5643_.

_____Karen P_____
(parent's signature)

The Daily Log

If your day-care center doesn't have a daily log system already set up, ask your child's provider if they would keep a daily log for your child. It is vitally important for you to have access to pertinent data such as fluid intake for infants, new foods your child may have tried, fitful naps, or small temperature spikes. This information can help you make a better, more informed decision on how to treat your cranky or sick child.

(If you know that she didn't take a nap, or tried a new food, or didn't eat a snack, you can provide a more direct cure.) To make it easy for your provider, review the Daily Log below, and then make a packet of copies of the Daily Log template in Chapter Ten or on the diskette in the day-care file and give them to your provider. To maintain the accuracy of the record (and keep it from being an onerous "end of the day" task), ask her to try to fill it in as the day progresses rather than all at once at the end of the day.

DAILY LOG

FOR: _Michael P._

(your child's name)

DATE: _June 17, 1995_

Meals

Breakfast   Time: _7:30 A.M._

Foods Eaten: _Cream of Wheat, 3 strawberries, milk_

Lunch   Time: _11:30 A.M._

Foods Eaten: _1/2 slice cheese pizza, apple, o.j._

Dinner   Time: _5:00 P.M._

Foods Eaten: _macaroni & cheese, milk_

Snacks   Time: _10:00 A.M._   Foods Eaten: _Yogurt_

Time: _3:00 P.M._   Foods Eaten: _5 Oreos_

Naps   Time: _10:30 A.M._   Length of Nap (min/hrs): _50 min._

Time: _2:00 P.M._   Length of Nap (min/hrs): _60 min._

Potty Time: _8:30 A.M._____ Type: _2_____

Time: _11:20 A.M._____ Type: _1_____

Time: _1:45 P.M._____ Type: _1_____

Time: _4:15 P.M._____ Type: _2_____

Medication Time: _____N/A_____ Type: _____

Activities (please list) _alphabet—can go up to m_____
_numbers—up to 10_____
_played in sandbox_____

MISC. NOTES: _Michael was cranky today—doesn't seem to be sleeping_
_very well._____

■ ■

Approved Pickup and Transportation Form

Because of the enormous liability involved, most day-care-center operators obtain written parental authorization before letting anyone other
than you or your spouse pick up your child. If your center does not have
an authorization form they already use, review the Approved Pickup and
Transportation form below, and then turn to the template in Chapter Ten
or click on the template in the day-care file on the diskette. Fill it out,
making sure that you include everyone who will be picking up your child
from school—for example, yourself, your spouse or partner, your mother
and sisters, and your nanny, among others. If your sister is an infrequent
visitor to the center, but is on the authorization form, ask her to keep
an eye out and see if anyone checks to see if she is authorized the next
time she picks up your child. Authorization forms are only effective if
the center really checks them!

APPROVED PICKUP AND TRANSPORTATION

For: _Michael P._

(your child's name)

The following persons are authorized to pick up _Michael P._ and drive him/her home from your facility:

Karen P.(mother)

Dan P. (father)

Nellie Smith (nanny)

Ann Brown (grandmother)

Signed:

Karen P.   _May 5, 1996_

(Parent's Name)   (Date)

CHAPTER NINE

Care for Your Older Child: Before and After School, School Holidays, and Summer Vacation

IN THIS CHAPTER:	*In-School Programs*
	Community Programs
	Independent Programs
	Summer Camps

AS YOUR CHILD GROWS . . .

You may think that child care becomes easier as your child gets older and enters school. This is true to some extent because your skills as both a parent and a child-care consumer have grown through experience, both good and bad. But the truth is that child care is somewhat of a moving target. Just when you think you have it right and everything is to your (and your child's) liking, something happens to change it. In this case that something is good: It's the fact that your child is growing up. But because of this your needs have changed and have become more complicated.

Older children bring a different set of needs and issues to the realm of child care. Most parents find that one of the differences is that older children have a longer day, and the activities they want to participate in (that still need to be supervised) tend to be expanding in both numbers and distance from their former small universe of their schools and neighborhoods. Sports activities are now organized leagues with away games across town and sometimes across the state. Computer and music lessons still have to be scheduled, whether you can ferry your child or not. If your workday starts at 7:30 A.M., but school doesn't start until 8:45 A.M., you'll need to find someone to take care of your child for an hour and then bring her to school. You'll also need someone else who can drive your child home from school. You may be lucky enough to find someone to care for your child in the afternoon, but it may be difficult to find a provider who wants to work for a only couple of hours in the early morning and then come back again for a couple of hours in the evening. Once your child is in kindergarten, where the hours are usually 8:30 A.M. to noon, how do you handle the rest of the day? You probably will be able to find a nanny, family day-care provider, or day-care center to cover for you until you get home from work, but what happens a year later when your child hits first grade? How do you get Janey from school to a private piano lesson and then home? Or how does Scott go from his after-school tutoring lesson to soccer practice? Can you find safe, reliable child care for a mere three hours a day—from 3:00 P.M., when school ends, until you get home from work at 6:00 P.M.?

If you can figure out how to handle these issues, how do you handle holidays—Christmas vacation, spring break, Martin Luther King, Jr. Day, snow days, parent-teacher days, or other holidays when many banks, government offices, and schools are closed, but you have to work? Even more problematic is summer vacation, when your child has three months of glorious freedom, but you are chained to your desk in an air-conditioned skyscraper downtown. It's bad enough that you have to work on beautiful, sunny, summer days, but who takes care of your child for the twelve or more hours you are commuting to your office, working, and then commuting back home?

Now that you see the scope of the problem, let me get more specific. As a parent of a school-age child, your child-care options may be limited by a new dynamic: the social, athletic, and extracurricular preferences of your child. Since your child is now older, she will expect to participate in making the choices about what she does, where she goes, and with whom she does her after-school activities. Parents are often handed an extra burden when finding care for older children in that they no longer have a passive infant or malleable toddler to find suitable and safe care for, but an older child with a definite personality who wants and needs to be part of the process. Once again, the fact that child care hasn't managed to keep up with the needs of family life in the nineties means that your family has to be creative and flexible. (Recently, however, the problems faced by parents of school-age children have been publicly acknowledged by various child-care advocacy groups, government agencies, foundations, and corporate entities, and some tentative steps are being taken to change the situation. One such step is a June 1995 $3.6 million grant from the DeWitt Reader's Digest Fund of New York City to the Wellesley College School-Age Child Care Project to strengthen and expand existing after-school programs in Seattle, Boston, and Chicago. Not only will this grant make current after-school projects far better, but one of the grant's goals is to encourage other communities to start ongoing after-school programs.)

IF YOU NEED CARE BEFORE OR AFTER SCHOOL

Family Day-Care Providers and Day-Care Centers

If your child is still young enough (in kindergarten or first grade), you may be able to find a family day-care provider or day-care center to care for your child before and after school. Many day-care centers now offer programs as early as 6:00 A.M., where you can drop off your child (some even provide breakfast) on your way to work. These day-care centers then shuttle your child to school by minivan or small school bus. Most of the centers that provide this service also pick children up at the end of the school day and bring them back to the center for afternoon playgroups or to start their homework. Even better, day-care centers that provide shuttle service to local schools tend to have the same holiday and vacation schedule as the school districts, so if you can find this type of service you will be covered during the same times that you are covered by school. And often, these same centers will provide child-care services during the summer, parts of the Christmas vacation, and spring break. They are also usually open for business on holidays when you need to go to work.

However, family day-care or day-care centers can be a complicated option because you need to think about transportation for your children if their after-school schedule requires more flexibility or if the day-care and family day-care centers in your area don't offer a shuttle service—or if the service doesn't meet your needs. How do you get your child from school to day care in the middle of the day when you are at work

30 miles away? A few family day-care providers may be willing to pick your child up from school. In addition, you may be able to find other parents with the same dilemma who would be willing to organize a car pool to a day-care center. But remember that car pools are built on parents cooperatively sharing the pickup and drop-off responsibilities. This might not work for some parents who cannot commit to a set schedule because their jobs include swing shifts or extensive travel. If these options don't work for you, or if you're having trouble setting them up, be persistent; ask around. Many parents are in the same position as you, and would be glad to work with you to figure it all out. If you can't participate in a car pool, look for a good trade. If one parent can drive your child to school Monday to Friday, maybe you can drive her kids to away-soccer games on the weekends. Poll other parents for things you might trade for weekly car pool duty.

Day-care centers and family day-care providers may also be more expensive than school-based after-school programs or programs run by community organizations, and they may not have the variety of programming that these groups do, such as art and music classes, athletics, and clubs. However, if you decide that a day-care center or family day-care provider is the right after-school option for your child, turn to Chapter Seven, "Finding and Hiring Family Day Care," and Chapter Eight, "Finding and Hiring Day-Care Centers" to get all of the information and templates you need to choose and manage this type of child-care service.

In-Home After-School Care

The most flexible, and potentially most expensive, after-school care is obtained when you hire a nanny. A nanny can pick your child up from school and care for her until you return home from work that evening. If your schedule is such that you need child care in the early mornings, you may be able to find a nanny willing to come to your house in the morning, feed your child breakfast, get her dressed and ready for school, and then drive her there. After taking a few hours off, or after doing errands and light housework if you can afford it, she can return to school in the afternoon to pick your child up. A nanny allows you to handle sick days, snow days, parent-teacher days, school holidays, and vacations with relative ease.

If a nanny seems like the most appropriate choice for your child, turn to Chapters Five and Six to get all of the information and templates you need to hire and manage an in-home provider.

In-School Programs

If your child is lucky enough to be in a school that has an after-school program, many of your problems will be solved. You won't need to worry about transportation of your child from school to the after-school program; most likely you'll be able to pick up your child from the program on your way home from work. Better yet, some school districts extend busing hours to accommodate after-school programming. In addition, your child will be with other children he knows, making his adjustment to the program easier. And depending on the program, your child will have the opportunity to participate in a wide range of organized, well-supervised extracurricular activities, like music lessons, art classes, drama, sports teams and other athletic pursuits, and clubs like Boy Scouts, Girl Scouts, Future Farmers of America, and 4-H.

The problem with in-school programs is that they are usually closed on those days that the school is closed, so you still need to have a backup plan for summer, holidays, snow days, and so on. Some operate only one or two days a week. And because of universal budget problems, many school districts can't predict what they'll be able to offer every year.

BACKGROUND CHECKS

If your district does offer an after-school program and you enroll your child in it, take a careful look at the teachers. Are they current, full-time instructors at the school? If so, you are in great shape. Full-time teachers in public schools undergo extensive background investigations by the state before they are allowed to teach. On the other hand, if your child's after-school program teachers are part-time, beware! In many states, part-time teachers are exempt from regulations requiring them to undergo the regular teacher background investigations.

While you're at it, find out whether your child's after-school coaches are full-time or part-time employees of the school district. If they are part-time, ask your school board to run them through the same background investigations required for full-time teachers and coaches. If they balk at this task, don't give up. Get other parents involved in the process. Circulate a petition. And go back to the board. Remember, only you can protect your child. Don't give up.

The same degree of vigilance should be applied to Boy Scout, Girl Scout, 4-H, and Eagle Scout leaders, and leaders of any other organizations who may or may not be employees of the school district. Over the past few years, the Boy Scouts in particular have had a public relations disaster on their hands as newspapers everywhere report that many Boy Scout leaders were found to have molested the young boys they were responsible for. Be sure that any organization your child wants to join does comprehensive background investigations on anyone who is responsible for caring for your child.

You have only a few options if you want to do a comprehensive, identity/education/employment verification and multijurisdictional criminal, civil, and driving check on a Boy Scout leader or other potential care provider for your child: (1) Do it yourself. (2) Hire a private investigator you know and trust. (3) Hire The ChildCare Registry or another preemployment screening company that can provide you with a packaged service and a legal release.

How to Do Your Own Background Check

I created The ChildCare Registry to provide parents with a service that provides legally released, comprehensive, state-of-the-art preemployment screening verifications and criminal, civil, and driving records that are completed within seven days. However, for parents who want to do the background check themselves, here is what I would do:

Get permission, in writing, from the care provider to do a background check.

Identity: In order to run a Social Security Index trace with the Social Security Administration, you will need the provider's name and a Social Security number and a valid federal Employer Identification Number. If you aren't hiring this person as an employee, and therefore don't need an identification number, ask to see a copy of the person's Social Security card and at least one more form of identification, preferably a picture ID. Make sure that the name, address, and other data correspond with the information you have and that all the ID is current and valid.

Employment: Get a complete list of all employers, including names of supervisors, with addresses and phone numbers for the last five years. Have the candidate include on the list her job position, starting and departing dates, and salary for each employer. Call each employer, indicate that you want to verify a person's previous employment, and cross your fingers because this can be ticklish. Personal employers are often hard to reach because you may not have their work numbers (I'm not sure you should call there, anyway) which means you will have to call in the evening. So, you may need to be persistent, but other parents are a gold mine of information, so don't get discouraged. Business employers, like day-care centers, or other previous employers, need to be called during business hours, so take the information with you to work and call during lunch or a break. This gets complicated if you don't reach anyone who can help you and you need to be called back. If you can get calls at the office, great—leave that number; but if you can't and you need to leave your home number, be sure to leave an appropriate message on your home answering machine encouraging the party to leave a detailed response for you. Some employers may chafe at this and refuse to leave a message with sensitive employment data on a home answering machine.

Education: Have your provider give you detailed information on each education claim. Get the full name, address, phone number, dates attended, and highest grade or graduation date for each institution. If you want to verify the provider's high school graduation, you can probably do that over the telephone by calling the administration office of the school during business hours. Colleges, universities, and other places of higher learning are trickier. Some require an authorization and release faxed to them. Others charge a fee, like $3, and insist on everything in writing, by mail. Many require the graduate's full name (watch out for name changes, like maiden names), date of birth, or Social Security number to ascertain identity and make sure you are talking about the same person. You will need to have all of this information handy when you call, so be sure to have a complete file on hand.

Driving Records: You will want to verify not only that the provider has a valid driver's license, which indicates his ability to get insurance, but that his driving record is also clear of any moving violations, driving under the influence, or other more serious issues, especially if he will be driving your child around. You would be surprised at how many people drive using a suspended driver's license! Also, keep in mind that in many states, even drivers whose licenses have been suspended can drive to and from work. So it is important to understand and verify his license status. How can you get a copy of his driving record? You can't, but he can. Once again, if you can get access to a public records database company that will accept your version of an authorization and release and sell "retail," you may be able to get a copy of his driving record. However, the only sure-fire way of getting a copy is to have him go to the local DMV, pay a fee (in California it's $5), and get a *dated copy* of his driving record. But be careful. It is easy to alter, fabricate, and counterfeit documents. Laser printers and high-resolution copiers have revolutionized the fine art of document manipulation, so it is critical that you can authenticate any document received by you. Insist that the DMV record be very fresh and current—I would recommend that it be dated within one week of your examining it.

Criminal History Records: This is really a tough one. Though no one will argue the need to be aware of any type of criminal record in the background of a person who is responsible for the care of your child, individual citizens are pretty much precluded from direct access to this information. The ChildCare Registry has access through a network of private investigators armed with sophisticated releases. Private investigators that you may hire can facilitate the same type of public-record courthouse search, but you will have to provide them with a seamless residential history, as the ChildCare Registry application does, so that they can know which county courthouses to search. Statewide criminal history databases do exist, but in only a few states, so it will be necessary to have detailed data on your candidate in any event. California offers parents an option called Trustline, which is a database that lists child-care provider applicants whose backgrounds have been verified against the California Department of Justice criminal histories records and the state's substantiated child-abuse files. The search is of California records only, so if the person lived outside of California four years ago, the record will not reflect the other jurisdiction's data. The process takes 4 to 6 weeks and costs $85.

Civil Courthouse Record Searches: Although a civil courthouse record search is considered an extra service and rarely provides the type of inflammatory data that might preclude a provider from working in child care, it is the one place where extremely pertinent information can hide from view. Did you know that many child molesters are often sued in civil court by the victim and their families for recovery of damages to pay for psychotherapy for the victim? Many times this is the only relief a victim and his/her family can find in the legal system, especially if the molester is not successfully prosecuted in criminal court or if the prosecutors don't go for an indictment because the facts are murky or victims are considered too young to testify. Civil courthouse records cannot be directly accessed by private citizens. However, they can be accessed by private detectives and should be done in each county of residence for five years. These searches need to be authorized and released by the provider and can be expensive because the private detectives will more than likely charge by the hour. Depending on how many jurisdictions in which the provider has lived, this can add up. Additionally, you can expect a document fee for each courthouse of at least $10.

Does the background-check process sound discouraging, time-consuming, and expensive? Still want to do this yourself? It's up to you. The whole time I spent writing this I felt like a car mechanic describing how easy it is to change your car's oil at home. Sure, you can do it, and maybe you can save money, but what a mess! Now that you know the components of a background check and some of the little dirty secrets of this industry, you can choose to go it alone. Just keep in mind that you need to protect yourself and the child-care provider by having complete authorization and a legal release to do this investigation—and the time to do it or the time to wait until all the pieces are verified.

A ChildCare Registry information packet, which includes everything a parent needs to request a background check including the CCR application, authorization and release, parent release and payment form can be ordered by calling (800) CCR-0033.

COMMUNITY AFTER-SCHOOL PROGRAMS

Community organizations like the YMCA, YWCA, Jewish Community Center, Big Brothers/Big Sisters, local churches and synagogues, and many local colleges and universities offer after-school programs at their facilities that include art and music lessons, athletics, and academic tutoring for your child. Appendix 2 has phone numbers and addresses of each national organization's headquarters. Call for information, then visit the programs yourself—without your child—to check them out.

Evaluating After-School Programs
The Telephone Prescreen
When you call an in-school, community, or independent after-school program for information, be sure to work through the After-School Program Telephone Prescreen Questions found in the template in Chapter Ten or in the Older-Child file on the diskette. Before you turn to the template, review the sample telephone prescreen questions and answers.

AFTER-SCHOOL PROGRAM TELEPHONE PRESCREEN QUESTIONS

1. What are the program hours? <u>2:30 p.m. to 7:00 p.m.</u>

2. How much does the program cost? <u>$10 a day.</u>

3. Can a child go every day of the school week or just a few days? <u>Every day of the week is fine.</u>

4. What kinds of organized activities does the program offer? <u>help with homework, art projects, softball, basketball, and other outdoor games when the weather is good, storytelling when the weather is bad, ongoing science projects.</u>

5. Are all ages mixed together, or all activities organized according to age? <u>activities are organized according to age.</u>

6. Do the children have any free, unscheduled time, or is it all taken up with the formal activities? [Some children need a break after a long day at school.] <u>At least one-quarter of the child's time is free.</u>

7. Is there quiet time for homework and is tutoring available? <u>No formal tutoring, but we will help with homework.</u>

8. Are nutritious snacks available? <u>yes</u>

9. How many children attend the program and what are their ages? [Make sure that plenty of children your child's age are enrolled.] <u>6 first graders, 5 second graders, and 10 third graders are in our program.</u>

10. What is the adult–child ratio? [Make sure that there are enough adults around so that your child receives some individual attention.] <u>1:4 for all age groups.</u>

11. How are the teachers selected? What are their qualifications, and have they undergone thorough background investigations? <u>all are teachers with over 2 years experience who are chosen after an extensive interview process—we have checked their backgroun and references.</u>

12. Are all of the teachers certified in CPR and first aid? <u>yes</u>

13. Does the program offer transportation from local schools? <u>yes— public schools only.</u>

14. If transportation is provided, do the drivers have clean driving records? Are seat belts required at all times? <u>All drivers have clean records and seat belts are required at all times.</u>

15. Is the program fully licensed with the state? <u>yes</u>

16. Is the program fully insured? *Yes*

17. Can you give me the names and phone numbers of two parents I can call for references? *Yes*

Comments: *The activities seem just right, but my child goes to private school, so I need to deal with transportation. Could be a problem. Next program....*

■ ■

THE ON-SITE VISIT

Once you identify a program that appears to have all your baseline requirements, it's time to visit. Review the After-School Program On-Site Visit Checklist below.

■ ■

AFTER-SCHOOL PROGRAM ON-SITE VISIT CHECKLIST

Safety

Is the neighborhood safe?	☑ yes	☐ no
Program facility secure?	☑ yes	☐ no
Facility well maintained?	☑ yes	☐ no
Smoke detectors working *(check to see if light indicating charged battery is on)*?	☑ yes	☐ no
Fire extinguishers current *(check date on canister or attached card)*?	☑ yes	☐ no
Electrical outlets covered?	☑ yes	☐ no
Adequate first-aid kit?	☑ yes	☐ no
Screened windows?	☑ yes	☐ no
Secured electrical cords?	☑ yes	☐ no
Evacuation plan/emergency drills?	☑ yes	☐ no

Sanitation/Cleanliness

Passes the "Sniff Test"?	☑ yes	☐ no
Does facility appear clean/organized?	☑ yes	☐ no

continued

Play area clean/organized?	☑ yes	☐ no
Surfaces clean?	☑ yes	☐ no
Toys/games clean?	☑ yes	☐ no
Food preparation areas clean?	☑ yes	☐ no
Bathroom clean/sanitized?	☑ yes	☐ no

Indoor Play Area

Is it cheerful/engaging?	☑ yes	☐ no
Are toys in good repair?	☑ yes	☐ no
Enough age-appropriate toys/games?	☑ yes	☐ no
Enough crafts/art supplies?	☑ yes	☐ no
Art work is displayed?	☑ yes	☐ no
Can adults see the entire room at once?	☑ yes	☐ no
Water available?	☑ yes	☐ no
Easy access to bathrooms?	☑ yes	☐ no
Adequate light/ventilation?	☑ yes	☐ no

Outside Play Area (if any)

Enough space?	☑ yes	☐ no
Grass/plants/flowers?	☑ yes	☐ no
Enclosed and secure?	☑ yes	☐ no
Adult can see entire play area at once?	☑ yes	☐ no
Sandboxes covered?	☑ yes	☐ no
Thick pads under play equipment?	☑ yes	☐ no
Play equipment in good repair?	☑ yes	☐ no

Program Operator and Staff

Warm/friendly?	☑ yes	☐ no
Smiles?	☑ yes	☐ no
Positive and open?	☑ yes	☐ no
Made you feel at home?	☑ yes	☐ no
Good communicators?	☑ yes	☐ no
Clean?	☑ yes	☐ no
Organized/under control?	☑ yes	☐ no
Truly like children?	☑ yes	☐ no

Program

Daily schedule posted for parents?	☑ yes	☐ no
Nutritious meals/snacks?	☑ yes	☐ no
Television allowed?	☐ yes	☑ no
Enough activities to keep your child engaged and interested?	☐ yes	☑ no
Plenty of other children that are your child's age?	☐ yes	☑ no

Administration

Written prices and policies?	☑ yes	☐ no
Fully insured (ask to see documentation)?	☑ yes	☐ no
Parents welcome at all times?	☑ yes	☐ no
Authorized persons only may pick up children?	☑ yes	☐ no

Additional comments: _I didn't realize this program was so far from home. The drive home will take 30 minutes—too long. Try to find another program closer to home._

■ ■

INDEPENDENT AFTER-SCHOOL PROGRAMS

If you can arrange transportation for your child from school to the program and have a little extra money to spend, you can find plenty of classes, lessons, sports teams, and other activities to fill your child's after-school hours. Your child can play on the local baseball, football, basketball, soccer, or swim teams; learn to ride horses at a nearby stable; take tennis lessons at the local tennis club; learn how to play golf at the local country club; take dance or gymnastics at a health club; or get extra help in math, reading, science, and languages from retired teachers or teachers who want to earn extra money after hours. In addition, there are many artists who enjoy earning extra cash teaching children how to draw, paint, or sculpt. Your local art store or gallery may offer art classes geared to children. If you have the money to spend and can figure out how to get your child there, you can find an activity to keep him safe, happy, and occupied.

As with any person you entrust with your child, be sure to thoroughly investigate the situation and the teacher, coach, or trainer before you drop your child off. Many Y's across the country are now starting to do comprehensive background checks, as they're just starting to realize how very important it is. But you must still do your homework. Insist on a comprehensive, national background check. Just follow the background check procedure described in the section above. Also, be sure to ask for references and check them carefully using the professional Reference Report template below. Sit in on a class or two, if possible, before you enroll your child. Make sure you feel good about the instructor.

Checking References

Remember, your child's instructor must have the following personal qualities:

- personal maturity
- responsible/dependable/reliable
- adaptable
- fun-loving
- warm/caring
- even-tempered

When you reach one of the instructor's references, introduce yourself and explain that you are considering enrolling your child in the instuctor's class. Then, ask all of the questions on the Reference Report below. The questions are designed to elicit as much information as possible about the instructor's personal qualities from the reference. Feel free to ask any additional questions you would like and be sure to listen carefully. Review the sample Reference Report below for an art teacher. Then, turn to the template in Chapter Ten or in the software under the Older Child icon.

■ ■ ■ ■ ■ ■ ■ ■ ■ ■ ■ ■ ■ ■ ■ ■ ■ ■ ■ ■ ■ ■ ■ ■ ■ ■ ■ ■ ■ ■ ■ ■

REFERENCE REPORT

Instructor: _Louise Bleu_

Parent Contacted: _Ann Leslie_

Address: _222 Westwind Rd., Newark, NJ 02114_

Phone Number: _(201) 555-2222_

How would you rate his/her overall teaching performance on a scale of 1 to 10 with 10 being excellent? _9_

What were his/her strengths? _Wonderful painter, really gets the kids enthu-siastic about painting, warm, capable, extremely responsible_

What were the areas that you would recommend improvements (weaknesses)?

a little shy with adults—obviously a true artistic personality, so it was hard to communicate with her

Would you let your child take his/her class again?   ☑ yes   ☐ no

Additional questions: _____

_____

_____

_____

_____

■■

IF YOU NEED CARE FOR YOUR CHILD DURING THE SUMMER

If you have decided that a full-time nanny is for you, summers won't be a problem. Likewise, if your child has been going to a day-care center or family day-care provider who is open during the summer, you can increase the number of hours your child is at the center every day, and summer will be solved.

However, if your child is too old to go to a day-care center or family day-care provider, and if your child is ready, one of the best ways to handle the summer months is to find a good summer camp. Because there are so many different types of day and resident summer camps, it is very likely that you can find one that fits your child's interests and your family's budget.

Day Camps

According to the American Camping Association, attendance at day camps throughout the United States is increasing every year. Day camps offer a variety of programs and activities for children ages five to fifteen, and are designed to increase a child's personal and social skills. Most day camps are coed and offer a fun mix of summertime activities—swimming, boating, hiking, horseback riding, tennis, and so on. Some camps focus on certain athletic pursuits—sailing and tennis are popular choices—where your child can spend up to six hours a day training for an end-of-summer regatta or developing a killer backhand. Recently, many day camps around the country have become more academically oriented; the study of science, astronomy, and desktop publishing are top choices. These camps offer in-depth academic instruction balanced with more traditional summertime fun, like swimming and softball. And finally, to make your life easier, many day camps now offer transportation for your child to and from the camp each day.

Some of the Activities Offered at Day and Resident Camps Across the United States

Hiking/backpacking	Horseback riding
Leadership training	Mountaineering
Climbing/Rappeling	Outdoor living skills
Drama	Dance
Music	Physical Fitness
Religion	Nutrition
Aquatics	Water-skiing
Canoeing	Rowing
Sailing	Windsurfing
Scuba Diving	Computers
Arts/Crafts	Cycling
Environmental Education	Farming/Ranching
Individual Sports—archery, riflery, tennis, gymnastics, tumbling	Team sports—baseball, basketball, football, soccer, hockey, softball

Resident Camps

Your child can attend a resident camp for a few days, a week, two weeks, or up to eight weeks. Usually, she will sleep in a cabin, tent, tepee, or other form of rustic shelter and participate in a wide range of supervised activities, including sailing, tennis, horseback riding, archery, and art and music classes. Like day camps, many resident camps are specializing. Depending on her interests, your child can attend a space camp for future astronauts and Star Trek fans; desktop publishing camp for the graphic designers of the future; weight-loss camp; Hebrew language camp; Bible study camp; environmental education camp; camps for children with low motivation and self-esteem; camps for children with diabetes; and many others. If you want it, you can find it!

Is My Child Ready for a Resident Camp?

The general rule of thumb for assessing a child's readiness for a resident camp is an honest evaluation by a parent of the child's ability and maturity to deal with homesickness, new people, new environments, and the loss of their normal routine. A good gauge in assessing these issues is the child's previous experience at a day camp, sleep-overs, or long weekends with friends or relatives. If your child is less than enthusiastic about the prospect of leaving home for any length of time, try a day camp again this year. One idea for helping the transition from day camp to resident camp is to find a friend to buddy up with so that the experience isn't totally alien. And be sure that the camp you choose is appropriate for your child in that it caters to younger, newer campers and that it has plenty of activities earmarked for those first few days when homesickness is likely to strike. Be sure to acquaint yourself with the camp's policy for calling home, and if this experience turns out to be a bad idea with mosquitoes, can you get a partial refund?

The American Camping Association (ACA) offers parents the following tips to determine whether their child is ready for resident camp:

- Has your child expressed an interest in going to camp?
- Has your child had previous sleep-over experiences?
- Did previous sleep-overs involve any "rescue" calls to Mom and Dad?
- Has your child already attended day camp?
- Did your child have a positive experience in day care?

The Cost of Camp

Independent, privately run camps cost about $35 to $100 a day according to the American Camping Association (ACA). Camps operated by nonprofit agencies, youth groups, and public agencies range in price from $15 to $55 per day. In addition, some camps charge extra fees for certain programs and activities, like horseback riding and scuba diving.

If the price of camp seems out of reach, some camps offer scholarships for partial or full tuition. Girl Scouts, Boy Scouts, church-affiliated camps, and city- or county-sponsored camps usually offer some sort of financial aid if you need it.

Questions to Ask a Camp Director

The most important factor determining the quality of a day or resident camp is management—how the activities are operated. A camp can have a beautiful brochure and offer every activity under the sun, but if you have the slightest suspicion that it is poorly managed, you should steer clear.

Get to know the camp director personally through telephone conversations and on-site visits. The ACA recommends that you ask the questions included in our Camp Telephone Prescreen Questions template. Be sure to include any additional questions you may have at the end of the template. Review the sample questionnaire below before you get on the phone.

CAMP TELEPHONE PRESCREEN QUESTIONS

1. What is the camp's overall philosophy? _Everyone participates, everyone is safe, learns new skills, and has fun._

2. Does the camp promote competition and healthy rivalry among teams, or is the camp focused on noncompetitive, cooperative learning? _Noncompetitive._

3. How is that philosophy carried out by the staff? _Lots of individual attention, especially when kids are learning new skills._

4. What are the different activities campers can participate in? _Swimming, horseback riding, tennis, gymnastics, painting, sculpture, music lessons._

5. What does a camper's day look like? _Up at 7 A.M., showers, clean cabins, breakfast. Then a choice of many different morning activities that will_

take approx. 2 1/2 hours, lunch, then 2 hours of free time, then a choice of afternoon activities that last for 2 hours, back for dinner, group time by the campfire until lights out at 9:00 P.M.

6. Is the camp accredited by the ACA? [for more on their regulations, see below] *yes*

7. What is the background of the director? *professor of physical education at Ohio State during school year. Summer camp counselor for 10 years. Camp director for 5 years.*

8. What is the ratio of counselors to campers? *1:5*

9. What are the ages of the counselors? *all over 18*

10. Do the counselors have previous experience caring for children? *yes, all are teachers during the school year.*

11. How does the camp recruit counselors? How are they screened? Does the camp require comprehensive background checks that include review of a criminal record? *recruit by word of mouth all are thoroughly interviewed, background checked, and reference checked.*

12. How are the counselors trained? Are they certified in CPR and first aid? *All are licensed teachers and certified in CPR and first aid.*

13. How does the camp handle special needs, including allergy and insulin medication, restricted diets, etc. Is there a nurse on staff? *Nurse is on staff and any special needs will be taken care of in a professional manner by the nurse.*

14. How are behavior and disciplinary problems handled? *Restrict children that are having discipline problems to the cabin for 1 hour. If too many problems occur, parents are notified and child is asked to leave.*

15. If the camp transports children to and from camp for various camp activities, how are the drivers screened? Do they have valid driver's licenses? Have their driving records been reviewed? *All drivers have valid driver's licenses with records that are thoroughly reviewed before camp starts.*

16. Can I speak to two parents who have enrolled their child in the camp in the last year? *yes*

ACA-Accredited Camps

If you choose a camp that has been accredited by the ACA, you are choosing a camp that must comply with more than three hundred national health, safety, and program-quality standards, including criteria for living areas, food service, emergency preparedness, program practices, health care, personnel, transportation, and administrative procedures. These standards do not guarantee that nothing will go wrong, but they do assure you that the practices of the camp have been reviewed and measured against a national standard. At least once every three years, teams of two or more trained camp professionals observe a camp's operations while the camp is in session and compare the camp's practices to the national standards.

The mandatory standards include:

- Emergency transportation available at all times, provided by the camp or community emergency services, with whom prior arrangements have been made in writing.

- First-aid facilities and staff available at all times when campers are present. The staff member must have one of the following qualifications: licensed physician, registered nurse, emergency medical technician, paramedic, or a person certified in American Red Cross Standard First Aid (minimum requirement), medic first aid, or equivalent.

- Aquatic programs must be supervised by staff meeting one of the following certifications: American Red Cross Lifeguard Training; YMCA Lifeguard; Boy Scouts of America Lifeguard; Royal Life Saving Society Bronze Medallion; or equivalent certification.

- Health histories for all campers and staff that meet the following requirements: record of prior medical treatment, immunizations, allergies (except for nonmedical religious camps), and description of any health conditions requiring special consideration.

- Emergency exits from second-floor sleeping quarters.

- At least one emergency exit in addition to the main door or entrance.

Note that the ACA does not require criminal background checks of the camp director, employees, or counselors.

CHRONOLOGICAL
LIST OF TEMPLATES

CHAPTER TEN

■ ■ ■ ■ ■ ■ ■ ■ ■ ■ ■

TEMPLATES

■ ■

Template 1
YOUR HOUSEHOLD PROFILE

A. _____

   Parent Name   *Parent Name*

B. _____

   Child Name/Age   *Child Name/Age*

_____

   Child Name/Age   *Child Name/Age*

_____

   Child Name/Age   *Child Name/Age*

C. List all existing household employees, their duties, and salaries.

_____

   Name   *Duties*   *Salary*

_____

   Name   *Duties*   *Salary*

D. List all nonsalaried child-care help you may currently use, their duties, and hours. (For example, if Grandma or Aunt Lisa regularly sits with the kids on Wednesday nights, or if there is a neighborhood mom who sits for you in exchange for your sitting for her, please list it here.)

_____

   Name   *Duties*   *Hours*

_____

   Name   *Duties*   *Hours*

■ ■

215

Template 2
YOUR FAMILY'S CALENDARS

	Weekly Planner			MONTH		YEAR	
SUNDAY	**MONDAY**	**TUESDAY**	**WEDNESDAY**	**THURSDAY**	**FRIDAY**	**SATURDAY**
7AM	7AM	7AM	7AM	7AM	7AM	7AM
8	8	8	8	8	8	8
9	9	9	9	9	9	9
10	10	10	10	10	10	10
11	11	11	11	11	11	11
12NOON	12NOON	12NOON	12NOON	12NOON	12NOON	12NOON
1	1	1	1	1	1	1
2	2	2	2	2	2	2
3	3	3	3	3	3	3
4	4	4	4	4	4	4
5	5	5	5	5	5	5

	Weekly Planner			MONTH		YEAR	
SUNDAY	**MONDAY**	**TUESDAY**	**WEDNESDAY**	**THURSDAY**	**FRIDAY**	**SATURDAY**
7AM	7AM	7AM	7AM	7AM	7AM	7AM
8	8	8	8	8	8	8
9	9	9	9	9	9	9
10	10	10	10	10	10	10
11	11	11	11	11	11	11
12NOON	12NOON	12NOON	12NOON	12NOON	12NOON	12NOON
1	1	1	1	1	1	1
2	2	2	2	2	2	2
3	3	3	3	3	3	3
4	4	4	4	4	4	4
5	5	5	5	5	5	5

Template 3
IN-HOME CARE NEEDS ASSESSMENT

Basic Requirements

1. The position is
   - ❏ full-time (25 to 40 hours)
   - ❏ part-time (up to 25 hours)

2. The provider will
   - ❏ live in (accommodations, room, board, and salary)
   - ❏ live out

3A. The provider will be required to drive and be the holder of a valid driver's license and be insured or insurable:
   ❏ yes   ❏ no

B. If the provider is required to drive, who will provide car?
   ❏ parent   ❏ provider

C. If parent's car is used, may provider use it in the provider's off-duty hours?   ❏ yes   ❏ no

D. If provider drives own car
   - ❏ proof of insurance will be required
   - ❏ parents will provide insurance or add provider to family policy

E. Will the provider be compensated for gas use while on the job? (The current rate is $.29 cents per mile.)
   ❏ yes   ❏ no

F. Will there be a policy for small cash expenditures and reimbursement for gas and other incidentals?
   ❏ yes   ❏ no

G. If you answered yes to question 3F, will you provide a list of "cleared" expenditures along with a simple expense form and payment policy?
   ❏ yes   ❏ no

Duties and Qualifications

4. The provider will report to

   _____ .
   Name of parent or parents

5. The provider will have responsibility for these children:

Child's name	Age
_____	_____
_____	_____
_____	_____
_____	_____
_____	_____

6. Please check the following areas of responsibility/duty:
   - ❏ light cleaning
   - ❏ cooking meals for children
   - ❏ driving
   - ❏ bathing
   - ❏ children's laundry
   - ❏ adhere to nap/bedtime schedule
   - ❏ adhere to dietary restrictions
   - ❏ reinforce family rules
   - ❏ carry I.D., medical forms/releases at all times

7. Please check the following minimum qualifications:
   - ❏ high school degree
   - ❏ college/advanced degree
   - ❏ previous child-care experience
   - ❏ previous infant-care experience
   - ❏ English speaking
   - ❏ infant/child CPR certification
   - ❏ nonsmoker
   - ❏ 7-year, national background check including civil, criminal, and driving
   - ❏ U.S. citizen or legal alien

Salary, Holiday, and Sick Day Policy

8A. The salary will be based on:
   - ❏ fixed hourly rate
   - ❏ flat monthly rate

B. The rate amount will be: $_____

C. The salary will be paid:
   ❏ weekly   ❏ bi-weekly   ❏ monthly

9. Will there be any paid benefits?
   - ❏ medical insurance
   - ❏ dental insurance
   - ❏ life insurance

continued

10A. Will there be paid holidays (nonwork days where the provider still receives a salary)? ❑ yes ❑ no

B. If yes, which holidays?
❑ all federal holidays
❑ all federal and bank holidays
❑ the following list of holidays:
   ❑ New Year's   ❑ Labor Day
   ❑ Memorial Day ❑ Thanksgiving
   ❑ July 4   ❑ Christmas
❑ no holidays will be paid unless by previous agreement, and each holiday will be assessed for child-care needs.

11A. Will sick days be paid? ❑ yes ❑ no

B. If yes, how many sick days per year?
❑ 1–3   ❑ 3–5

C. If yes, what is paid sick-day policy?
❑ sick days paid after 90-day employment review
❑ sick days paid after ____-day employment review

12. If the provider is due one week's paid vacation scheduled at a mutually agreed-upon time, then the vacation will be after:
❑ 6 months of employment and favorable review
❑ 9 months of employment and favorable review
❑ other

Accommodations

13. If you have chosen a live-in provider, please check the following features that best describe the provider's living arrangement:
❑ private bedroom/bath
❑ separate kitchen/eat alone
❑ share kitchen/eat alone
❑ eat with family
❑ private telephone
❑ shared telephone
❑ television in room
❑ share laundry

Work Hours and Scheduling

14. The provider's regular work hours will be:_____A.M. to _____ P.M.

15. The provider will be required to work:
❑ evenings ❑ weekends

16. If evenings and weekends are required, and are over and above regular work hours (40 hours a week), how will the provider be compensated? (Keep in mind that you are not required by law to pay overtime to a live-in employee.)
❑ at normal rate per hour
❑ at 1.5 times the normal rate
❑ other

17. Will the provider be required to travel with the family? (Remember, travel with the family is not a substitute for paid vacation.) ❑ yes ❑ no

18A. Will the provider have guest privileges?   ❑ yes   ❑ no

B. If yes, in what areas of the home will these privileges be allowed?
❑ provider's quarters
❑ family area
❑ by mutual agreement

C. Will the live-in provider be allowed to have overnight guests?
❑ yes ❑ no
❑ by mutual agreement

Child-Care Management

19A. Will there be regularly scheduled meetings between provider and parent(s)? ❑ yes   ❑ no

B. If yes, how often?   ❑ weekly
❑ bi-weekly ❑ monthly

C. When will the provider get her weekly work schedule?
❑ at previous week's meeting
❑ as needed

D. Will there be other management/provider communication, other than at meeting? ❑ yes ❑ no

E. If yes, please check the other types of communication you will require from the provider on a regular basis:
❑ daily diary ❑ weekly report

NOTES: _____
_____
_____
_____

218

Template 4
FAMILY DAY-CARE NEEDS ASSESSMENT

Basic Requirements

1A. The operator must allow drop-off from:
❑ 6:00–7:00 A.M. ❑ 7:00–8:00 A.M.
❑ 8:00–9:00 A.M. ❑ after 9:00 A.M.

B. The operator must allow pick-up from:
❑ 4:00–5:00 P.M. ❑ 5:00–6:00 P.M.
❑ 6:00–7:00 P.M. ❑ after 7:00 P.M.

2. I want my child to attend:
❑ every weekday, all day
❑ three days a week, all day
❑ every weekday morning
❑ every weekday afternoon
❑ three days a week, mornings
❑ three days a week, afternoons
❑ other_____

3A. The provider must be near my:
❑ work ❑ home ❑ other

B. I would prefer the facility to be:
❑ in the owner's home
❑ in a facility other than the owner's home

4A. The provider must be open:
❑ 12 months a year
❑ 9 months a year (closed during summer)

B. The provider must be open:
❑ on the following holidays

_____

_____

5. The facility must have the following features:
❑ playground
❑ separate area for napping
❑ separate area for diapering
❑ plenty of toys/activities for infants
❑ plenty of toys/activities for toddlers

6. The maximum number of children the provider cares for must be:
❑ 1–3 ❑ 3–6 ❑ 6–10

7. Parents will be welcome to drop in any time: ❑ yes ❑ no

8. The provider will be licensed:
❑ yes ❑ no

9A. I can pay the following rate for family day–care services:
❑ less than $50 a week
❑ $50–$100 a week
❑ $100–$200 a week
❑ $200–$300 a week
❑ more than $300 a week

B. I can pay the provider:
❑ weekly ❑ monthly
❑ biyearly ❑ once a year

Teacher Qualifications

10A. The provider and all assistants will have the following minimum qualifications:
❑ high school degree
❑ college/advanced degree
❑ previous child-care experience
❑ previous infant-care experience
❑ English speaking
❑ infant/child CPR certification
❑ nonsmoker
❑ 7-year, national background check including civil, criminal, and driving

B. All members of the household with access to my child will be background-checked: ❑ yes ❑ no

Child-Care Management

11A. Will there be regularly scheduled meetings between provider and parent(s)? ❑ yes ❑ no

B. If yes, how often?
❑ weekly ❑ biweekly ❑ monthly

C. When will the provider get your weekly work schedule?
❑ at previous week's meeting
❑ as needed

D. Will there be other provider/parent communication, other than at meetings? ❑ yes ❑ no

E. If yes, please check the other types of communication you will require from the provider on a regular basis:
❑ daily log
❑ expense reports/weekly

F. Please check the following items you will provide the provider and update on a regular basis:
❑ emergency phone numbers
❑ approved transportation form
❑ medical forms/releases

NOTES: _____

Template 5
DAY-CARE NEEDS ASSESSMENT

Basic Requirements

1A. The center must open at:
- ❏ 6:00–7:00 A.M. ❏ 7:00–8:00 A.M.
- ❏ 8:00–9:00 A.M. ❏ after 9:00 A.M.

B. The center must close at:
- ❏ 4:00–5:00 P.M. ❏ 5:00–6:00 P.M.
- ❏ 6:00–7:00 P.M. ❏ after 7:00 P.M.

2. I want my child to attend:
- ❏ every weekday, all day
- ❏ three days a week, all day
- ❏ every weekday morning
- ❏ every weekday afternoon
- ❏ three days a week, mornings
- ❏ three days a week, afternoons
- ❏ other_____

3. The center must be near my:
- ❏ work   ❏ home   ❏ other

4A. The center must be open:
- ❏ 12 months a year
- ❏ 9 months a year (closed during summer)

B. The center must be open:
- ❏ on the following holidays

_____

_____

_____

5. The center must have the following features:
- ❏ playground
- ❏ separate area for napping
- ❏ separate area for diapering
- ❏ plenty of toys/activities for infants
- ❏ plenty of toys/activities for toddlers

6. The maximum number of children in my child's group must be:
- ❏ 1–3   ❏ 3–6   ❏ 6–9

7. Parents will be welcome in the center at any time: ❏ yes   ❏ no

8. The center will be licensed:
- ❏ yes   ❏ no

9A. I can pay the following rate for day-care services:
- ❏ $50–$100 a week
- ❏ $100–$200 a week
- ❏ $200–$300 a week
- ❏ more than $300 a week

9B. I can pay the center:
- ❏ weekly   ❏ monthly
- ❏ biyearly   ❏ once a year

Teacher Qualifications

10A. My child's teachers will have the following minimum qualifications:
- ❏ high school degree
- ❏ college/advanced degree
- ❏ previous child-care experience
- ❏ previous infant-care experience
- ❏ English speaking
- ❏ infant/child CPR certification
- ❏ nonsmoker
- ❏ 7-year, national background check including civil, criminal and driving

Child-Care Management

11A. Will there be regularly scheduled meetings between provider and parent(s)?   ❏ yes   ❏ no

B. If yes, how often?
- ❏ weekly   ❏ biweekly   ❏ monthly

C. When will the provider get your weekly work schedule?
- ❏ at previous week's meeting
- ❏ as needed

D. Will there be other provider/parent communication, other than at meetings?   ❏ yes   ❏ no

E. If yes, please check the other types of communication you will require from the provider on a regular basis:
- ❏ daily log

F. Please check the following items you will provide the provider and update on a regular basis:
- ❏ emergency phone numbers
- ❏ approved transportation form
- ❏ medical forms/releases

NOTES: _____

_____

Template 6
SCHOOL-AGE CHILD NEEDS ASSESSMENT

Basic Requirements

1. I need care for my school-age child from:
   ❑ 6:00–7:00 A.M. until school starts.
   ❑ 7:00 A.M. until school starts.
   ❑ when school ends until 5:00–6 P.M.
   ❑ when school ends until 6:00–7 P.M.
   ❑ when school ends until 7:00–8 P.M or later.

2A. I need someone to drive my child to school: ❑ yes ❑ no

B. I need someone to drive my child from school: ❑ yes ❑ no

3. I need someone to care for my child:
   ❑ on scheduled school holidays
   ❑ during Christmas vacation
   ❑ during spring break
   ❑ during summer vacation
   ❑ on sick days
   ❑ when school is closed because of snow, parent–teacher days, etc.

4. I would like to see my child involved in the following activities after school:
   ❑ art classes
   ❑ music lessons
   ❑ sports
   ❑ academic tutoring
   ❑ homework
   ❑ Boy Scouts
   ❑ Eagle Scouts
   ❑ Girl Scouts
   ❑ Brownies
   ❑ 4-H
   ❑ unscheduled, free time
   ❑ Other (list other activities below)

   _____

   _____

5. I can pay the following for before- and/or after-school child-care services:
   ❑ less than $50 a week
   ❑ $50–$100 a week
   ❑ $100–$200 a week
   ❑ $200–$300 a week
   ❑ more than $300 a week

6. My child is in:
   ❑ kindergarten ❑ first grade
   ❑ second grade or older

7A. If you require child care in the morning, someone to drive your child to school, and can pay $200 or more a week for child care, start by considering an in-home provider. Complete the In-Home Care Needs Assessment to be sure that this kind of care is right for you.

B. If you require after-school care, need someone to pick-up your child from school, and can pay $200 or more a week, consider an in-home provider or a family day-care provider. Complete the In-Home Care Needs Assessment or the Family Day-Care Needs Assessment.

C. If you require after-school care and can pay $50 a week, try a community center, etc.

Summer Vacation

8. During summer, my child needs care:
   ❑ 7:00 A.M.–7:00 P.M. M-F
   ❑ 9:00 A.M.–5:00 P.M. M-F
   ❑ A.M. M–F
   ❑ P.M. M–F
   ❑ Other_____

9. My child's summer vacation runs from (May, June)_____ to (August, September)_____.

10. My child is particularly interested in:
    ❑ art   ❑ music
    ❑ sports   ❑ other

11. My child is comfortable sleeping away from home: ❑ yes ❑ no

12. I can pay the following for a summer camp program:
    ❑ less than $50 a week
    ❑ $50–$100 a week
    ❑ $100–$200 a week
    ❑ $200–$300 a week
    ❑ more than $300 a week

Template 7
IN-HOME PROVIDER JOB DESCRIPTION

Basic Requirements

_____

_____

Duties and Qualifications

Duties _____

_____

_____

_____

Qualifications _____

_____

_____

_____

Salary, Holiday, and Sick Day Policy

_____

_____

_____

_____

Work Hours and Scheduling

_____

_____

_____

_____

Child-Care Management

_____

_____

_____

_____

Template 8
FAMILY DAY-CARE-CENTER DESCRIPTION

Basic Requirements

_____
_____
_____
_____
_____
_____
_____
_____
_____
_____

Provider Qualifications

_____
_____
_____
_____
_____
_____
_____
_____
_____
_____
_____
_____

Child-Care Management

_____
_____
_____
_____
_____
_____
_____
_____
_____
_____
_____
_____

Template 9
DAY-CARE-CENTER DESCRIPTION

Basic Requirements

_____
_____
_____
_____
_____
_____
_____
_____

Provider Qualifications

_____
_____
_____
_____
_____
_____
_____
_____
_____
_____
_____

Child-Care Management

_____
_____
_____
_____
_____
_____
_____
_____
_____

Template 10
SCHOOL-AGE CHILD-CARE DESCRIPTION

Basic Requirements

_____
_____
_____
_____
_____
_____
_____
_____

Provider Qualifications

_____
_____
_____
_____
_____
_____
_____
_____
_____
_____
_____

Child-Care Management

_____
_____
_____
_____
_____
_____
_____
_____
_____
_____
_____

Template 11
PLACEMENT AGENCY SCREENING QUESTIONS

1. "How long has your agency been in business?" _____

2. "Are you independently owned or part of a chain?" _____

3. "With whom will I be dealing and will it be the same person every time I call?"
   _____

4. "How do you recruit nannies?" ❏ advertise ❏ word of mouth
   ❏ affiliated with child-care group or nanny school
   ❏ other _____

5. "Do you verify the backgrounds and experience of your nannies?" [All will answer yes, so go on to the next question.]_____

6. "How extensive is the background check? Do you check criminal records, civil records, and driving records in every state that the nanny has lived in over the past 7 years?" _____

   _____

7. "Do you do background checks yourself or do you hire an independent, third party to investigate?" _____

8. "Will I see the written résumés on the nannies I am considering?" _____

9. "How do you check references? What questions do you ask former employers, and how do you really know they were former employers?" [Many people make up references. They have friends answer the calls who then tell potential employers everything they want to hear!]_____

   _____

10. "Do the nanny candidates sign with you exclusively?" _____

11. "Do they pay a fee to be represented by you?" _____

12. "Are your nannies certified in infant and child CPR and first aid?" _____

13. "Do you provide any training for your nannies?" _____

14. "What is your fee?" _____

15. "What form of payment will you accept? Check or credit cards?" _____

16. "Do you get paid up front or after placement?" _____

17. "Will you give me a refund if my nanny doesn't work out?" _____

18. "If my chosen nanny leaves me within a certain amount of time, do I get a refund or will you find me another nanny?" _____

Template 12
YOUR NEWSPAPER ADVERTISEMENT

Nanny Wanted: _____ , _____ for
_____Question 1_____   _____Question 2_____

_____ , _____ , _____ ,
_____Question 5_____   _____Question 3a to 3g_____   _____Question 7_____

_____ , _____ , _____ ,
_____Question 7_____   _____Question 7_____   _____Question 6_____

_____ , Call _____ .
_____Question 8_____   *Fill in your name, area code*
                                      and phone number and time
                                      available.

Template 13
TELEPHONE PRESCREEN QUESTIONS
FOR IN-HOME PROVIDERS

Candidate:_____

Phone Number:_____

Date of Call:_____

Start by describing the position, pay, and hours. Then ask:

1. "Would you be able to work at the proposed pay and number of hours a week?"
   ❏ yes   ❏ no

2. "Please give me an overview of your experience and qualifications for work in child care." _____

   _____

   _____

3. "Are you certified in CPR, infant CPR, and first aid?"

   _____

4. "Why did you leave your most recent job?"_____

   _____

   _____

5. "Tell me why you are interested in this job." _____

   _____

   _____

6. "What are your long-term plans or career goals?" _____

   _____

7. "Would you agree to a national investigation of your background?" ❏ yes ❏ no

8. Include any other questions you would like to ask in the following space or on another sheet.

   _____

   _____

   _____

IN-PERSON INTERVIEW

_____

Date: *Time:*   *Location:*

Template 14
IN-PERSON INTERVIEW QUESTIONS
FOR IN-HOME PROVIDERS

Candidate:_____

Date of Interview:_____

Once again, describe in detail the position, pay, and hours. Hand her the job description and run through all duties and responsibilities. Then ask:

1. "Do you have any questions or concerns about the position, pay, or hours?"
   _____

2. "What about the duties and responsibilities that this position requires?" __
   _____
   _____

3. "Tell me a little about your family background and education."_____
   _____
   _____

4. "What was your motivation for becoming a nanny?" _____
   _____

5. "Tell me why you believe you are the right person to care for my child." ____
   _____

6. "Run through a routine for a typical day with my child." _____
   _____

7. "Give me some examples of age-appropriate activities you would do with my child on a regular basis." _____
   _____

8. "How would you discipline my child?" _____

9. "How would you handle an emergency, for example a fire in the house?"____
   _____

10. "How would you handle a medical emergency, for example if my child was choking?" _____
    _____

11. "Do you have any health or medical problems that would interfere with your ability to work here?" _____
    _____

229

continued

12. Include any other questions you would like to ask in the following space or on another sheet. _____

RECORD YOUR IMPRESSIONS

Appearance:

_____
_____
_____
_____

Attitude:

_____
_____
_____
_____

Enthusiasm:

_____
_____
_____
_____

Intelligence:

_____
_____
_____
_____

Common Sense:

_____
_____
_____
_____

Interaction with your child:

_____
_____
_____
_____

Template 15
CHILD-CARE PROVIDER
PROFESSIONAL REFERENCE REPORT

Applicant: _____

Company/Parent Contacted: _____

Address: _____
_____

Phone Number: _____

Individual Contacted: _____

Reported: _____
_____

Dates of Employment _____

Starting Position _____

Ending Position _____

Salary _____

Reason for Leaving: _____

Results: _____
_____
_____
_____
_____

Dates of Employment	☐ VER	☐ INC	☐ CNV	☐ NR
Starting Position	☐ VER	☐ INC	☐ CNV	☐ NR
Ending Position	☐ VER	☐ INC	☐ CNV	☐ NR
Salary	☐ VER	☐ INC	☐ CNV	☐ NR
Reason for Leaving	☐ VER	☐ INC	☐ CNV	☐ NR*

How would you rate his/her overall job performance on a scale of 1 to 10 with 10
    being excellent? _____

Did he/she show improvement/growth in the position? _____

What were his/her strengths?_____

What were the areas that you would recommend improvements (weaknesses)?
_____

Would you reemploy?	☐ Y	☐ N
Any trouble with:		
Attendance	☐ Y	☐ N
Attitude	☐ Y	☐ N
Dependability	☐ Y	☐ N
Teamwork	☐ Y	☐ N

Additional Information:_____
_____
_____
_____
_____

*VER=VERIFIED; INC=INCORRECT; CNV=COULD NOT VERIFY; NR=NOT REPORTED

continued

Subjective Data

Did you enjoy having her in your home? _____

_____

Was she willing to put in extra effort or time when it was required?_____

_____

Is she a flexible person? Can she handle the chaos of everyday life with children?

_____

How did she handle constructive criticism? _____

_____

How would you rate her level of personal maturity? _____

How did your child feel when she left? _____

_____

Additional Questions: _____

_____

_____

_____

_____

You're Hired!

Template 16
YOUR CHILD'S EMERGENCY
MEDICAL AUTHORIZATION

To Whom it May Concern:

As the parent of _____, I hereby authorize
_____to approve emergency medical treat-
ment for our child. Our child's date of birth is_____.
He/she is allergic to _____. His/her
pediatrician is _____, who may be reached at
(   )_____. My child's blood type is _____.

Our child's insurance carrier is_____ and the policy
number is_____.

Our address is _____
and our phone number is (   )_____.

_____
(parent's signature)

Template 17
APPROVED PICKUP AND TRANSPORTATION

FOR _____
(your child's name)

The following persons are authorized to pick up _____ and
drive him/her home from your facility: *(your child's name)*

_____

_____

_____

_____

_____

Signed:

_____

(Parent's Name)   *(Date)*

Template 18
PROVIDER DAILY EXPENSE REPORT

Name:_____   Date: _____

Expense Detail

Breakfast:

Lunch:

Dinner:

Snacks:

Parking:

Entertainment:

Auto Mileage @ $.29/mile:

Telephone:

Other:

TOTAL EXPENSES:

Less Advance:

Balance Due Me:

The above is a true accounting of the costs I have incurred.

_____
(provider signature)

PLEASE ATTACH RECEIPTS

(For Parent: Date paid _____   Amount _____)

Template 19
DAILY LOG

FOR: _____

(your child's name)

DATE: _____

Breakfast Time: _____

Foods Eaten: _____

Lunch Time: _____

Foods Eaten: _____

Dinner Time: _____

Foods Eaten: _____

Snacks Time: _____

Foods Eaten: _____

Naps Time: _____

Length of Nap (min/hrs): _____

Potty Time: _____ Type: _____

Time: _____ Type: _____

Time: _____ Type: _____

Medication Time: _____ Type: _____

Activities (please list) _____

_____

_____

MISC. NOTES: _____

_____

_____

_____

Template 20
MEETING AGENDA

Meeting Date: _____ Meeting Time: _____

ITEM 1: _____
meeting notes: _____
_____
_____

ITEM 2: _____
meeting notes: _____
_____
_____

ITEM 3: _____
meeting notes: _____
_____
_____

ITEM 4: _____
meeting notes: _____
_____

ITEM 5: _____
meeting notes: _____
_____

ITEM 6: _____
meeting notes: _____
_____

NEXT MEETING: Date: _____ Time: _____

(Make two copies of this form—one for parent and one for provider)

Template 21
HOUSEHOLD INVENTORY ITEMS

I, _____, acknowledge that on _____, I have

(Name of Provider)   *(today's date)*

received the following items that are the property of _____.

                                                                                (parents' names)

_____

_____

_____

_____

_____

_____

_____

_____

_____

_____

These items are to be used by me in my capacity as an employee of
_____and are to be returned upon request, upon

(Parents' Names)

my voluntarily leaving their employ, or at termination. Additionally, I
agree not to duplicate any keys or to give any other party access to

_____.

_____   _____
   Provider Name   Phone Number

Template 22
QUARTERLY REVIEW

Date _____ Provider's name _____

How would you rate his/her overall job performance on a scale of 1 to 10 with 10
    being excellent? _____

    last quarter's rating _____

Issues: _____

_____

_____

_____

(This is where you copy and paste your "issues notes" from the weekly agenda
and the "needs improvement" section of last quarter's review.)

_____

_____

_____

_____

_____

_____

_____

_____

Is he/she showing improvement/growth in the position? _____

_____

_____

Any trouble with:
    attendance   ❏ yes ❏ no
    attitude   ❏ yes ❏ no
    dependability   ❏ yes ❏ no
    teamwork   ❏ yes ❏ no

Needs improvement: _____

_____

_____

_____

Future plans: _____

_____

_____

Provider's comments for future growth:_____

_____

Template 23
IS THERE A PROBLEM?

1. Is there any mention of this type of behavior from any previous employer?
   ❏ yes ❏ no
   If yes, add notes: _____

   _____

   (This is why it is critical to go back at least five years. If alcohol or substance abuse is the problem, it could be an old one and may have not been experienced by the last employer.)

2. Were there any issues regarding the provider's driving record? ❏ yes ❏ no
   If yes, when, where, and how did provider explain to your satisfaction during interview? _____

   _____

   (Another reason why a review of driving records is critical. No DUI's or DWI's is a good indication of sobriety but is only good until the date of the last record check.)

3. Any criminal convictions for alcohol- or substance-abuse-related issues?
   ❏ yes ❏ no
   If yes, when, where, and how did provider explain to your satisfaction during interview? _____

   _____

4. When did you notice a decline in work behavior or performance? _____

   _____

   _____

5. Was there a specific incident that precipitated your concern? ❏ yes ❏ no

6. Have you previously discussed issues with the provider that now appears to be precursor behavior? ❏ yes ❏ no
   If so, what does your Provider's Personal File reflect? _____

   _____

   _____

7. How is your provider's behavior affecting your child(ren)? _____

   _____

   _____

   Are you worried about their safety?   ❏ yes ❏ no
   Do they know or notice something is wrong?   ❏ yes ❏ no
   Is/Are your child(ren) reticent or anxious about being with the provider alone?
                                                     ❏ yes ❏ no
   Are your child(ren) acting or speaking out because they sense something about the provider has changed?   ❏ yes ❏ no

Template 24
PROVIDER TERMINATION CONTRACT

_____

_____

_____

(Date)

_____

_____

_____

Dear _____ :
　　　　　　(Nanny)

Effective _____, *your employment with* _____ *is*
　　　　　　(date)　　　　　　　　　　　　　　　*(employer)*
terminated. Your final paycheck for services rendered will be given to
you on _____. *(This paycheck will also include any severance pay-*
　　　(date)
ments which we have agreed to pay under the terms of your employment.)
We will provide you with a separate notice advising you in connection with
any continuing health benefits or other employee benefits programs which
may be available to you after termination, if any.*

We will meet you at _____*o'clock today to discuss exit arrange-*
　　　　　　　　　　(time)
ments connected with your termination. At that time you should return
the items listed on the attached Household Inventory Items list.

If you have any questions regarding the above or other aspects of
your separation from employment, please be prepared to discuss them
with us at your exit interview.

We wish you the best of luck in your future endeavors.

Very truly yours,

_____

Parent(s) signature(s)

*If parents are supplying health or other benefits, they should consult each
specific program for instructions regarding terminated employees' options for main-
taining coverage subsequently.

Template 25
PROVIDER EXIT INTERVIEW

Date: _____ Provider's Name: _____

Dates of Employment _____ to _____

Starting Position _____

Ending Position _____

Salary _____

Reason for Leaving _____

_____

_____

How would you rate his/her overall job performance on a scale of 1 to 10 with 10 being excellent? _____

Did he/she show improvement/growth in the position? _____

_____

_____

_____

What were his/her strengths? _____

_____

_____

_____

What were the areas that you would recommend improvements (weaknesses)? _____

_____

_____

Would you reemploy?   ❏ yes   ❏ no

Any trouble with:
   attendance   ❏ yes   ❏ no
   attitude   ❏ yes   ❏ no
   dependability   ❏ yes   ❏ no
   teamwork   ❏ yes   ❏ no

Additional information: _____

_____

_____

_____

_____

Template 26
FAMILY DAY-CARE TELEPHONE
PRESCREEN QUESTIONS

Family Day-Care Operator Name: _____

Location: _____

Phone Number: _____ Date of Call: _____

Start by telling the operator a little about your child—name, age, sex, etc., and describe what you are looking for, especially the days and number of hours a week you require care. Then ask:

1. "What days are you open and for what hours?" _____
   _____

2. "How much do you charge?" _____
   _____

3. "Do you have any openings now, or in the near future?" _____

4. (If your state requires licensing) "Is your center licensed?" _____

5. "Please give me an overview of your experience and qualifications for work
   in child care." _____
   _____
   _____
   _____

6. "Are you certified in CPR, infant CPR, and first aid?" _____

7. "How many children do you care for and what are their ages?" _____
   _____
   _____
   _____

8. "How many children do you care for at any given time?" _____
   _____
   _____
   _____

9. "Do you have any assistants?" _____
   _____
   _____
   _____

10. "Would you agree to an investigation of your background?" _____

11. (If the provider has assistants) "Would you agree to an investigation of your
    staff?" _____

continued

12. "Would you agree to an investigation of everyone who lives in your house and has access to my child?" _____

_____

_____

13. "Could you please describe your facility?" _____

_____

_____

_____

14. "Approximately how many square feet is the indoor space? _____
And the outdoor play area?" _____

15. "Describe a typical day my child would have in your center." _____

_____

_____

_____

_____

16. "Is there a secure outdoor area for the children to play?" _____

17. "Is there a napping space for infants and older children?" _____

18. "Is there storage space to keep my child's belongings?" _____

Include any other questions you would like to ask in the following space or on another sheet. _____

_____

_____

_____

_____

_____

_____

Template 27
FAMILY DAY-CARE ON-SITE VISIT CHECKLIST

Date: _____ Time: _____

Safety

Is the neighborhood safe?	❏ yes	❏ no
House/apartment secure?	❏ yes	❏ no
House/apartment well maintained?	❏ yes	❏ no
Smoke detectors working *(check to see if light indicating charged battery is on)*?	❏ yes	❏ no
Fire extinguishers current *(check data on canister or attached card)*?	❏ yes	❏ no
Medicines locked up?	❏ yes	❏ no
Household/cleaning products locked up?	❏ yes	❏ no
Electrical outlets covered?	❏ yes	❏ no
Adequate first-aid kit?	❏ yes	❏ no
Screened windows?	❏ yes	❏ no
Secured electrical cords?	❏ yes	❏ no
Evacuation plan/emergency drills?	❏ yes	❏ no
Kitchen equipment inaccessible?	❏ yes	❏ no
Stairs gated and inaccessible?	❏ yes	❏ no

Sanitation/Cleanliness

Passes the "Sniff Test"?	❏ yes	❏ no
House appears clean/organized?	❏ yes	❏ no
Play area clean/organized?	❏ yes	❏ no
Are sheets/blankets in nap room clean?	❏ yes	❏ no
Surfaces clean?	❏ yes	❏ no
Toys/games clean?	❏ yes	❏ no
Food preparation areas clean?	❏ yes	❏ no
Bathroom clean/sanitized?	❏ yes	❏ no

Indoor Play Area

Is it cheerful/engaging?	❏ yes	❏ no
Are toys in good repair?	❏ yes	❏ no
Enough age-appropriate toys/games?	❏ yes	❏ no
Enough crafts/art supplies?	❏ yes	❏ no
Art work is displayed?	❏ yes	❏ no
Can adults see the entire room at once?	❏ yes	❏ no
Water available?	❏ yes	❏ no
Easy access to bathrooms?	❏ yes	❏ no
Cubbyholes for each child?	❏ yes	❏ no
Adequate light/ventilation?	❏ yes	❏ no

Nap Area

Quiet/restful location?	❏ yes	❏ no
Adequate ventilation?	❏ yes	❏ no
Individual cots and cribs?	❏ yes	❏ no
Cots/cribs away from curtains with pull cords?	❏ yes	❏ no
Cots/cribs new and in good condition?	❏ yes	❏ no

continued

Cot/crib bolts and screws secure? ☐ yes ☐ no
Cot/crib mattresses in good condition? ☐ yes ☐ no
Crib side slats no farther than $2^3/_8$" apart? ☐ yes ☐ no
Distance from crib mattress to top of railing at least 22"? ☐ yes ☐ no
Crib corner posts are less than 1" high? ☐ yes ☐ no

Outside Play Area (if any)

Enough space? ☐ yes ☐ no
Grass/plants/flowers? ☐ yes ☐ no
Enclosed and secure? ☐ yes ☐ no
Adult can see entire play area at once? ☐ yes ☐ no
Sandboxes covered? ☐ yes ☐ no
Thick pads under play equipment? ☐ yes ☐ no
Play equipment in good repair? ☐ yes ☐ no
Garden tools inaccessible? ☐ yes ☐ no

If No Outside Play Area

Is outside time scheduled every day? ☐ yes ☐ no
Is a park nearby? ☐ yes ☐ no
Is the park safe? ☐ yes ☐ no

Operator

Warm/friendly? ☐ yes ☐ no
Smiles? ☐ yes ☐ no
Positive and open? ☐ yes ☐ no
Pleasant tone of voice? ☐ yes ☐ no
Made you feel at home? ☐ yes ☐ no
Good communicator? ☐ yes ☐ no
Clean? ☐ yes ☐ no
Organized/under control? ☐ yes ☐ no
Truly likes children? ☐ yes ☐ no

Program

Set daily schedule? ☐ yes ☐ no
Posted for parents? ☐ yes ☐ no
Adequate play time? ☐ yes ☐ no
Adequate nap time? ☐ yes ☐ no
Nutritious meals/snacks? ☐ yes ☐ no
Television allowed? ☐ yes ☐ no
Access to pets? ☐ yes ☐ no

Administration

Written pricing/policies? ☐ yes ☐ no
Additional staff? ☐ yes ☐ no
Family member access to children? ☐ yes ☐ no
Licensing documents in order? ☐ yes ☐ no
Fully insured (ask to see documentation)? ☐ yes ☐ no
Parents welcome at all times? ☐ yes ☐ no
Daily log? ☐ yes ☐ no
Authorized persons only may pick up children? ☐ yes ☐ no
Regular meetings with parents? ☐ yes ☐ no

Additional Comments: _____

■■■

246

Template 28
FAMILY DAY-CARE ON-SITE VISIT
INTERVIEW QUESTIONS

1. "How would you discipline my child?" _____
   _____
   _____
   _____

2. "What indoor activities do you generally encourage?" _____
   _____
   _____
   _____

3. "What outdoor activities do you encourage?" _____
   _____
   _____
   _____

4. "How do you handle mealtimes?" _____
   _____
   _____
   _____

5. "What would you do if my child became ill at your house?" _____
   _____
   _____
   _____

6. "How do you handle situations where one child needs special attention, such
   as one child needing to go potty, or a child who has hurt himself and needs
   medical attention? What do you do with the other children?" _____
   _____
   _____
   _____

7. "Do you have any regular visitors to your home during child-care operating hours?
   Who are they and what is their relationship to you?" _____
   _____
   _____
   _____

continued

8. "What is the average length of time you provide child care for your families?"

_____

_____

_____

9. "What is the biggest challenge you face every day?" _____

_____

_____

_____

10. "How do you keep yourself refreshed and enthusiastic about this type of work?"

_____

_____

_____

11. "How do you handle days when you are too ill to care for the children?" ___

_____

_____

_____

Additional questions specific to your child's age: _____

_____

_____

_____

_____

Template 29
DAY-CARE TELEPHONE PRESCREEN QUESTIONS

Name of Center: _____

Name of person you spoke with: _____

Title: _____

Location: _____

Phone Number: _____ Date of Call: _____

Start by telling the provider a little about your child—name, age, sex, etc., and describe what you are looking for, especially the days and number of hours a week you require care. Then ask:

1. "What days are you open and for what hours?" _____

2. "How much do you charge?" _____

3. "Do you have any openings now, or in the near future?" _____

4. "Does your center comply with all state regulations? Can I review your licensing documents?" _____

5. "What type of experience, training, and qualifications are your providers required to have?" _____

   _____

6. "Are all of your providers certified in CPR, infant CPR, and first aid?" _____

7. "What is the teacher–child ratio for children my child's age?" _____

8. "How many children are enrolled in your center and what are their ages?"

   _____

9. "Can parents drop in at any time?" _____

10. If your state requires it, ask: "Do all of your employees meet the state's requirements on in-service training?" _____

11. "Have all of your providers been background-checked by the state or by an independent investigative service, and if so, could I review the dossiers of providers who would care for my child?" _____

12. If your state requires it, ask: "Are all of your employees properly immunized?"

   _____

13. "Could you please describe your facility?" _____

   _____

14. "Describe a typical day my child would have in your center." _____

   _____

   _____

15. Include any other questions you would like to ask on another sheet.

Center Visit

Date: _____ Time: _____

249

Template 30
DAY-CARE ON-SITE VISIT CHECKLIST

Safety

Building secure?	❏ yes	❏ no
Building well maintained?	❏ yes	❏ no
Smoke detectors working *(check to see if light indicating charge battery is on)*?	❏ yes	❏ no
Fire extinguishers current *(check date on canister or attached card)*?	❏ yes	❏ no
Electrical outlets covered?	❏ yes	❏ no
Adequate first-aid kit?	❏ yes	❏ no
Dangerous supplies inaccessible?	❏ yes	❏ no
Screened windows?	❏ yes	❏ no
Secured electrical cords?	❏ yes	❏ no
Evacuation plan/emergency drills?	❏ yes	❏ no
Stairs gated and inaccessible?	❏ yes	❏ no

Sanitation/Cleanliness

Passes the "Sniff Test"?	❏ yes	❏ no
Does center appear clean/well organized?	❏ yes	❏ no
Play area clean/organized?	❏ yes	❏ no
Are sheets/blankets in nap room clean?	❏ yes	❏ no
Surfaces clean?	❏ yes	❏ no
Toys/games clean?	❏ yes	❏ no
Food preparation areas clean?	❏ yes	❏ no
Bathroom clean/sanitized?	❏ yes	❏ no

Indoor Play Area

Is it cheerful/engaging?	❏ yes	❏ no
Are toys in good repair?	❏ yes	❏ no
Enough age-appropriate toys/games?	❏ yes	❏ no
Enough crafts/art supplies?	❏ yes	❏ no
Art work is displayed?	❏ yes	❏ no
Can adults see the entire room at once?	❏ yes	❏ no
Water available?	❏ yes	❏ no
Easy access to bathrooms?	❏ yes	❏ no
Cubbyholes for each child?	❏ yes	❏ no
Adequate light/ventilation?	❏ yes	❏ no

Nap Area

Quiet/restful location?	❏ yes	❏ no
Adequate ventilation?	❏ yes	❏ no
Individual cots and cribs?	❏ yes	❏ no
Cots/cribs away from curtains with pull cords?	❏ yes	❏ no
Cots/cribs new and in good condition?	❏ yes	❏ no
Cot/crib bolts and screws secure?	❏ yes	❏ no
Cot/crib mattresses in good condition?	❏ yes	❏ no

Crib side slats no farther than 2⅜" apart? ☐ yes ☐ no
Distance from crib mattress to top of railing at least 22"? ☐ yes ☐ no
Crib corner posts less than 1" high? ☐ yes ☐ no

Outside Play Area

Enough space? ☐ yes ☐ no
Grass/plants/flowers? ☐ yes ☐ no
Enclosed and secure? ☐ yes ☐ no
Adult can see entire play area at once? ☐ yes ☐ no
Sandboxes covered? ☐ yes ☐ no
Thick pads under play equipment? ☐ yes ☐ no
Play equipment in good repair? ☐ yes ☐ no

Center Operator

Good communicator? ☐ yes ☐ no
Accessible? ☐ yes ☐ no
Professional? ☐ yes ☐ no
Organized? ☐ yes ☐ no
Does center appear to be well managed? ☐ yes ☐ no

Provider who will care for your child

Warm/friendly? ☐ yes ☐ no
Smiles? ☐ yes ☐ no
Positive and open? ☐ yes ☐ no
Pleasant tone of voice? ☐ yes ☐ no
Made you feel at home? ☐ yes ☐ no
Good communicator? ☐ yes ☐ no
Clean? ☐ yes ☐ no
Organized/under control? ☐ yes ☐ no
Truly likes children? ☐ yes ☐ no

Program

Set daily schedule? ☐ yes ☐ no
Posted for parents? ☐ yes ☐ no
Adequate play time? ☐ yes ☐ no
Adequate nap time? ☐ yes ☐ no
Nutritious meals/snacks? ☐ yes ☐ no

Administration

Written pricing/policies? ☐ yes ☐ no
Provider background checks available for review? ☐ yes ☐ no
Regulatory documents in order? ☐ yes ☐ no
Fully insured (ask to see documentation)? ☐ yes ☐ no
Parents welcome at all times? ☐ yes ☐ no
Daily log? ☐ yes ☐ no
Authorized persons only may pick up children? ☐ yes ☐ no
Regular meetings with parents? ☐ yes ☐ no

Additional Comments: _____

Template 31
DAY-CARE ON-SITE VISIT INTERVIEW QUESTIONS

1. "How would you discipline my child?" _____
   _____
   _____
   _____

2. "What indoor activities would you engage in with my child?" _____
   _____
   _____
   _____

3. "What outdoor activities would you engage in with my child?" _____
   _____
   _____
   _____

4. "What kind of background and experience do you bring to your job here?"
   _____
   _____
   _____

5. "What is the biggest challenge you face every day?" _____
   _____
   _____
   _____

6. "How do you keep yourself refreshed and enthusiastic about this type of work?"
   _____
   _____
   _____
   _____

   Additional questions specific to your child's age: _____
   _____
   _____
   _____
   _____
   _____
   _____
   _____

Template 32
AFTER-SCHOOL PROGRAM TELEPHONE
PRESCREEN QUESTIONS

For school age children using programs not operated by licensed day care or local schools.

1. What are the program hours? _____

2. How much does the program cost? _____

3. Can a child go every day of the school week or just a few days? _____

   _____

4. What kinds of organized activities does the program offer? _____

   _____

   _____

5. Are all ages mixed together, or all activities organized according to age? ___

   _____

6. Do the children have any free, unscheduled time, or is it all taken up with the formal activities? [Some children need a break after a long day at school.]

   _____

7. Is there quiet time for homework and is tutoring available? _____

   _____

8. Are nutritious snacks available? _____

9. How many children attend the program and what are their ages? [Make sure that plenty of children your child's age are enrolled.] _____

   _____

10. What is the adult–child ratio? [Make sure that there are enough adults around so that your child receives some individual attention.] _____

    _____

11. How are the teachers selected? What are their qualifications, and have they undergone thorough background investigations? _____

    _____

12. Are all of the teachers certified in CPR and first aid? _____

13. Does the program offer transportation from local schools? _____

14. If transportation is provided, do the drivers have clean driving records? Are seat belts required at all times?_____

15. Is the program fully licensed with the state? _____

16. Is the program fully insured?_____

continued

17. Can you give me the names and phone numbers of two parents I can call for references? _____

_____

COMMENTS: _____

_____

_____

_____

Template 33
AFTER-SCHOOL PROGRAM ON-SITE VISIT CHECKLIST

Safety

Is the neighborhood safe?	❏ yes	❏ no
Program facility secure?	❏ yes	❏ no
Facility well maintained?	❏ yes	❏ no
Smoke detectors working (*check to see if light indicating charged battery is on*)?	❏ yes	❏ no
Fire extinguishers current (*check date on canister or attached card*)?	❏ yes	❏ no
Electrical outlets covered?	❏ yes	❏ no
Adequate first-aid kit?	❏ yes	❏ no
Screened windows?	❏ yes	❏ no
Secured electrical cords?	❏ yes	❏ no
Evacuation plan/emergency drills?	❏ yes	❏ no

Sanitation/Cleanliness

Passes the "Sniff Test"?	❏ yes	❏ no
Does facility appear clean/organized?	❏ yes	❏ no
Play area clean/organized?	❏ yes	❏ no
Surfaces clean?	❏ yes	❏ no
Toys/games clean?	❏ yes	❏ no
Food preparation areas clean?	❏ yes	❏ no
Bathroom clean/sanitized?	❏ yes	❏ no

Indoor Play Area

Is it cheerful/engaging?	❏ yes	❏ no
Are toys in good repair?	❏ yes	❏ no
Enough age-appropriate toys/games?	❏ yes	❏ no
Enough crafts/art supplies?	❏ yes	❏ no
Art work is displayed?	❏ yes	❏ no
Can adults see the entire room at once?	❏ yes	❏ no
Water available?	❏ yes	❏ no
Easy access to bathrooms?	❏ yes	❏ no
Adequate light/ventilation?	❏ yes	❏ no

Outside Play Area (if any)

Enough space?	❏ yes	❏ no
Grass/plants/flowers?	❏ yes	❏ no
Enclosed and secure?	❏ yes	❏ no
Adult can see entire play area at once?	❏ yes	❏ no
Sandboxes covered?	❏ yes	❏ no
Thick pads under play equipment?	❏ yes	❏ no
Play equipment in good repair?	❏ yes	❏ no

continued

Program Operator and Staff

Warm/friendly?	❏ yes	❏ no
Smiles?	❏ yes	❏ no
Positive and open?	❏ yes	❏ no
Made you feel at home?	❏ yes	❏ no
Good communicators?	❏ yes	❏ no
Clean?	❏ yes	❏ no
Organized/under control?	❏ yes	❏ no
Truly like children?	❏ yes	❏ no

Program

Daily schedule posted for parents?	❏ yes	❏ no
Nutritious meals/snacks?	❏ yes	❏ no
Television allowed?	❏ yes	❏ no
Enough activities to keep your child engaged and interested?	❏ yes	❏ no
Plenty of other children that are your child's age?	❏ yes	❏ no

Administration

Written prices and policies?	❏ yes	❏ no
Fully insured (*ask to see documentation*)?	❏ yes	❏ no
Parents welcome at all times?	❏ yes	❏ no
Authorized persons only may pick up children?	❏ yes	❏ no

Additional Comments _____

_____

_____

_____

_____

_____

Template 34
REFERENCE REPORT

Instructor: _____

Parent Contacted: _____

Address: _____

_____

_____

Phone Number: (____) _____

How would you rate his/her overall teaching performance on a scale of 1 to 10 with 10 being excellent? _____

What were his/her strengths? _____

_____

_____

_____

What were the areas that you would recommend improvements (weaknesses)?

_____

_____

_____

Would you let your child take his/her class again?   ❏ yes   ❏ no

Additional questions: _____

_____

_____

_____

_____

_____

Template 35
CAMP TELEPHONE PRESCREEN QUESTIONS

1. What is the camp's overall philosophy? _____
_____
_____

2. Does the camp promote competition and healthy rivalry among teams, or is the camp focused on noncompetitive, cooperative learning?
_____
_____

3. How is that philosophy carried out by the staff? _____
_____
_____

4. What are the different activities campers can participate in? _____
_____
_____
_____

5. What does a camper's day look like? _____
_____
_____
_____

6. Is the camp accredited by the ACA?_____
_____

7. What is the background of the director? _____
_____

8. What is the ratio of counselors to campers? _____

9. What are the ages of the counselors? _____

10. Do the counselors have previous experience caring for children?_____
_____
_____

11. How does the camp recruit counselors? How are they screened? Does the camp require comprehensive background checks that include review of a criminal record? _____
_____
_____

12. How are the counselors trained? Are they certified in CPR and first aid?___
_____
_____

13. How does the camp handle special needs, including allergy and insulin medication, restricted diets, etc.? Is there a nurse on staff? _____

_____

_____

14. How are behavior and disciplinary problems handled? _____

_____

_____

15. If the camp transports children to and from camp or various camp activities, how are the drivers screened? Do they have valid driver's licenses? Have their driving records been reviewed? _____

_____

_____

16. Can I speak to two parents who have enrolled their child in the camp in the last year? _____

_____

_____

Legal Kit

LIMITATIONS

This child-care packet is intended to provide useful legal and management information that will enable you to safely avoid the major landmines that await the unwary child-care employer. We believe that this kit accomplishes such a purpose. Unfortunately, however, state laws vary significantly with respect to many of the legal concepts that will govern the relationship between you and the person you hire to provide child-care services for you. Additionally, space limitations and the scope of this packet preclude the discussion of many other important areas of state and federal law that may affect such relationships. As a result, the use of any information or of any forms contained herein is your responsibility; and you are encouraged to consult a licensed lawyer in your state to make sure that such information and forms are applicable to your particular situation.

You should also recognize that the information contained herein is relevant as of the current date and that laws change, sometimes significantly. Make sure that the information provided herein is current and relevant at the time of its use by you. Again, consultation with a licensed lawyer in your state is encouraged.

INTRODUCTION

Although many child-care relationships are entered into orally, without obtaining suitable background checks and without complying with legal formalities, it should be recognized that these arrangements amount to little more than playing "Russian Roulette" with a precious commodity— your child. These informal arrangements can result in very serious legal problems, including fines and penalties from both federal and state governments. They may also result in your being liable for willful or negligent acts of your child-care provider (to your child or perhaps even to another child who is in your child-care provider's hands).

While following all of the suggestions contained in this kit will not guarantee that your experience with child care will be free from problems, at least the "Russian Roulette" scenario can be converted into a process that involves reasonable risks commensurate with your need for child care. You and your child-care provider will also develop a more clear understanding of what is expected from the relationship.

Part I of this kit will deal with the legal contract between you and your child-care provider. To simplify this potentially otherwise intimidating process, the sample legal contract form is followed by a section in which each paragraph of the contract is explained in such a way that you will be able to understand its relevance in a general legal context and, more importantly, to your particular situation.

After you have selected an appropriate child-care provider and have signed your child-care contract, you will be required to comply with a myriad of state and federal laws, some of which will require you to prepare and file forms and other information with the federal government and one or more of your state agencies. Part II of this kit will guide you through this maze of paperwork in easy to understand how-to language.

Part III contains a list of each Internal Revenue Service (IRS) form you will require. You will also find a brief description of each form or publication and its purpose.

There are circumstances for which the sample form of legal contract included in this kit may not be appropriate, although much of the information discussed herein with respect to the hiring process and the legal contract should still prove useful. For example, if you intend to use the resources of a day-care center outside your home (which could be a large chain or a smaller provider using a home-based facility to care for a limited number of children), you should expect that those child-care providers will ask you to sign a contract form prepared by them. Before accepting their contract, review the one provided in this kit to make sure you are aware of areas you need covered.

PART I   THE LEGAL CONTRACT

Now that you have successfully navigated the hiring process and located an acceptable candidate to provide your child care, you will need to attack the formidable task of defining the legal relationship between you and your provider. This daunting task can be simplified greatly by reading and using the following materials.

While these materials should provide you with the necessary tools to accomplish this task, consultation with a legal adviser in your state should always be considered. In no event should you use any "form" without clearly understanding all of its implications.

Now, for the contract. As you begin to focus on the terms of the contract, you should consider doing each of the following:

- Have a preliminary discussion with your child-care provider to clearly define the most important contract issues, such as duties, hours of work, pay, etc.

- Always retain at least one "clean copy" of the blank form of legal contract (and the other forms that are included in this kit) so that you can make extra copies or use the forms again. See pages 264–269 in this appendix for the blank contract form.

- Prepare a draft contract for your review and then edit that contract appropriately before submitting it to your child-care provider. After you are satisfied with its content, submit the contract in draft form to your child-care provider and have a face-to-face discussion about the draft contract so that each of you fully understands what is expected.

- Prepare a final contract that includes as few handwritten changes or other interlineations to the typed version as possible. When changes must be made, use the Contract Addendum that is attached as Schedule 2 to the sample contract (see page 270 in this appendix). Each page of the Contract Addendum should be initialed by you and your child-care provider to indicate agreement and then affixed to the primary contract form. If it should be necessary to use handwritten modifications or other interlineations in the final contract, both you and your child-care provider should initial each of these modifications and interlineations.

- Both you and your child-care provider should sign at least two copies of the entire contract. One of these signed copies should be retained by your child-care provider and the other signed copy should be retained by you and filed in your safekeeping files.

- Make sure that you have received all of the certificates and other information that your child-care provider is required to deliver to you pursuant to the legal contract (such as driver's license information, insurance certificates, CPR certificates, etc.) and establish a bookkeeping system to make sure that this information is current at all times.

- Determine the requirements that will be applicable to your child-care arrangements (e.g., amount and frequency of payments after required deductions) and institute an effective bookkeeping system to provide payments and to document such payments to meet sufficiently your state and federal law requirements, particularly those administered by the IRS.

- Make sure all employment-related information and forms to be filed by you and your child-care provider have been identified, completed, and filed with the appropriate state and federal regulatory agencies. Also make sure that your bookkeeping system provides a "tickler" system to remind you of the ongoing filing requirements and the scheduled changes in the forms (such as changes in tax calculations required by inflation adjustments).

- Finally, take a step back and realize that your considerable efforts should reward you with a safe trip through the perilous minefield.

The Legal Contract

The blank sample contract appears below. See pages 101–105 in Chapter Five for a sample completed contract illustrating the type of information that *may* be included in your particular contract. Following these forms, there is a discussion of each paragraph of the contract and the contract schedules; and, when appropriate, instructions for completing the blank spaces in the form contract and contract schedules.

Contract for Child Care

THIS CONTRACT FOR CHILD CARE (the "Contract") is made and entered into on the 1st day of _____ 19_____ between _____ ("Employer") and _____ ("Employee") and contains the terms and conditions of Employee's engagement by Employer to provide the child-care services herein described. The following sets forth those terms and conditions:

1. Term.

This Contract shall commence on _____, 19_____, and shall continue indefinitely thereafter until either Employee or Employer shall provide written notice to the other of such party's notice of termination. Any such notice of termination, and all rights and obligations of the parties under this Contract shall be effective immediately upon the delivery of such notice personally by one party to the other or upon the deposit of such written notice in the United States Mail, certified mail, return receipt requested, addressed to the party to whom such notice is to be delivered at the address for such party set forth below. Employee expressly acknowledges and agrees that this Contract is a contract terminable at will by either party at any time, without notice (other than the limited notice described above) and with or without cause, and that, except as may be specifically provided for in Paragraph 10 below, upon termination, Employee shall not be entitled to receive any severance pay, vacation pay, sick pay or any other compensation or benefits. Employee hereby releases Employer from making any such payments or providing any such benefit, to the fullest extent permitted by law.

2. Children.

Employee agrees to provide child-care services for the following children ("the Children"):

_____	_____
Name	*Date of Birth*
_____	_____
Name	*Date of Birth*
_____	_____
Name	*Date of Birth*

3. Location and Schedule of Hours.

The Employee will provide child care to the Children at _____, except to the extent that the responsibilities of Employee as specified in this Contract require Employee to provide transportation for the Children or otherwise render child care at remote locations. The Employee shall either: *(check appropriate box)*

❏ A. Provide child-care services on a live-in basis, in which event full-time lodging and regular meals will be provided to Employee by Employer; or

❏ B. Provide child-care services during the hours _____ to _____ on _____, with such variations thereof as Employer may from time to time reasonably request, but generally including at least the same number of hours of work as contemplated by the regular schedule specified herein.

Employee also acknowledges that Employer's child-care needs may from time to time require Employee to work on holidays or hours that may substantially exceed the hours included in the regular schedule specified above, and Employee agrees to make every effort to accommodate Employer's reasonable requirements in this regard.

4. Responsibilities.

The child-care duties of Employee shall generally include the responsibility of supervising and attending to the physical and emotional health, safety, and well-being of the Children at all times during which Employee is performing the child-care services contemplated hereby. Without limiting the foregoing general overall responsibilities of Employee, Employee's specific duties shall include the following: *(check all appropriate boxes and provide details)*

❏ A. Cooking and cleaning:_____

❏ B. Bathing and personal care: _____

❏ C. Health and medical care: _____

❑ D. Social and recreational: _____

_____

❑ E. Transportation: _____

_____

❑ F. Shopping and errands: _____

_____

❑ G. Educational: _____

_____

❑ H. Ironing and Laundry: _____

❑ I. Other Responsibilities and Special Instructions: See Schedule 1 attached hereto (Description of Additional Child-Care Responsibilities and Special Instructions).

In the event that Employee's duties shall include providing transportation for the Children, Employee shall furnish his or her own automobile and shall keep it maintained and repaired in good driving condition. Employee shall maintain automobile insurance on the automobile with such coverages and in such amounts as Employer may reasonably require and certificates shall be delivered to Employer from time to time as may be necessary to confirm the existence and effectiveness of such insurance. All costs associated with the automobile, including the insurance, shall be the responsibility of Employee without reimbursement or additional compensation to Employee, except to the extent that the parties shall specify otherwise in the Contract Addendum referred to in Paragraph 12 below.

5.   Payment Terms.

A. Employee will be paid: *(check appropriate box)*

❑ $ _____ per hour

❑ $ _____ per week

❑ $ _____ per month

❑ Other: _____

B. Employer will deduct the following from Employee's paycheck: *(check all appropriate boxes)*

❑ Social Security and Medicare taxes

❑ Federal income taxes

❑ State income taxes

❑ Other taxes: _____

❑ Long distance or toll phone charges: _____

❑ Other deductions *(specify)*: _____

C. The Employee acknowledges that Employer has advised Employee that Employee may be entitled to earned income credit ("EIC"). By checking the following box, Employee represents that Employee is eligible to receive advance payment of EIC, that Employee has provided Employer with a copy of a completed Form W-5 (Earned Income Credit Advance Payment Certificate) and Employee requests that Employer include the appropriate amount of EIC in Employee's paychecks:

❑ Employee is to receive advance payment of the EIC.

D. Employee will be paid at the following specified intervals and dates:

❑ Once a week on every _____

❑ Twice a month on every _____

❏ Once a month on _____
❏ Other: _____

E. Employer and Employee shall review Employee's compensation payable hereunder, in the event of Employee's continued employment hereunder, not less frequently than annually, but Employee acknowledges and agrees that Employer shall have no obligation to increase such compensation at the time of any such review, or otherwise.

6. Overtime.

If Employee works more than forty hours in any single week (and is not engaged hereunder to perform child-care services on a live-in basis), Employee shall be entitled to receive overtime pay at the rate of one and one-half times Employee's then hourly rate. No overtime pay shall be paid to Employee if Employee performs the child-care services hereunder on a live-in basis, regardless of the number of hours worked. No overtime pay shall be payable solely because Employee works on any one or more holidays or on Saturday or Sunday or for working more than eight hours in any single day, unless then applicable law shall require any such payments, or unless provided for in Paragraph 7 below.

7. Benefits.

Employer will provide Employee with the following benefits: *(check all appropriate boxes)*

❏ A. Meals: _____.
❏ B. Room and board: _____
❏ C. Sick leave:_____
❏ D. Vacations: _____
_____
_____
❏ E. Holidays: _____
_____
_____
❏ F. Health insurance: _____
❏ G. Transportation: _____
❏ H. Worker's Compensation: _____
❏ I. Other: _____

8. Licenses and Certificates.

In connection with the performance of Employee's duties hereunder, Employee has provided Employer with appropriate documentation to establish the following: *(check all appropriate boxes)*

❏ A. Valid Driver's License
❏ B. Evidence of CPR proficiency
❏ C. Evidence of Life Saving proficiency
❏ D. Evidence of First Aid proficiency
❏ E. Evidence of Health Insurance
❏ F. Evidence of Automobile Liability and other Insurance
❏ G. INS Form I-9

continues

❑ H. Form W-4
❑ I. Form W-5
❑ J. Other: _____

Employee agrees to promptly notify Employer of any change in status that would render any one or more of the foregoing (which have been checked as being applicable) inaccurate or not current.

9.   Employment Application.

Employee has completed and provided to Employer an Application for Employment ("Employment Application") in connection with Employee's employment hereunder. Such Employment Application contains a variety of facts, statements and references provided by Employee and Employer has relied upon the accuracy thereof in hiring Employee. Employee represents and warrants to Employer that all information contained in the Employment Application is true and correct in all respects and that the discovery by Employer of the falsity or inaccuracy of any such information will subject Employee to immediate termination by Employer.

10. Severance.

In the event Employee's employment is terminated at any time after Employee has worked hereunder for at least _____, and such termination of Employee is not for cause (including any termination pursuant to Paragraph 9 above), Employee shall be entitled to severance in the amount of $_____.

11. Return of Materials.

Upon termination of this Contract, regardless of how termination is effected, or whenever requested by Employer, Employee shall immediately return to Employer all of Employer's supplies, computer and other equipment, all cards, disks, tapes and other media, all educational and entertainment materials, and all other property of Employer used by Employee in rendering the child-care services hereunder, or otherwise, and which is in Employee's possession or under Employee's control.

12. Additional Terms and Provisions.

Employer and Employee recognize that certain changes in the working relationship contemplated hereby may occur from time to time and that such changes may necessitate modification of this Contract. Schedule 2 attached hereto contains a form of Contract Addendum that may be utilized by the parties to memorialize any such changes. Each such Contract Addendum that is completed and signed by the parties hereto, together with all other schedules and agreements executed by the parties pursuant hereto, shall be deemed to be incorporated in this Contract for all purposes as if set forth in full herein. No agreement, amendment or modification of this Contract shall be effective unless it is in writing and signed by both parties hereto.

13. Governing Law.

This Contract is executed and delivered by the parties in the State of_____ and shall be construed in accordance with and governed by the laws of such State.

_____

(Employer)
Employer's Address

_____

_____

(Employee)
Employee's Address

_____

_____

SCHEDULE 1: DESCRIPTION OF ADDITIONAL CHILD-CARE RESPONSIBILITIES AND SPECIAL INSTRUCTIONS

The undersigned parties have entered into a Contract for Child Care, dated _____, 19_____ (the "Contract"), pursuant to which Employee has been engaged to perform certain child-care services for Employer. Capitalized terms used herein that are defined in the Contract shall have the same meanings herein that are applicable to such terms in the Contract. The Contract contemplates that the parties have agreed upon certain duties and responsibilities relative to the child-care arrangements contemplated by the Contract or that special instructions are needed which may be more conveniently described in this Schedule. Accordingly, the following sets forth the agreements of the parties with respect to such matters:

14. Additional Child-Care Responsibilities.

_____
_____
_____
_____
_____
_____
_____
_____
_____

15. Special Instructions.

_____   Dated: _____

_____   _____

_____   (Employer)

_____   Dated: _____

_____   _____

_____   (Employee)

continued

SCHEDULE 2: CONTRACT ADDENDUM

The undersigned parties have entered into a Contract for Child Care, dated
_____, 19_____ (the "Contract"), pursuant to which Employee has been
engaged to perform certain child-care services for Employer. Capitalized terms
used herein which are defined in the Contract shall have the same meanings herein
which are applicable to such terms in the Contract. The Contract contemplates that
the parties may have agreed upon additional terms and conditions at the time of
execution of the Contract which may be more conveniently described in this Schedule or that certain changes or additions to the Contract may be necessary or appropriate following the execution of the Contract to reflect evolving circumstances or
needs. Accordingly, the following sets forth the agreements of the parties with
respect to such matters.

16. Contract Additions.

The following additions to the Contract have been agreed upon by the parties and
are hereby made a part of the Contract:

_____

_____

_____

_____

_____

_____

_____

_____

_____

_____

_____

17. Contract Amendments.

The following changes or amendments to the Contract have been agreed upon by
the parties and are hereby made a part of the Contract:

_____

_____

_____

_____

_____

Except as specifically modified by this Contract Addendum, the Contract shall remain in full force and effect.

Dated: _____

_____

(Employer)

_____

(Employer)

Dated: _____

_____

(Employee)

Taking the Legal Contract Apart

Parties.

This unnumbered introductory paragraph contains the date the agreement is signed and the names of the contracting parties, you as the "Employer" and your child-care provider as the "Employee." After inserting the date on which you sign the contract in the first blank space, you will complete this section of the contract by inserting your name in the second blank space (formatted as either Dan and Karen P., or Mr. and Mrs. Dan P.) and the name of the child-care provider in the final blank space. You will be referred to as the "Employer" and your child-care provider will be referred to as the "Employee" throughout the remainder of the contract. By using the terms "Employer" and "Employee," you will avoid the necessity of using your name and the name of the child-care provider each time a reference is needed. This same concept of using defined terms, following the first usage of a term in a contract, is common practice in legal documents and makes the drafting process less cumbersome. You will see this concept used throughout the contract for other defined terms.

1. Term.

This paragraph specifies when the term of the arrangement begins (which may be different from the date at the beginning of the contract, which merely refers to the date of signing), and how long the term is to continue. Although you can specify a term of days, months, or even years, you will probably want the option to terminate the arrangement at any time for any reason. If you specify a finite term, you may have to pay your child-care provider for the entire period of the contract. *Therefore, it is very important not to contract for a specific period of time in order to avoid incurring legal liability for any remaining time following discontinuation of the arrangement, for whatever reason.* The sample form indicates that you can terminate the arrangement at any time for any reason. The sample contract form indicates that your child-care provider has the corollary right to terminate the arrangement at any time, which is necessary if you wish to have such right. You should also note that the sample contract provides for severance payments, *at your option*, by referring to Paragraph 10 of the contract, where these arrangements are detailed. Finally, this paragraph contains release language that is designed to limit the child-care provider's ability to make legal claims for severance payment, vacation pay and/or other damages resulting from the termination of the arrangement. The enforcement of this type of provision may vary from state to state.

2.   Children.

To complete this section, you will need merely to list the name and birth date of each child who is to be the subject of the child-care services contemplated by the contract.

3.   Location and Schedule of Hours.

You will need to specify the location at which the child-care services will be performed. Normally this will be your residence, so you would simply insert your address in the blank space. The remaining portion of this section deals with the child-care provider's schedule, such as 8:00 A.M. to 5:00 P.M., weekdays. You may generally schedule the days and number of hours that you and your child-care provider may agree upon as part of your arrangement. However, see discussion under *Overtime* in Paragraph 6 below for the circumstances under which overtime must be paid to your child-care provider. You will note that the sample contract provides for a choice of schedule options, one of which contemplates a live-in arrangement (the first box) and the other of which contemplates a specific schedule (the second box). You will need to check the appropriate box and, if you select the second box, you will also need to complete the information in the blank spaces next to that box to specify the agreed upon schedule. It may become necessary to alter the schedule from time to time to meet your evolving family needs; such changes can be incorporated into a signed Contract Addendum in the form of Schedule 2 to the sample form contract.

4.   Responsibilities.

This section of your contract is one of the most important sections and should be reviewed carefully with your child-care provider. *It is very important, both from a legal point of view, and otherwise, to make sure that you and your child-care provider have a clear understanding of the scope of the duties that are contemplated by the arrangement.* The sample contract form contains only a few broad categories of typical child-care duties and it is likely that you will need to utilize Schedule 1 to the sample contract to further describe the specific duties that you expect your child-care provider to perform. Simply complete that Schedule to provide for any additional duties.

You will note that the sample contract form contemplates that your child-care provider may be required to transport your children to various events, and that your child-care provider will provide such transportation, and carry and provide evidence of liability insurance. If significant transportation duties are anticipated, you may need to pay your child-care provider additional compensation, perhaps based upon mileage. The sample contract contemplates that such a payment, if desirable, will be provided for in the Contract Addendum attached to the sample form of contract as Schedule 2. The Schedule 2 Contract Addendum can also be used to provide any specific guidelines regarding care of your children, such as instructions relating to medical needs.

5.   Payment Terms.

You will need to complete this section to spell out clearly the amount of and frequency of the payments that you will be making to your child-care provider. If your child-care provider lives in your home, you will probably pay that person a fixed monthly salary (which, of course, may be broken into two equal semimonthly, or even weekly, payments). If your child-care provider will be working at your home but will not be living there, you may either pay an hourly wage, or a fixed salary, but you must always pay (except for casual baby-sitting under certain circumstances) at least the minimum wage for each hour worked. Except for minimum wage considerations, the amount of hourly wage or fixed salary that you pay your child-care provider will most likely be determined by what your local market typically pays for such services, taking into consideration such things as the number and ages of your children, the number of hours to be worked, incidental benefits that you will be providing, and the scope of duties contemplated.

To complete this section of the contract you will need to determine the method and frequency of the payment, check the appropriate box in the sample contract, and fill in the amount of hourly wage or salary. The *Other* category provides a convenient box to check and complete for special compensation such as automobile expense reimbursement.

After completing the payment information section, you will need to check all appropriate payroll deduction boxes, such as Social Security, Medicare taxes, and state and federal income taxes. (See Part II below for guidance on these deductions.) You may also need to provide for additional deductions not specified in a particular category (such as health insurance premiums). To do this, merely check the *Other deductions* box and specify the nature of the additional deduction(s). The sample form also has a box to check if your child-care provider is to receive advance payment of earned income credit. That box should be checked if your child-care provider establishes eligibility and requests such credit. The amount of the credit can be determined by referring to the appropriate tables in IRS Publication 15 *(Circular E, Employer's Tax Guide)*, and should be paid with each paycheck from the Social

Security, Medicare, and income taxes that otherwise would have been withheld from your child-care provider's pay. See Part II below for guidance in handling the earned income credit.

The final part of this section requires you to check the box and complete the frequency of payments that you and your child-care provider have agreed upon as appropriate for your arrangement. The last paragraph states that you and your child- care provider will have at least an annual salary review but that you will not be obligated to give your child-care provider any raises. You may, of course, determine that such raises are appropriate, either because of good performance or because of local market conditions.

6.   Overtime.

This section of the contract doesn't require any completion on your part and essentially recites the current law with respect to the minimum requirements applicable to overtime payments.

As described in Part II below, current federal law requires that domestic employees who do not live in your household must be paid extra pay when they work overtime (generally in excess of 40 hours per week). Overtime pay rate, when applicable, is the greater of one and one-half times the employee's regular hourly rate, or one and one-half times the minimum wage for each hour worked.

Live-in child-care providers are generally exempt from overtime pay requirements, but must be paid at least the minimum wage for each hour worked overtime. Also, to be eligible for the exemption, you must give your live-in child-care provider complete freedom for reasonable periods of time to sleep, eat meals, and simply enjoy personal pursuits without child-care responsibilities. See Part II below for additional information regarding the payment of overtime.

Current law may not require the payment of overtime to your child-care provider in many instances in which overtime payments might be customary in other businesses. You may, of course, choose to pay overtime in any of those instances you consider fair and appropriate. If you elect to do so, you will either need to modify Paragraph 6 of the sample contract or provide for the appropriate changes in the Schedule 2 Contract Addendum or cover such matters in the *Benefits* paragraph below.

7.   Benefits.

As described above, even though you may not be required under current law to pay for vacations, provide sick pay, or make premium payments for weekend or holiday work (unless it is overtime work), you may wish to do so as a matter of fairness to your child-care provider. This section of the contract allows you to provide for these optional benefits as well as certain other benefits that might be particularly applicable to a child-care provider who lives in your home, such as meals and room and board.

To provide for a specified benefit, all you need do is to check the appropriate box and complete the blank space with the appropriate information. For example, as provided in the sample completed contract, you may wish to pay for vacations after your child-care provider has worked for you for a specified period of time, such as a year. This can be accomplished by simply checking the box by *Vacation* and inserting "you will be entitled to one week of paid vacation for each full year that your employment hereunder continues, the specific time of which must be approved by Employer" in the blank space. You may also wish to pay for certain holidays, without requiring your child-care provider to work on those days, or to pay overtime to your child-care provider for actually working on those holidays. Again, to do this, simply check the box next to *Holidays* and insert the appropriate information in the accompanying blank space.

The *Other* box should be checked when no specific category conveniently describes the fringe benefit that you wish to provide. For example, you may wish to provide for a separate telephone line for your child-care provider or you may allow your child-care provider to have limited personal use of one or more items of your property, such as your automobile. These benefits, as with all other benefits that you choose to provide, should be described in concise language so that you and your child-care provider can avoid what might be unpleasant misunderstandings about matters that are supposed to be incentive-oriented.

8.   Licenses and Certificates.

This section provides a checklist of many of the important matters that you should have considered during the hiring process. Many of these boxes will need to be checked if your child-care provider is adequately qualified, although you may have decided to employ someone even if some of the licenses or certificates described in this section were absent. For example, if you don't have a swimming pool at your home or do not need your child-care provider to drive, it would be less important for your child-care provider to have life-saving training or a driver's license. It is also possible that your child-care provider will not need to provide a particular certificate because of its inapplicability (for example, your child-care provider may not need to provide a Form W-4 because no withholding is contemplated, or a Form W-5 because no earned income credit is available). In any event, you will need to check the appropriate boxes for those applicable licenses and certificates and specify any additional licenses and certificates in the blank space next to *Other* after checking the corresponding box.

9. Employment Application.

This section of the contract merely requires that the child-care provider affirm the accuracy of the information contained in the Employment Application. This affirmation has practical utility by making you and your child-care provider focus on the information contained in the Employment Application. This section has legal utility by creating a potential claim against your child-care provider if you should sustain any damage or liability as a result of any false statement contained in the Employment Application. This section would most likely be useful in defending claims made against you by your child-care provider, or by third parties as a result of the negligence or other actionable conduct on the part of your child-care provider. For example, you could be held liable under theories of "negligent hiring" for damages caused to a neighbor's child who was involved in an automobile accident while being transported by your child-care provider, perhaps along with your child, to a school soccer game. The degree of care that you exercised in hiring your child-care provider (some of which may be evidenced by the Employment Application and the reliance thereon in Paragraph 9 of the contract) may be very important in avoiding or limiting liability in such circumstances.

10. Severance.

As described above under *Term,* the contract contemplates a termination-at-will arrangement by either party, and that no severance will be required. However, after a lengthy period of employment, it is often considered fair and customary to provide for at least some severance. Providing for severance under these circumstances may also provide a useful incentive in retaining a desirable employee and may in any event be necessary to compete in your local market. If you choose to pay severance, then simply complete the first blank with the specific period of time required to "earn" severance (for example, six months) and complete the second blank with the amount of the severance (for example, two weeks' pay, or $1,000).

11. Return of Materials.

This section of the contract does not require any action on your part and merely requires your child-care provider to return all of your materials to you after the employment arrangement is terminated. This section serves primarily as a reminder to make sure that you account for these items at the end of the contract.

12. Additional Terms and Provisions.

This section provides for the basic mechanics to amend and modify the primary contract form through the use of the Schedule 2 Contract Addendum. The Contract Addendum provides a convenient way to add additional terms and conditions that you and your child-care provider may consider appropriate for your specific circumstances but do not quite fit the prescribed categories or language contained in the primary contract. As circumstances change, you will also find that the Contract Addendum can be used to incorporate these changes without the necessity of re-writing the entire contract. In other words, the Contract Addendum is a sort of "living" document that can evolve with your needs.

13. Governing Law.

You complete this section by inserting the state law that you wish to govern your employment arrangement. Absent special circumstances, this state will normally be your state of residence, especially if the child-care services are also to be performed there. Assuming you have made a valid choice of law in this paragraph (either your state or another state having a significant interest in the transaction, such as a state where the services are to be performed, if not in your state), that state law will be applied by any court having reason to construe your contract for most purposes, whether or not that particular court is located in the same state as that selected by you.

Analyzing a Day-Care Center or Family Day-Care Home Contract

Placing your child in a day-care center rather than employing a personal employee to care for your child in your home will eliminate the need to comply with the record-keeping and tax requirements. However, if you determine that the day-care center or family day-care home is the best choice for your child-care needs, you should still be concerned about your legal arrangements. The typical day-care or family day-care operator will ask you to sign a contract covering the essentials of your arrangements. You will also generally be asked to provide medical and emergency information and a medical authorization form to permit the operator to obtain medical care for your child in the case of an emergency. If such information is not requested, you should provide it anyway, and insist that the center utilize the information if necessary.

Among other matters, which your provider or operator contract should cover, are the following:

1. You should have a clear understanding of the fee arrangements. The arrangements should allow you flexibilty to terminate the arrangement without incurring large minimum payments and should in any event be terminable by you on limited notice.

2. You will need to provide for appropriate arrangements to care for your child when emergency situations prevent you from picking up your child at the scheduled time. These arrangements may comtemplate extended arrangements with the center, alternate sources provided by the center, or friends or relatives being contacted by the center to pick up your child in your absence. Back-up plans for your child are essential and should be given priority in your contract with your day-care center.

3. You should provide in your contract for documentation of all required licenses, permits, and safety and other inspection reports. This may be accomplished by adding a paragraph such as follows: "Attached hereto are copies of all licenses and permits regulating [the day-care center or family day-care home] or under whose authority [the day-care center or family day-care home] operates, together with all safety and similar inspection reports received by [the day-care center or family day-care home] within the past twelve months. Such licenses and permits are currently in force and [the day-care center or family day-care home] is not in default under or in violation of any of such licenses or permits."

4. Your contract should specify the type and amount of insurance that the day-care center or family day-care home will be required to maintain in reasonable amounts in the case of liability.

5. Your contract should specify that the day-care center, family day-care home, and all the employees thereof will at all times meet state requirements for day-care employees, that suitable background checks have been conducted on all employees, that all employees have attained a level of education at least equivalent to a high-school degree, and that all employees have received day-care training commensurate with the work to be performed. You may

also wish to request specific résumé information on the day-care employees.

6. Your contract should clearly specify whether the day-care center or family day-care home may transport your child away from the primary facility (such as on a field trip) and under what conditions such transportation may take place.

7. Your contract should specify that you may visit the day-care center or family day-care home at any time during reasonable business hours with or without notice.

In addition to assuring that you have made adequate contract arrangements, you should also make a careful physical inspection of the day-care center's or family day-care home's facilities as described in Chapters Seven and Eight. You should make sure that the inside and outside areas are adequate, that sufficient equipment and materials are available, that safety precautions have been taken, and that reasonable sanitary conditions exist.

PART II   THE PAPERWORK BLIZZARD

Now that you have hired your child-care provider, what about all the paperwork? Well, there's a bunch, so let's get started.

Defining the Employment Arrangement

In connection with the hiring process and the signing of your legal contract, you will be determining the nature of the working arrangement, specifically whether your child-care worker is considered to be an independent contractor or your employee. The Federal Insurance Contribution Act (FICA) and the Federal Unemployment Insurance Act (FUTA) withholding provisions are applicable and must be compiled with in the case of employees but are inapplicable to independent contractors. FICA taxes are used to fund obligations with respect to Social Security, the Disability Insurance Trust Fund, and Medicare. FUTA taxes are used to fund benefits payable under the unemployment insurance system, which generally provides for payments to employees that are terminated through no fault of their own. See Chapter Three for a definition of what makes someone an independent contractor or employee.

If your child-care worker is considered an employee, you will have to comply with substantial paperwork requirements imposed by the federal government and by one or more of your state agencies. You will first be required to verify that your child-care worker is legally eligible to work in the United States. After that determination is made, you will need to be concerned about FICA and FUTA taxes and compliance with federal and state laws regarding minimum wage, overtime payments, and perhaps worker's compensation.

You will also need to keep good records, especially if your child-care worker is classified as an employee. This process begins with your obtaining an employer identification number from the federal government by filing Form SS-4 (*Application for Employer Identification Number*). Simply complete this form and file it with your regional IRS center, the location of which is indicated in the instructions to the SS-4. Use this number on all filings made with the IRS and the Social Security Administration. For additional information about your employer identification number, and for copies of Form SS-4, call your local IRS office, or the IRS toll free at (800) TAX-FORM ([800] 829-3676) and ask for IRS Publication 1635 (*Understanding Your Employer Identification Number*). You may also obtain the other IRS forms and publications mentioned herein by calling the same toll-free number.

For your next order of business, you should establish a carefully organized employee file that will contain the Employment Application and all other relevant hiring materials, such as the background check report, the results of any special testing conducted by you, driver's license information, all other licenses and certificates obtained by you in connection with the hiring of your child-care provider, and all payment and tax information. Under federal law, records relating to employment taxes and similar information must be retained for at least four years (generally from the due date of the corresponding tax return), and many state laws significantly extend this period of time for state-required employee records. *Your failure to comply with the various laws and record-keeping requirements may result in your being assessed substantial fines and penalties.*

With all the red tape and legal implications that result from the classification of your child-care worker as an employee, why not simply treat your worker as an independent contractor? Unfortunately, it is not that easy. If you have the right to control not only what your child-care worker does, but also how he or she does it, you and your child-care worker will generally be classified as an employer and employee, at least for IRS and state tax purposes. A worker is treated as an independent contractor when the employer controls only the *result* of the work, but not the means by which that result is accomplished. Although the IRS considers at least twenty separate factors in evaluating employee status, your child-care worker will most likely be considered an employee, rather than an independent contractor, particularly if your child-care worker provides the agreed-upon services in your home. IRS Publication 937 (*Employment Taxes*) contains specific information on how to determine whether an individual providing services is an employee or an independent contractor. Also, you may use Form SS-8 (*Determination of Employee Work Status For Purposes of Federal Employment Taxes and Income Tax Withholding*) to request that the IRS determine whether your child-care worker is an employee.

This kit is supposed to make the hiring process easy, right? Well, when does it start getting easy? The answer is right now. The following paragraphs will tell you exactly what you have to do about your new employee and exactly when you have to do it.

Federal Taxes

In addition to securing your employer tax identification number from the IRS (by filing Form SS-4, as described above) you will need to obtain the required federal domestic employee tax forms. IRS Publication 926 *(Household Employer's Tax Guide)* contains a relatively complete summary of all of the federal tax requirements applicable to domestic employees. IRS Publication 15 *(Circular E, Employer's Tax Guide)* contains tax tables and other important employer-employee information. You should obtain a copy of these publications and the tax packet for domestic employees described in IRS Publication 926 from your local IRS office or by calling the IRS toll free at (800) TAX-FORM ([800] 829-3677). You may also call your local IRS office during regular business hours at the local number in your telephone directory or at the toll free number, (800)829-1040, to ask any tax questions.

As noted above, some of the information which you will be receiving, relates to your FICA tax obligations. For example, if your employee earns more than $1,000 during the year 1996, both you and your employee will be required to pay FICA taxes of 7.65 percent (6.2% for Social Security taxes and 1.45% for Medicare tax) on your employee's Social Security and Medicare wages. You are responsible for the payment of your employee's share of these taxes as well as your own. You can either withhold your employee's share from his or her wages, or pay it from your own funds. Any Social Security and Medicare taxes paid for the employee by you must be included in the employee's wages for income tax purposes. Beginning in 1995, Social Security and Medicare taxes should be reported on Schedule H to your Form 1040 or 1040A income tax form and should be paid by you at the time you file that form. These payments were required to be paid quarterly under prior law.

Also, as noted above, you will be required to pay FUTA taxes for your employee if you pay wages to your employee totaling $1,000 or more in a calendar quarter during the year. These taxes may also now be paid annually with your IRS Form 1040 or 1040A and, for 1995, are payable at the rate of 6.2 percent on the first $7,000 of gross wages paid to your employee. However, if you also pay state unemployment tax (which will generally be the case) you may subtract, in 1995, 5.4 percent from the FUTA taxes otherwise payable, with the result that the effective FUTA rate being paid is 0.8 percent. *FUTA taxes must be paid by you and should not be deducted from your employee's wages.* Until 1998, you may pay domestic employment taxes in full at the time you file your own tax return without incurring any interest or penalties. Beginning in 1998, however, you will be required to increase your quarterly estimated tax payments to take into account employment taxes owed on domestic workers. FICA and FUTA taxes are also subject to adjustment on an annual basis to reflect future inflation.

When determining the amount of wages that is subject to taxation, it is important to remember that calculations are generally based upon gross pay (salary before any deductions or withholding) including the reasonable value of all noncash compensation, except that certain incidental noncash items—such as meals (if they are being provided for your convenience), uniforms, and lodging (if it is a condition of employment)—may be excluded in determining gross pay.

IRS Publication 926 explains how to calculate these domestic taxes using current tax rates, and should be consulted for this purpose.

Withholding Taxes and Earned Income Credit

Under current law you do not have to withhold federal income tax from your employee's pay unless your employee specifically requests such withholding. If withholding is requested, your employee must sign a Form W-4 (*Employee Withholding Allowance Certificate*) and you must withhold from any pay, before you deduct any amounts for other withheld taxes, an amount computed in accordance with the IRS withholding tax tables based upon the filing status and exemptions shown on your employee's Form W-4 (See IRS Publication 15). As of 1995, these taxes, if withheld by you, must also be reported on Schedule H to your Form 1040 or 1040A income tax return and are to be paid by you at the time such return is filed.

Your employee may also be entitled to an earned income credit (EIC), which may be paid in advance in certain circumstances. If applicable, this credit reduces your employee's tax, or allows your employee to receive a payment from the IRS if no tax is owed. Your employee would have been required to provide you with a completed IRS Form W-5 in order to certify eligibility for advance EIC. If your employee is eligible, you should deduct the appropriate amount (which may be determined from the EIC tables in IRS Publication 15) from Social Security and Medicare taxes and withheld income taxes. If applicable, advance EIC must be paid to your employee in each paycheck. *Do not pay more than the amount of Social Security and Medicare taxes and withheld federal income tax that your employee would otherwise need to pay to the IRS.* If no income tax is withheld, you must still inform your employee that he or she may have the right to EIC, but not to the advance payment. You may give notice either by providing your employee with (1) IRS Form 797 (*Possible Federal Tax Refund Due to the Earned Income Credit*), (2) your own written statement containing the same wording as IRS Form 797, (3) the IRS Form W-2 (described below), which has the required statement about the EIC on the back of Copy C, or (4) a substitute Form W-2 with the same EIC statement on the back of the employee's copy that is on Copy C of the IRS Form W-2.

If you must file Form W-2 for your employee and you file in a timely manner, no further notice is necessary, provided the Form W-2 has the required statement about the EIC on the back of the employee's copy. If a substitute Form W-2 is given on time but doesn't contain the required statement, you must give your employee notice within one week of the date the substitute Form W-2 is delivered. If Form W-2 is required but you do not give it to your employee on time, you must give your employee notice on Form 797 (or by your statement containing the same language) by the date that the Form W-2 is required to be given. If Form W-2 is not required, you must give your employee notice by February 7 of that year.

The W-2 Form

Under current law, you must provide your employee with copies B, C, and 2 of IRS Form W-2 (wage and tax statement) on or before January 31 of each year with respect to the prior year's compensation and provide to the Social Security Administration, on or before the last day of February of each year, copy A of the W-2 Form. Completion of Form W-2 should be self-explanatory, although IRS Publication 926 contains additional information that you may find useful regarding the completion and filing of the W-2 Form.

Minimum Wage and Overtime

With limited exceptions, such as casual baby-sitting, under current federal law, you must pay the minimum wage to your employee if he or she works at least eight hours in a work week, or if you pay your employee wages of at least $50.00 in any calendar quarter. Also under current federal law, you must generally pay extra compensation if your employee works overtime and does not live in your home as part of the child-care arrangement. If your employee does live in your home, you generally will not have to pay overtime, but you must pay at least the minimum wage for each hour worked. *To avoid paying overtime to your live-in employee, however, you must give your employee periods of complete freedom for sleeping, eating, and purely personal pursuits free from all child-care responsibilities.* When applicable, the overtime pay rate is the greater of one and one-half times your employee's regular hourly wage, or one and one-half times the minimum wage rate, for each hour worked in excess of forty hours per week. Under current federal law, you do not have to pay your employee any premium compensation for Saturday, Sunday, or holiday work, or for hours worked in excess of a usual number of hours on any particular day (although California and certain other states may, under certain circumstances, require premium pay in such cases). Some states may also require minimum wage payments that are greater than the amount required under federal law; and if you are in one of those states, you must pay your state-mandated higher amount.

Worker's Compensation and State Law

Some form of worker's compensation insurance program is applicable in all states for the purpose of providing payment for medical expenses and lost wages to employees who are injured at work. Many states exempt domestic workers from their worker's compensation system altogether, although voluntary participation may be allowed in certain states. Where it is not allowed, private worker's compensation insurance may be required. Normally, participation in a state-sponsored worker's compensation program, whether directly, or indirectly through private insurers, will provide protection against work-related claims exceeding certain specified limits. If your state does not require you to carry worker's compensation and you don't otherwise insure against such liability, or if your state does require such coverage and you fail to provide it, you could be liable for payment of potential damages to your employee that may be substantially higher than would be the case when worker's compensation payments are made pursuant to a state program with which you are in compliance. You should always provide a safe working environment for your employee (e.g., make all required repairs to your home) and discuss your insurance coverage with your insurance agent or other knowledgeable representative.

State Tax Requirements

You should contact the department of labor and/or the other agencies of your state of residence that administer your state income taxes, unemployment insurance programs, worker's compensation programs, and other state tax and insurance programs relating to domestic employees to obtain specific information about your state requirements. State law requirements vary significantly from state to state.

Worker's Eligibility

In addition to all of the paperwork referred to above with respect to state and federal tax compliance, you must also satisfy the Immigration and Naturalization Service (INS) that your employee is eligible to work in the United States. It is unlawful for you to knowingly hire or contract to employ an alien who cannot legally work in the United States. At the time you hire your employee, he or she must complete the employee portion of the INS Form I-9 (*Employment Eligibility Verification*). You will need to complete the remaining portions of the INS Form I-9. You do not have to file this form with the government, but you must retain a completed copy in your files for at least three years after the date of hire, or one year after the date of termination, whichever is later. At the time you hire your employee, you must also examine the originals (except for a birth certificate, which may be a certified copy) of documents presented by your employee to establish employment eligibility. Your employee, not you, must determine which documents to provide. If you demand to see a specific document, you may create a claim for an unfair immigration-related employment practices case. Generally, an eligible employee must either be a United States citizen, or a national of the United States, or a legal alien who is authorized to work in the United States. The documents that may be provided to you to verify eligibility status include a U.S. passport (valid or expired), a driver's license issued by a state or possession of the United States (which contains information similar to the typical state driver's license), a Social Security card issued by the Social Security Administration, and a variety of other documents evidencing U.S. citizenship or legal alien status. A complete list of the acceptable documents can be found in the instructions to INS Form I-9.

Two copies of INS Form I-9 are also contained in the *INS Handbook for Employees*, which contains additional useful information about eligibility requirements. You may obtain a copy of this handbook (and additional copies of INS Form I-9) by calling the INS toll free, at (800) 755-0777.

PART III   LIST OF FORMS YOU MAY NEED AND THEIR DESCRIPTIONS

Throughout the preceding discussions are references to various state tax, federal tax, and related forms that you or your child-care provider will need to utilize or file with a state or federal agency. It is essential that you fully understand these forms and file them when required to avoid possible penalties or other sanctions. The following section lists the various forms that should be obtained by you as part of your child-care arrangements.

Contract for Child Care	Use this form to create the legal arrangements between you and your child-care provider. See pages 264–269 in this appendix for a blank sample of this form.
Schedule 1 to Contract for Child Care	(*Description of Additional Child-Care Responsibilities and Special Instructions*) Use this Schedule to specify any additional duties or instructions that are not easily included in the sample legal contract. See page 269 in this appendix for a blank sample of this form.
Schedule 2 to Contract for Child Care	(*Contract Addendum*) Use this Schedule to add supplemental provisions to the legal contract at the time the contract is signed and to modify and change the contract terms as your family needs evolve. See page 270 in this appendix for a blank sample of this form.
Employment Application	Obtain a completed Employment Application from each candidate you interview and retain a copy of the application for your employee.
INS Form I-9	(*Employment Eligibility Verification*) This one-page form needs to be completed (but not filed with the government) to assure that your child-care provider can legally work for you. The back of the INS Form I-9 contains instructions for its completion.
IRS Form SS-4	(*Application for Employer Identification Number*) This form is filed with your regional IRS office

to obtain an employer identification number, which you must have if you employ a domestic worker.

IRS Form SS-8	(*Determination of Employee Work Status for Purposes of Federal Employment Taxes and Income Tax Withholding*) This form may be used by you (and may be requested from you by the IRS) to request that the IRS determine whether your child-care worker is an employee or an independent contractor.
Form W-4	(*Employee Withholding Allowance Certificate*) This form will be used if your child-care provider wants federal income taxes withheld from his or her paycheck.
Form W-5	(*Earned Income Credit Advance Payment Certificate*) This form must be completed by your employee if your employee is eligible and wants to receive advance earned income credit.
Form 797	(*Possible Federal Tax Refund Due to the Earned Income Credit*) This form contains information regarding the earned income credit and may be used to provide required notice of earned income credit to your.
IRS Publication 926	(*Employment Taxes for Household Employees*) This publication explains how to calculate and pay FICA and FUTA taxes.
Form 940-EZ	(*Employer's Annual Federal Unemployment (FUTA) Tax Return*)
Form W-2	(*Wage and Tax Statement*) This report is used to report the wages paid to your employee. Copy A is filed with the Social Security Administration, and copies B, C, and 2 are given to your employee (use Form W-3 if you have more than one employee during the calendar year).
IRS Publication 1635	(*Understanding Your Employer Identification Number*) This publication contains general information about how the IRS uses your nine-digit tax identification number (which you obtain by filing Form SS-4 with the IRS) to identify your tax accounts.

IRS Publication 937

(*Employment Taxes*)   This form is informational only and provides a list of distinctions that the IRS considers important in classifying workers as independent contractors or employees.

IRS Publication 15

(*Circular E, Employer's Tax Guide*)   This publication contains tax tables and other general employer-employee information.

APPENDIX 2

■ ■ ■ ■ ■ ■ ■ ■ ■

Resources

Here are some important phone numbers to keep on hand for your child-care needs.

Child Care Aware .. (800) 424-2246
Will give you the phone number of your local resource and referral agency.

The ChildCare Registry .... (510) 248-4100
Will provide legal, comprehensive seven-year background checks on your provider.

The Children's Foundation .... (202) 347-3300
Can answer your questions about licensing and child-care regulations.

Center for Research on Women: School-Age Childcare Project .... (617) 283-2543

American Red Cross .... (800) 442-5980
Offers classes in First Aid and CPR (adult, child, and infant).

Atlanta .... **(404) 881-9800**
Los Angeles .... **(213) 729-5200**

Chicago .... **(312) 440-6600**
New York .... **(212) 787-1000**

Dallas .... **(214) 871-2175**
San Francisco .... **(415) 202-0600**

Denver .... **(303) 778-2580**
Seattle .... **(206) 323-2345**

Child Molester Identification Line (900) 463-0400
Will provide a listing of sex offenders registered statewide for California residents only.

The following national day-care organizations can provide you with a local referral:

KinderCare .... (800) 633-1488

La Petite Day Care .... (913) 345-1250

Kids R Kids Quality Learning Centers .... (800) 297-0033 .... or (404) 297-7777

And the following organizations may be helpful in caring for your older child:

American Camping Association .... (800) 428-2267

National Camping Association .... (800) 966-2267

Girl Scouts of the USA .... (800) 223-0624

Boy Scouts of the USA .... (214) 580-2000

Boys & Girls Clubs of America .... (404) 815-5700

BIBLIOGRAPHY

American Camping Association. *1995/96 Guide to Accredited Camps.* Martinsville, IN: American Camping Association, 1995.

American Camping Association. *Standards for Day and Resident Camps.* Martinsville, IN: American Camping Association, 1993.

American Public Health Association and American Academy of Pediatrics. *Caring For Our Children.* Ann Arbor, MI: American Public Health Association and American Academy of Pediatrics, 1992.

Auerbach, Stevanne. *Keys To Choosing Child Care.* New York: Barron's, 1991.

Bananas Guide for Parents and Children. Berkeley, CA: Wingbow Press, 1982.

Berezin, Judith. *The Complete Guide to Choosing Child Care.* New York: Random House, 1990.

Buhler, Danalee. *The Very Best Child Care and How to Find It.* Rocklin, CA: Prima, 1989.

Civardi, Anne and Stephen Cartwright. *Going to School.* London, England: EDC Publishing, 1993.

Clayman, Charles B. *The American Medical Association Encyclopedia of Medicine.* New York: Random House, 1989.

Dargatz, Jan. *52 Ways to Evaluate Your Childcare Options and Gain Peace of Mind.* Nashville, TN: Thomas Nelson Publishers, 1994.

Denton, Judy. *My Mom Made Me Go to School.* Pictures by Lisa McCue. New York: Bantam Doubleday Dell, 1993.

Draper, Wanda. *Is There a Nanny in The House?* Oklahoma City, OK: Macedon Productions, 1992.

Fuller, Elizabeth. *Nannies: How I Went Through 18 Nannies for One Little Boy Before I Found Perfection in a Former Marine Sergeant Named Margaret.* New York: Primus, 1993.

Johnson, J. and J. McCracken, eds. *The Early Childhood Career Lattice: Perspectives on Professional Development.* Washington, DC: National Association for the Education of Young Children, 1994.

Kettmann, Susan. *Every Question to Ask Before You Choose Family Friendly ChildCare.* Waco, TX: WRS Group, 1994.

Merriam, Eve. *Mommies at Work.* Illustrated by Eugenie Fernandes. New York: Little Simon, 1989.

Nash, Margaret, Costella Tate, Sandra Gellert, and Beverly Donehoo. *Better Baby Care: A Book for Family Day Care Providers.* Washington, DC: The Children's Foundation, 1993.

O'Connell, Dorothy R. *Babysitting Safe and Sound.* New York: Fawcett, 1990.

Pelletier, Elaine S. *How to Hire a Nanny.* Englewood, CO: Andre & Lanier, 1994.

Price, Susan C. and Tom Price. *The Working Parents Help Book.* Princeton, NJ: Peterson's Guides, 1994.

Rothenberg, Mikel A. and Charles F. Chapman. *Barron's Medical Guide*, 3rd ed. Hauppauge, NY: Barron's Educational Series.

Zuspan, Frederick P., William F. Rayburn, and Jeanne T. Fitzgerald. *The Women's Health and Drug Reference.* St. Louis, MO: GW Graphics and Publishing, 1993.

Studies

Helburn, Suzanne. *Cost, Quality, and Child Care Outcomes in Child Care Centers.* Denver, CO: University of Colorado, 1995.

U. S. Department of Labor. *Care Around The Clock: Developing Child Care Resources Before 9 and After 5.* Washington DC: U.S. Department of Labor, 1995.

INDEX